READING IN THE PRIMARY SCHOOL YEARS

**Pauline Harris, Jan Turbill,
Phil Fitzsimmons & Barbra McKenzie**

Social Science Press
Australia

Published in 2001, reprinted in 2001 by
SOCIAL SCIENCE PRESS
PO Box 624
Katoomba NSW 2780
(A Division of David Barlow Enterprises Pty. Limited
ABN 76 001 943 200)
Telephone: (02) 4782-2909 ✱ Fax.: (02) 4782-5303
Email: socsci@ozemail.com.au
Web Site: http://www.ozemail.com.au/~socsci

ISBN 1 876633 21 2

PRINTING BY:
Ligare Pty Ltd
138 Bonds Road
Riverwood NSW 2210

Contents

This book is dedicated to the memory of my mother

Mary Therese Harris
1927 – 2000

My first reading teacher, along with Dad,
and
an avid reader who always could read between the lines
and never falter at taking a stand and voicing her views.

P.H.

Acknowledgements

The authors gratefully acknowledge the following people who made important contributions to this book:

The work of Peter Freebody and Allan Luke, which has yielded significant insights into reading practices and which provides the framework for this book

Brian Cambourne, for his longstanding research on language and learning and his specific contribution to Chapter One on language and learning

Lynn Banbrook, for her informative feedback on the E.S.L. sections in our book

Wilma Vialle, for her initial encouragement and guidance in getting this book project launched

John Daley, Library Services Co-ordinator at Wollondilly Shire Council, for his generous expert input on library services and partnerships with schools which benefit children's reading

J. Sara Paulk of Tifton-Tift Library, Tifton County, Georgia, U.S.A., for allowing us to include aspects of their Sister Library relationship with Wollondilly Shire Library

St Anthony's Primary School, Picton, for allowing us to include their wonderful experiences of reporting their Olympic/Paralympic experiences over the internet to audiences far and wide

Celine Bernhardt and the children of KB at Hurstville Public School, for allowing us to use their photos on the cover of this book

Terry McGoldrick, for allowing us to use his example of developing text analysts in his Year 5 classroom

Silva Bramblett, for her unerring proof reading with eyes that saw what we were too close to see ourselves

Our first year language students of 2000, who were our initial pilot group for reshaping content and trialling new strategies and whose responses to our innovations have helped shape this book

And last and in no way least, our families, friends and colleagues who get us through with unfailing support, loads of patience and the odd glass of wine.

About the Authors

Pauline Harris is Senior Lecturer and Course Director of Early Childhood in the Faculty of Education at the University of Wollongong, Australia. She began her teaching career several years ago as an early years teacher in Sydney schools. Over the years, she found herself teaching in a diverse range of social, cultural and linguistic settings. Pauline undertook her postgraduate studies overseas at The University of California, Berkeley, and on completing her Doctoral thesis on reading in the early school years, she took up her present position at the University of Wollongong. There, she teaches in language and literacy, as well as play, curriculum and classroom research methodologies. Her research interests continue to rest with young children's reading, which in recent years has been funded by the Australian Research Council. Of current research interest is the nexus between reading and information technology.

Jan Turbill is currently a Senior Lecturer in the Faculty of Education at the University of Wollongong, Australia. She began teaching in 1964 for the Department of School Education in New South Wales, teaching Kindergarten-Grade Two children for 12 years, working a as Literacy Consultant for 9 years, before moving to the academic world of the University in 1985. Jan's research ranges from early literacy development to the professional development of teachers. More recently she has been researching the use of technology as a support for literacy learning in the early years of schooling and as a medium for professional learning for teachers.

Phil Fitzsimmons currently lectures in language education in the Faculty of Education at the University of Wollongong. His research interests include preschool critical literacy development, use of information technology in preschool settings, referential communication, and the use of humour in classrooms. His teaching career spans 16 years in the classroom and eight years teaching at the tertiary level.

Barbra McKenzie worked in the corporate sector before turning to primary teaching. Her minor thesis work involved the role that non-verbal communication plays in classroom management. She currently lectures in language and literacy in the Faculty of Education at the University of Wollongong and is completing a Ph.D. Her major research interest lies in exploring the nexus between professional development and classroom practice.

Introduction

I remember years ago reading a text which likened the act of reading to a 'gymnast's struggle'. As I sat to write this introduction, those words came back to me vividly – and more so now that we have just reached the end of what for me was a very enjoyable Sydney 2000 Olympics.

Reading **is** like a 'gymnast's struggle', with many twists, turns and challenges along the way. How a gymnast functions is determined by their apparatus, skills, and the contexts in which they train and perform. Reading is not so different in this respect – how we read is shaped by the skills we have developed in particular contexts and by the kinds of texts we read.

Reading in the Primary School Years is framed by a wholistic view of language and literacy learning in sociocultural contexts. We draw on a model of reading which has been put forward by Alan Luke and Peter Freebody. It is a model which portrays reading as a set of social practices. It is our view that each of these sets of practices is equally important and so we have tried to provide a balanced view of these practices in our book.

Our book begins with a look at language learning in general terms – for we view reading as part of language. Here we look at how children learn, for this provides us with a basis for thinking about how teachers might best support and foster reading development in children.

We then move in Chapter Two to a focus on reading. We provide an overview of a number of different ways of thinking about reading. It is always important to acknowledge different ways of thinking about reading, to show there is indeed more than one way, and to encourage you to reflect on these and what your own views are. This chapter then moves to a more detailed examination of the model which frames our book - a model which portrays reading as a set of social practices.

Chapter Three takes us into the classroom. Because this book is about reading in the Primary school years, we need to provide a description of that context and how we view reading in classrooms.

Chapters Four, Five, Six and Seven each examines one of four sets of reading practices: code breaking practices (Chapter 4); text participant practices (Chapter 5); text user practices (Chapter 6); and text analyst practices (Chapter 7). Each of these chapters defines and explains the set of reading practices in question. We introduce each set of practices, examine the kinds of knowledge and skills readers need to have to carry out these practices, relate these practices to information technology and library use, provide information on developmental trends and related classroom practices, examine how teachers support readers from diverse cultural and linguistic backgrounds and describe assessment procedures.

We close our book with a chapter which brings all that has gone before together in terms of the bigger picture of classroom practice and programming.

We have included a number of key features which we hope will encourage your critical reflection on what you read between these covers and elsewhere. Each chapter starts with a quote which frames what follows. A preview is provided, so as to clarify the chapter's purpose and focus and to enable you, the reader, to activate what you may already know about the topic at hand. This is further served by focal questions which follow each chapter preview.

At the end of each chapter, we have provided a summary, as well as a list of key concepts. We have not defined these concepts, for we are leaving that to you, the reader. We want to flag terms which we believe you need to understand and which you are likely to encounter elsewhere in what you read about reading.

Throughout each chapter we have included tasks which we encourage you to do. Perhaps you might keep these in a portfolio which you can revisit as you study and reflect on what you have written, what you understand, what puzzlements might remain, and what connections you make to classroom practices.

Tutorial activities are provided at the end of each chapter, as are further readings. We do not pretend to provide the definitive, ultimate text on reading. Rather, we have attempted to provide a detailed overview of reading practices, and we encourage you to follow up points of interest by pursuing further reading such as we suggest here.

Now, let the games begin - on to the 'gymnast's struggle' of reading.

Pauline Harris

Chapter 1

WHAT IS LANGUAGE?

*'... she discovered I was literate and looked at me with more
than faint distaste. Miss Caroline told me to tell my father not to
teach me any more, it would interfere with my reading.*

*"Teach me?" I said in surprise. "He hasn't taught me anything,
Miss Caroline. Atticus ain't got time to teach me anything," I
added, when Miss Caroline smiled and shook her head. "Why he's
so tired at night he just sits in the living room and reads."'*
(Harper Lee, *To Kill a Mockingbird*, 1968, p.30)

Chapter Preview

This initial chapter explores what language is and the optimal conditions
for language learning. It forms the basis for all that follows both theoretically
and in practical terms, and how the beliefs highlighted in the following
pages can be translated into classroom practice.

Focal Questions

- What is language?
- How is it best learned? *demon, lmmer, expectat⁻ etc.*

Introduction: The Beginning of the 'Doubting Game'

This book focuses on reading and as you will come to realise as you make your way
through the ensuing chapters, it will naturally contain elements of bias that all texts
contain. Desmond Ford (1980) believes that this is naturally compounded once authors
who deal with beliefs and practice pull their text together because they tend to deal in
what he terms 'academic incest', social intercourse with those of a like mind.

Therefore we want you the reader to undertake what Elbow (1973) calls the 'doubting
game'. We want you to read with a critical eye, doubting and disputing any elements
that seem to be at odds with what you believe. Only by confronting what we believe
and reflecting on what you believe will you become a teacher who can match what you

philosophically believe with what you practise in the classroom. Teachers who can do this appear to be the most empowered.

And so now read on.

How reading is learned and how it is best taught are two arguments that have been debated for many decades and have formed part of what many have termed the 'literacy wars'. Right from the start we want you to know that while we are not trying to keep the battle raging, we do have a particular point of view on how reading 'works' and how it is best learned that has emerged from our research and reading over the years. We will deal with the former in the next chapter; the latter is the focus of this chapter. Before you read what our particular focus is, we want you to begin to try and crystallise your understanding. Take a few minutes to answer the following questions and see how your reflections then match what we have to say with what you have written.

TASK

How do children learn in general?

How do children learn language?

What do you think is the relationship between learning to speak and learning in general?

What do you think is the relationship between learning to speak and learning to be literate?

How did you learn to read? Do you think you are a 'good' reader? Why/ Why not?

Who is the best reader you know? Why do you think this person is a 'good reader'?

Is this different from the way you read?

What does this tell you about this aspect of reading and how it might be effectively taught in classrooms?

These questions are intended to start you thinking about what is the nature of language and its relationship to reading. If you were to read textbooks from other disciplines, such as psychology or linguistics, you would find many definitions of reading, literacy and language learning in general. While there may be similarities in these definitions, there are also many differences. As you continue in your studies and read in the area you will find that there are some views about language, learning and learning to read in particular that are quite contradictory. While this may at first seem confusing it is also quite common in all domains of knowledge. One only has to watch the current affairs type television shows to see and hear the different views in areas of medicine, science, child rearing, finances and so on. There is no 'one view' or 'right view' and we acknowledge that others will have different views from ours and from those espoused in this book.

We believe that learners take an active role in their learning, whether that learning be riding a bike or learning a language. We need to examine two questions: what is language and how do children learn a language? These are fundamental questions as we believe that both reading and writing are also language processes. Wherever we use the term language, we are actually referring to <u>reading</u>, <u>writing</u>, <u>speaking</u> and <u>listening</u>.

We believe that because reading is a language process it is learned in a similar fashion to the way in which children learn to speak. That is, the language knowledge that learners need to learn and use as readers and writers is very similar to the knowledge that speakers and listeners of that language use. We are not advocating that print on a page is the same as talk written down. We recognise that there are significant differences between oral and written language, but what we are saying is that there are also similarities in the way that both are learnt as well as the purposes for learning them.

What is Language?

Various disciplines have studied language and language use for quite a considerable time, and therefore a myriad of definitions and applications have arisen. However, in this book we have taken the perspective that language is functional and as such is a 'resource for making meaning' (Halliday, 1975). Before we espouse our definitions, we want you to take time to undertake the following reflective tasks.

TASK

Consider these scenarios, and jot down your responses to the questions posed at the end of each.

1.   You are a proficient speaker of English who finds yourself standing on an underground Russian metro station. You do not speak Russian, nor do you read and write the Russian script. You need to find your way to your hotel that is on one of the many railway lines that run through this busy downtown station. Why are you so 'lost' in this setting? What can you do?

2.   You walk into a lecture a little late. You get out your notebook and pen ready to take notes. You listen, yet you do not understand. You hear words you know but it seems that the words are making no sense to you at all. Yet you know you need to understand what you are hearing the lecturer say ...   ☞

> *'The economies and cultures or New Times rely upon discourses and texts – retro and nouveau, official and face to face – as principal modes of work, consumption, leisure and everyday exchange. Discourse and texts are forms of capital for exchange in these economies'* (excerpt taken from Luke 2000, p.449)
>
> Why can't you get meaning from the language coming at you? What can you do?
>
> 3.   You meet your friends for lunch after the lecture.
>
>   'What was that about?'
>
>   'Not sure, but I think that it's all written in a book somewhere.'
>
>   'Where can we get the book?'
>
>   'He said it was in Special Reserve in the Library.'
>
>   'What ya going to have for lunch? I'm going to buy something. Anyone want a drink?'
>
> You breathe a sigh of relief. You understood everything that was being said here. Why?
>
> What does this tell you about this aspect of reading and how it might be effectively taught in classrooms?

Now let's consider what was happening in these scenarios from a language perspective.

In the first scene you were not a 'native to the culture'. While you might be able to hear the sounds of the Russian language being spoken around you and see the script written on walls and boards you could not 'crack the code'. You could not work out the grammar of the language or bring any meaning to anything that you heard or saw. In language terms you had no understanding of the sounds or 'phonemes' of Russian, nor the symbols or 'graphemes' of the language. In other words you had no 'graphophonic knowledge' to bring to the setting. Nor had you any understanding of word order, what were nouns, verbs and other structures of the language. Therefore you had no 'syntactic knowledge'. Finally, although you may have had many experiences with train travel you were unable to match your experiences to the Russian language used around you. Thus you were not able to take meaning away from the language you were hearing and seeing. You had no 'semantic knowledge'.

In the second setting, you were aware that it was English being spoken. You could 'see' the words written in English on the overhead transparency being shown. So you were able to bring your knowledge of the sounds and symbols of English to this setting (your graphophonic knowledge). And you had some idea of the grammar of the language being used (your syntactic knowledge) yet you had little if any previous knowledge of the content or topic being talked about. You had no semantic knowledge to bring to the setting and thus you were not able to understand much (if anything) or what was being said. Although this was an English speaking setting you still could not be said to be a 'native to that culture'. To become part of the culture you needed background information about the topic, about the content being shared. As you begin to gain this knowledge you will begin to understand the language being used and even begin to use it yourself. You will become a 'member of the culture'.

In the final setting, you were able to bring your semantic (prior experiences and knowledge), your syntactic (knowledge of the grammar) and your knowledge of the sounds of English together to gain meaning from what was being said. You were using language to 'make-meaning' as well as to understand the meaning being made.

These scenarios help us understand language and its use as a meaning-making resource. As language users we use language to get our needs met and to make sense of the world around us. We never stop learning language as different settings and 'cultures' use specific language forms and structures. Language is therefore a meaning-making system that can be said to be made up of interconnecting sub-systems which all need to be operating for meaning to be maintained. As you will see this view of language depicts both the oral and written forms of language. When drawn as a model these subsystems look like this:

Figure 1

Three Cueing Systems of Language

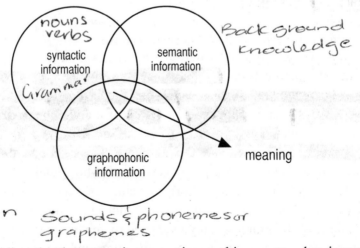

The understanding that language is a meaning-making system has important spin-offs for teaching generally, and for the teaching of reading specifically, as we will see in the next chapter.

TASK

Take a few minutes to think of your own schooling. Were all of the reading and writing lessons meaning-driven? Did you always see the meaning behind each lesson? We're sure that most people have either seen or had to endure meaningless lessons even though they were in the language of their culture.

What does this tell you about this aspect of reading and how it might be effectively taught in classrooms?

To sum up we want to reiterate the following key points:
- *language in any mode (spoken or written) is always a meaning-driven undertaking*. Even speaking to oneself or reading in bed at night is meaning-driven. However, the previous activity reveals that only those who are 'natives to the culture' can understand the language use in that culture.
- *language is a code or set of symbols*. Speech or written words are the symbolic construction we use to represent our environment and the properties of our daily lives. However, these symbols also allow us to operate beyond what we see in front of us. We can use our language in very creative ways, describing and discussing events, objects and places that are removed from us in both time and space. Our language allows us to be extremely creative beings. Not only do we use language to communicate and exchange information, but we also use it to reflect, to persuade, clarify, predict and a whole host of other functions. As Britton (1970, p.31) has said,

> '... we use language as a means of organising a representation of the world – each for himself – and that the representation so created constitutes the world we operate in, the basis of all our predictions by which we set the course of our lives.'

As seen in the previous tasks, language is culturally derived and bound. By this we mean that the language that we each use is specific to the culture into which we were born or choose to live. That language also serves as a boundary to that culture. This is most evident when one moves across the border of say France and Italy. In this instance one moves from one language to another and clearly from one culture to another.

Another example that is not so evident is when an Aboriginal child enters the school setting or culture. The language the Aboriginal child uses derives from and is bound by the culture of the Aboriginal community in which the child lives. When that same child enters the school culture the language used by that culture can be quite different. Thus the potential for language to become a 'meaning-making' resource is inextricably linked to the culture in which it is used. Another way of saying this is that language is a *cultural resource*, it has the potential to serve each of us well in the culture (or cultures) in which we find ourselves.

Language becomes a meaning-making resource when the sound and symbols of that language are arranged in a known structure or predictable pattern. This is often termed 'syntax' or 'grammar' of the language. The limited number of grammatical rules allows humans to organise their language into virtually an unlimited array of forms of interaction and exchanges. As children grow and develop linguistically (i.e. develop in their language ability and use) they learn the patterns of grammar that are accepted and not accepted by the community and culture they are growing up in. Grammar is one of the key systems that allows human interaction to be creative, inventive and yet still remain understood.

The component of language that carries the meaning are the sounds and symbols of language, called phonemes and graphemes. The 26 letters of the English language can be joined together to make up approximately 45 of these basic sound units.

- *language is functional*

We have alluded to this concept throughout. However, we believe that it is such an important concept that we need to discuss it a little more fully. Here we rely on the work of the linguist Michael Halliday and his theory of 'Functional Systemic Linguistics' (Halliday, 1978, 1980, 1985). Halliday refers to his theory of language as 'functional' because his focus is on understanding and explaining what language enables us to **do** (i.e. 'function') in everyday, real world human things, such as sharing and transmitting information, expressing feelings and attitudes, constructing knowledge, making sense of and understanding the world, arguing, getting our needs met, reflecting, finding out, entertaining, instructing, persuading and so on.

The important implications of Halliday's work can be summarised thus:

- He has helped us view language differently. Instead of viewing language simply as a medium for communication, he has helped us understand that it is also *a resource for making meaning, for coming to know about our world.*
- His work has also helped us understand that the ability to make meaning is really a *cultural resource* that allows us to achieve successfully what we want to achieve in our culture and the wider society.
- It has also helped us understand how meaning, language, thinking, knowing, understanding, learning and problem-solving are related. For example, different fields of knowledge such as mathematics, science, law and other content areas have idiosyncratic ways of using language. Halliday's work shows that such ways of using language are at the core of understanding the concepts and ideas within different domains of knowledge and content. Thus if one wants to think, learn, understand, 'know' and problem-solve like a mathematician, one must have control over the ways of using language that mathematicians have internalised. And so it is for law, science, and all of the curriculum areas. If one wants to become a member of the law profession one must first internalise the way that lawyers use language. This in turn will enable them to think like lawyers,

analyse evidence like lawyers, argue like lawyers and identify and solve problems like lawyers.

- Halliday has also helped us understand that some forms of language or 'genres' are highly valued in different contexts. For example, being able to use the language of academic argument is highly valued in some academic circles, just as being able to write a persuasive essay in a history exam, or an 'objective' scientific report in a science exam are highly valued in most secondary history and science classrooms.

- Another spin off from Halliday's work has helped us become aware of the relationship between audience, purpose and linguistic choice and how this knowledge can be used to help our students become aware of the way that language choice changes as the audience and purpose for that language change. For example, the choice of words used by a journalist to describe a football match or netball game to friends over a few drinks after the game would differ from those chosen to describe the same match in the written newspaper article the journalist later wrote. In this case the audience impacts on the journalist's linguistic choice used to describe (purpose) the same game (topic).

- Finally, Halliday's work has given us a new concept, *text*, defined as meaningful stretches of written and spoken language. He argues that when we use language in the everyday world, the level at which we think and operate is NOT the isolated sound or word level, but at the level of the whole text. If we need to respond to such texts in terms of its success or failure in making the meanings which are appropriate for the audience and purpose (which is important in school learning, as well as for social and economic survival in most societies), then we need to start attending to the language in the text so that we can identify the linguistic devices being used. We can then make some judgement about the agendas of those who created the text. Are they genuine? Are they trying to con us by putting a 'spin' on the meanings they are constructing for potentially sinister purposes?

- On the other hand we can also use such linguistic devices to help us create texts that will enable us to show that we can think and understand like a lawyer, like a scientist, or that will increase the probability that we can persuade others to meet our needs.

In summary, Halliday's model gives us both a framework and a language for understanding how texts 'work'. (For further reading see Derewianka, 1990.)

How Do Children Learn Language?

As we see it, there are several principles that underpin this question. These are:

- ***language learning is a social process*** – In all societies children learn to use language in what Halliday (1975) terms 'that little coterie known as the family'. From the outset children learn to speak as the result of being part of a social and cultural fabric. Halliday (1980) proposes that we 'learn language, learn through language and learn about language simultaneously as we use language. Language cannot be learned in isolation from others. As soon as children are born they enter a world that is full of sounds and talk. From the first moment children enter the world they find themselves to be a part of adult conversations. For the most part 'motherese' (see Vialle, Lysaght & Verenikina 2000, p.74), is an extremely small part of the language children hear. The overwhelming majority of the language forms in the children's immediate culture and environment is framed in adult conventions without any attempt to simplify. As parents and others care for the daily needs of children they chatter to the child, asking questions ('Who's a pretty baby? Did you have a big sleep?'), they share family stories ('Grandma's coming today and we are going shopping') and they use language that they neither expect the child to understand or respond to at this stage. Families include children in their language acts as they gather around their new offspring. And all this time there is a myriad of background talk emanating from radios, televisions, computers and often other siblings. While this language may often seem to be a jumble of noise and sounds, there is always one constant in play: meaning is being developed through social interaction. This is the driving force that will operate throughout the initial years in each child's language development and beyond (Vialle, Lysaght & Verenikina 2000, p.66).

- ***language learning is a mutual process*** – Children are not passive passengers in the language that surrounds them. Young children can understand a great deal a long time before they can actually vocalise any recognisable words. As active participants in the everyday interactions of life, gradually children realise that they can get things done with sounds and then words. Somewhere around two years of age children have begun the path of genuine interaction with the use of recognisable words and begin to negotiate their own way through the world. They are not left to their own devices in this learning process but are supported by their family members. The 'significant others' in their lives help the child by scaffolding (see reference to Vygotskian concept of' scaffolding' in Vialle, Lysaght & Verenikina 2000, p.36; also Bruner 1983, 1998) the learner with crucial language aid and support. This learning process is neither formal nor deliberate. Learning to use the language into which one is born is however expected!

- *language learning is an **active process*** – Language learning occurs continually from the moment children enter the world. As children mature they gain an ever increasing control over their language through the mutual help and support of their parents and others in their lives. Brian Cambourne has formalised this active learning process into a theory known as 'The Conditions of Learning' (1988,1995). In summary Cambourne believes that these conditions operate synergistically and aid barrier-free learning.

In what follows we have asked Brian Cambourne to share with you his 'theory of learning'.

Dr Brian Cambourne[1] :

I have spent the past 25 year of my academic life exploring how children learn and in particular how they learn language. My research has led me to believe that there are a set of conditions which I claim make complex learning possible. The categories I have identified are not exclusive or 'set in concrete'. They are simply the end product of my research in the area over many years. They evolved thus:

- the motivation to seek a more relevant theory of learning, emerged when I was a young teacher, because I continually encountered non-mainstream students who repeatedly demonstrated that they were capable of the most complex kind of learning outside of the classroom setting, yet seemed unable to learn even the most simple concepts of reading writing, spelling, maths that I tried to teach them.

- this led me to question the relevance of the mechanistic models of learning which I'd been trying to apply to my teaching. I was attracted to Frank Smith's concept of the brain as an 'organ of learning'. This concept helped me make these links between the brain, learning and evolution.

Thus if the brain is the organ of learning then:

- the ability to learn and the processes involved, must have played an important role in species-survival

- therefore it had to evolve in ways that increased the probability that crucial survival skills and knowledge were consistently, regularly, successfully, and easily learned by each new generation

- learning to use and understand the language of the culture into which one was born was a universal example of this complex 'species-survival' learning.

- I set out to understand this kind of learning by systematically observing toddlers in experimenter-free settings as they learned language. I observed (i.e. 'bugged' and unobtrusively took field notes) as these toddlers listened to, and responded to language with care-givers, siblings, relatives, neighbours, friends in different settings. As a consequence of both this research and the literature I'd reviewed on language acquisition, I concluded that because certain conditions always seemed to be present

---

1. This extract has been taken with permission from Turbill, J., Butler, A. & Cambourne, B. (1999) 4th ed. Frameworks: Literacy and Learning Staff Development Program: Readings.

in the environment in which language was being used (and therefore 'learned'), these conditions could be considered 'necessary' conditions for such learning to occur.

- I identified the following conditions:

Immersion

Demonstration

Engagement

Expectations

Responsibility

Employment

Approximations

Response

Immersion – The state of being saturated by, enveloped in, flooded by, steeped in, constantly bathed in, that which is to be learned. From the moment of birth young language learners are immersed in the medium they are expected to learn. It is therefore a necessary condition for learning to talk, one which is denied pre-lingually deaf children and 'feral' children.

Demonstration – Multiple opportunities to observe (see, hear, witness, experience, feel, study, explore) actions and artefacts. All learning begins with a demonstration of some action or artefact (Smith, 1981). Father asking at the breakfast table, 'Will you pass the butter please?' and the subsequent passing of it is not only a demonstration of what that particular sequence of sound means, but also a demonstration of what language can be used for, how it functions, how it can be tied to action, what kind of language is appropriate for the setting we call breakfast and so on. Young learners receive thousands of these demonstrations. They are the raw data that must be used to tease out how language is structured and used. This notion of demonstration can be generalised to all learning. Potential horse riders need demonstrations of how a horse is ridden before they can begin learning to ride. The same applies to tying shoelaces, riding bikes, and singing, as well as to reading, writing and spelling.

Engagement – While immersion and demonstration might be *necessary* conditions for learning to occur, they are not *sufficient*. Potential learners must first engage with the demonstrations which immersion provides. Engagement depends on active participation by the learner which in turn involves some risk taking; learners can only actively participate if they are prepared to 'have-a-go'. Children learn to talk because they engage with the demonstrations of talking and language use that are constantly occurring around them. If students do not engage with the demonstrations which immersion provides, little or no learning will occur.

Expectations – are essentially messages that significant others communicate to learners. They are also subtle and powerful coercers of behaviour. Young learner-talkers receive very clear messages that not only are they expected to learn to talk but also that they are capable of doing it. They are not given any expectation that it is 'too difficult' or that they might fail – quite the opposite. Try asking the parents of very young children whether they expect their offspring to learn to talk. Pay attention to the kind of response that you get.

Responsibility – When learning to talk, learner-talkers are permitted to make some decisions (i.e. take responsibility) about what they will engage in and what they will ignore. Nature does **not** provide language demonstrations that are specially arranged in terms of simple to complex. No one decides beforehand which particular language convention or set of conventions children will attend to and subsequently internalise. Learners are left some choice about what they will engage with next. Learners are able to exercise this choice because of the consistency of the language demonstrations occurring in the everyday ebb and flow of human discourse. Such demonstrations:

- are always in a context that supports the meanings being transacted
- always serve a relevant purpose
- are usually wholes of language
- are rarely (if ever) arranged according to some predetermined sequence.

Significant others in young learners' environments communicate very strong expectations that the learning task will ultimately be completed successfully, while simultaneously providing deep immersion with meaningful demonstrations. But the learners themselves decide the nature of the engagement that will occur.

Approximations – When learning to talk, learner-talkers are not expected to wait until they have language fully under control before they are allowed to use it. Rather they are expected to 'have-a-go' (i.e. to attempt to emulate what is being demonstrated). Their childish attempts are enthusiastically, warmly, and joyously received. Baby talk is treated as a legitimate, relevant, meaningful and useful contribution to the context. There is no anxiety about these unconventional forms becoming permanent fixtures in the learner's repertoire. Those who support the learner's language development expect these immature forms to drop out and be replaced by conventional forms. And they do. What is more, they have been doing so for as long as children have been learning to talk.

Employment – This condition refers to the opportunities for use and practice that are provided by children's caregivers. Young learner-talkers need both time and opportunity to employ their immature, developing language skills. They seem to need two kinds of opportunity, namely those that require social interaction with other language users and those that are done alone. Parents and other caregivers continually provide opportunities of the first type by engaging young learners in all kinds of linguistic give-and-take, subtly setting up situations in which they are forced to use their under-developed language for real and authentic purposes. Ruth Weir's (1962) classic study of the pre-sleep monologues of very young children is an example of the second kind of opportunity. Her work suggests that young learner-talkers need time away from others to practise and employ (perhaps reflect upon) what they have been learning. As a consequence of both kinds of employment children seem to gain increasing control of the conventional forms of language which they are working towards. It is as if in order to learn language they must first use it.

Response – This condition refers to the feedback or information that learner-talkers receive from the world as a consequence of using their developing language knowledge and skills. Typically, these responses are given by the significant others in the learners' lives. When the learner-talker says, as he/she points to a glass on the table, 'Dat glass', the response from the parent if it is true (i.e. it is a glass) typically goes something like this, 'Yes, that's a glass.' Exchanges like these serve the purpose of sharing information about the language and the degree of control that the learner has over it at any one time. The parent is supplying the missing bits of the child's approximation. The child is supplying the parent with an example of what he/she is currently capable of doing. It's as if the parent intuitively understands the importance of responsibility and says to herself/himself, 'I've no way of deciding which aspect of this learner's approximation is in need of adjustment just now. Therefore I'll demonstrate the conventional version of what I think was intended and leave the responsibility for deciding what is salient in this demonstration to the learner.'

These conditions can be represented graphically thus:

Figure 1

A Model of Classroom Literacy Learning

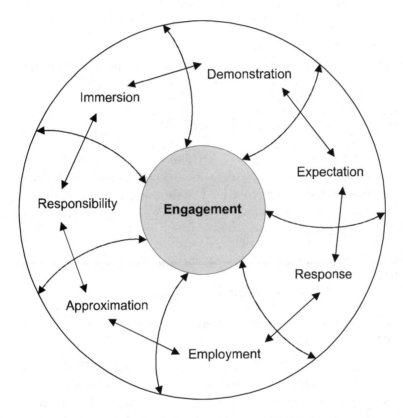

This representation shows very clearly that 'Engagement' lies at the core of any learning situation. The factors which affect the degree to which learners will engage with demonstrations can be summarised below.

Principles of Engagement

- learners are more likely to engage deeply with demonstrations if they believe that they are capable of ultimately learning or doing whatever is being demonstrated.
- learners are more likely to engage deeply with demonstrations if they believe that learning whatever is being demonstrated has some potential value, purpose, and use for them.
- learners are more likely to engage with demonstrations if they are free from anxiety.
- learners are more likely to engage with demonstrations given by someone they like, respect, admire, trust, and would like to emulate.

So what?

What are the implications of the above set of conditions? What does it mean for the way we think about the teaching and learning of literacy? There are several:

- the Conditions of Learning are very similar to what we discover about how we all go about learning something new. Just think about a time when you learned something new and consider whether these conditions applied to your learning.
- if we could apply these conditions to our literacy classrooms it might make it possible for more of our students to acquire literacy.
- this raises the question: What kinds of things can teachers do to implement these conditions in their classrooms?

We will explore the questions posed here by Brian Cambourne in later chapters.

Summary

Language learning is an active process which is shaped by the learner's interactions with others in their environment as well as learner engagement with their environment. Several key conditions, as identified by Cambourne, come together to nurture this learning. These conditions have relevance to learning to read and to the kinds of reading environments teachers might provide in their classrooms.

Key Concepts

- language as a meaning-making system
- conditions of learning:
  - immersion
  - demonstration
  - engagement
  - expectations
  - responsibility
  - employment
  - approximations
  - responses

Tutorial Activity

1. A Language Experience.

    Consider the following language experiences. Discuss with a partner or in small groups the language you would use in each of these experiences. Reflect on why you chose to use the language you did. Consider how the audience and purpose for using the language impact on the language you would choose to use.

    a. You need a new video recorder and player. You decide to 'let your fingers do the walking' and 'shop' over the phone. What language would you use to achieve the purpose of buying the video you want?

    b. You and a friend decide to take a trip to the winery countryside. You decide to rent a car and unfortunately you get a flat tyre on a back isolated dirt road. What language would you use to achieve the purpose of changing the tyre and getting on your way again?

    c. You are fed up with the pollution at the nearby beach that you frequent. You decide to write to the Council to request that they do something about it. What language would you use to achieve your purpose?

Further Reading

Cambourne, B. 1988, *The Whole Story: Natural Learning and the Acquisition of Literacy*, Ashton Scholastic, Auckland, New Zealand.
Derewianka, B. 1990, *Exploring How Texts Work*, Primary English Teaching Association, Sydney.

References

Bruner, J. 1983, *Child's Talk: Learning to Use Language*, W.W. Norton and Company, New York.
Bruner, J. 1998, *The Culture of Education*, Harvard University Press, Cambridge, MA.
Cambourne, B. 1988, *The Whole Story: Natural Learning and the Acquisition of Literacy*, Ashton Scholastic, Auckland, New Zealand.
Cambourne, B.L. 1995, 'Towards an educationally relevant theory of literacy learning: Twenty years of inquiry', *The Reading Teacher*, vol.49, no.3, pp.182-192.
Derewianka, B. 1990, *Exploring How Texts Work*, Primary English Teaching Association, Sydney.
Halliday, M.A.K. 1978, *Language as a Social Semiotic: The Social Interpretation of Language and Meaning*, Edward Arnold, London.

Halliday, M.A.K. 1980, 'Three aspects of children's language development: learning language, learning through language, learning about language', Paper presented in Master of Education Course, Sydney University, Australia.

Halliday, M.A.K. 1985, *An Introduction to Functional Grammar,* Edward Arnold, London.

Turbill, J., Butler, A. & Cambourne, B. 1999, 4th ed. *Frameworks: Literacy and Learning Staff Development Program*, University of Wollongong, Wollongong and Wayne-Finger Lakes Board of Co-operative Services, Newark, New York.

Vialle, W., Lysaght, P. & Verenikina, I. 2000, *Handbook on Child Development,* Social Science Press, Australia.

Weir, R. 1962, *Language in the Crib,* Mouton and Co, The Hague.

Chapter 2

WHAT IS READING?

*'... to completely analyse what we do when we read
would almost be the acme of a psychologist's achievements,
for it would describe some of the most intricate workings of
the human mind'.*
(Huey, 1968, cited in Harris & Hodges, 1995, p.206)

Chapter Preview

In this chapter we explore three major questions: What is reading? How
does reading 'work'? How is reading best learned? To answer these
questions we need to consider how proficient readers make meaning from
texts and the complexities involved in this process. We will explore the
reading theories that have influenced the teaching of reading over the past
forty years. Finally we will provide a framework for the teaching of reading
that reflects current theory and research.

Focal Questions

- What is reading?
- How does reading work?
- Why do we need reading theories?
- What is our model of reading?

What is Reading?

Reading is just one of the components of our language system by which we
communicate and make meaning. These components are:
- Reading
- Writing
- Speaking
- Listening

Reading is linked often with writing and called 'literacy'. At the same time, 'speaking'
and 'listening' are linked and commonly called 'oracy'. However, more recently educators
are suggesting that to be literate involves the interaction of all four language modes.

'Literacy is the ability to read and use written information and to write appropriately in a range of contexts. It is used to develop knowledge and understanding, to achieve personal growth and to function effectively in our society.

Literacy involves the integration of speaking, listening and critical thinking with reading and writing'. (Australia's Language and Literacy Policy, 1991, p.9)

While the purpose of this book is to focus on *reading,* we need to acknowledge that we too believe that reading is not separate from writing, speaking and listening. We also acknowledge that when people talk about reading they often mean different things. Thus we need to have a common working definition so that we are all talking about the same thing, when we ask the question: what is reading? A fairly broad, functional definition of reading that we believe most will accept is:

READING IS UNDERSTANDING WRITTEN TEXT.

By defining reading as understanding written text (such text may be include print and visual texts, book-based, environmental and digital texts) we simply mean that the end result of any act of engagement with a written text should be comprehension of that text. For comprehension to occur readers must first construct a meaningful message inside their heads. Without such understanding or 'comprehension' it is difficult to argue that reading has actually occurred. Of course, some readers will appear to read it, that is understand it, better than or differently from others depending on the experiences they bring to the text. We will explore this point in more detail later in this chapter.

How Does Reading 'Work'?[2]

We are going to respond to this question in two ways. Firstly, we will consider what we as proficient readers do as we try to 'read' texts. Secondly, we will explore the reading theories that try to explain how reading works, i.e. how readers go about the process of making meaning from texts. Then in the later chapters in this book we will explore how a reader goes from being a non-reader to a reader and the implications of all this for teachers.

Let us begin with what we as proficient readers do. In other words, let us develop our own personal theory of how reading works.

We will do this by experiencing a series of short activities that we will then reflect on, drawing on our own personal experiences as readers.

---

2. This section has been adapted with permission from Turbill, J., Butler, A. & Cambourne, B. 1999, 4th ed. *Frameworks: Literacy and Learning Staff Development Program.*

TASK

Read this piece of text through aloud with fluency:

> *Pokarekare ana*
> *Nga wai o Rotorua*
> *Whiti atu koe hine*
> *Matino ane e*
>
> *Ehine e*
> *Hoki mai ra*
> *Ka mate ahau*
> *I te aroha e.*

How did you fare? Would you say that you could 'read' this text?

What does this tell you about this aspect of reading and how it might be effectively taught in classrooms?

If asked, some of us might be able to say aloud the words of this well known Maori traditional song. Those of us who knew the tune would probably be able to sing it if we were not too shy. But how many of us could convince someone that we had *read* it in the sense implied by our definition? That is, we had gained some meaning from the text; we understood it; we comprehended it. Unless we happen to speak the Maori language, we were not able to understand this text, even if we were a fluent reader of other texts. So, according to our definition of reading, (i.e. reading is understanding written text) reading has not occurred. Why? Simply because comprehension of what the author intended has not occurred.

So what does this mean? To begin to understand what is happening, we need to understand something about the language processes (which we introduced in Chapter 1) that we bring to and use when reading. You will remember from Chapter 1 that we suggested that one way of looking at language processes (and thus reading) is to understand that language can be seen as comprising three subsystems. These are:

- A graphophonic system. Sometimes this term is broken into two: the graphology or visual and the phonology or sound systems. The sound/symbol relationships (the phonology and graphology systems) of the written language are referred to as the graphophonic system of language. This includes what we call 'phonics'.
- A semantic system. The background knowledge or 'knowledge of the field' is referred to as the semantic system.
- A syntactic system. The grammar of the language, the structure and word order is what is known as the syntactic system.

To be proficient language users we need knowledge of all three of these systems; that is, we use the knowledge of these three sub-systems of language simultaneously to compose meaning from texts. Writers also use the same cues or language information to compose meaning into texts.

The following venn diagram depicts the relationship between the cueing systems.

Figure 1

Three Cueing Systems of Language

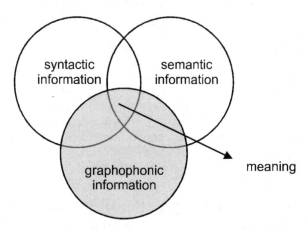

If we now consider the language information or cues that we could use when trying to 'read' Po Karekare, most of us could only indicate that we were using our graphophonic knowledge. Since we neither had any understanding of the meaning of the words nor the grammar of the language, we were not able to draw on any information from the other two sub-systems. Therefore while we may have been able to identify the sounds and pronounce them (in some way), we had not gained meaning from this text.

TASK

Jot down what information you would need to be able to read Po Karekare; that is, to understand the written text.

know the language, grammar,

What does this tell you about this aspect of reading and how it might be effectively taught in classrooms?

Let us carry out another short task. The following has been adapted from a daily newspaper.

TASK

ANZAC TEST

... Referee Bill Gordon referred the matter to the video ref. Replays revealed double movement and the ref disallowed the try. Twelve minutes later Gordon pulled back a forward pass from Vagras to second rower Mick Tiri which saw the Storm forward roaring into the clear from inside his own half. A couple of tackles after the ensuring scrum win, skipper Brendon Kay took a pass from Watson and threw a dummy before darting past Vagras to a try. Ritter scored within close range. Five eight Kay kicked and winger Verekina muffed his attempt to field it, the ball finishing in the in-goal.

Now that you've attempted to read ANZAC Test, think about these three questions:

1. Apart from names how many of the words of this text are totally new print items; That is you have never seen them in print before?

2. Apart from names, how many words do you need help with pronouncing?

3. How many words could you not use in a sentence of some kind or other?

Jot down some of the things that would help you to understand this piece of text, 'Anzac Test'.

What does this tell you about this aspect of reading and how it might be effectively taught in classrooms?

As you considered these questions most of you would have agreed that:
- You had all seen the overwhelming majority of words in print at some time in your reading careers.
- You could pronounce all of the words perhaps excluding some names.
- You could use all of the words in a sentence of some kind.

Let us look at our model of the Three Cueing Systems again and consider which of these systems we were able to use as a reader when trying to 'read' Anzac Test.

Figure 2

Three Cueing Systems of Language

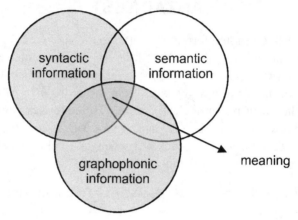

We could decode the text and pronounce all the words. So you were using your graphophonic system for information. And we also now could identify nouns, verbs and other grammatical words; that is, we could get a sense of the word order of the sentences for we were using our syntactic system. But how many of us had the background, or field knowledge of rugby league football? How many could draw on their semantic information? Without that information then it was difficult to gain the meaning from the text that the author intended.

So, how many of us can honestly claim to be able to understand and explain the meanings in this piece of written text in ways that show that we have actually read it according to our definition? This does not mean to retell it from memory, but to explain what it means to someone else while the text is there in front of our eyes.

While there would be some who could understand this text to the extent that you could picture what was going on and, given the opportunity could probably retell the scene or draw it, however there would be also many who would be hard pressed to show that they have read this piece of text; that is read it in terms of how we defined reading. Does this mean that these people have a reading problem? If they were to be given some intensive drill on each of the words in the text until they could recognise every word in isolation instantly would that help them understand it? Of course it would not, because all of us can already recognise the majority of words in the text. What if they were given some intensive 'phonic drill? Would that help? That would not help either. Most of you previously admitted that you were able to pronounce all the words, so why would you need to be given any phonic drill? Nor would dictionaries be of much help. How can we help people who can say the words, but still not understand the text? If we can imagine that this text about rugby really had to be known and understood for an important test or assignment what kind of help would be needed for them? How could an effective teacher help students deal with this piece of text?

If readers are to understand texts like this, they must be able to go beyond the words on the page. They need to understand that there is much more to reading, as we have defined it, than merely being able to recognise the words and say them. Whilst this is important there is more. A reader must also have a great deal of background knowledge about the content of the text being read and must also have control of the jargon, or the specialist language used in the text. With respect to the text we have just been working with we needed to know at least that a game of rugby league was being reported and that rugby league is played in a certain way with particular objectives, rituals, rules, conventions and that certain words and phrases have quite unique meanings in the context of the game. If we have such knowledge we know what an 'Anzac Test' is, what a 'try' is (and that it is OK for this word to be a noun), what a 'video ref' is, we would know what 'muffing an attempt' means and that a ball can end up 'lying in in-goal'.

Yet what about those students who do know about rugby league but who still would not be able to read the text? As well as needing prior knowledge and specialist language, potential readers must also be in control of the strategies which make the construction of meaning possible. Proficient readers all have and use these strategies quite subconsciously. It is important if we are to understand reading that we make strategies consciously. These reading strategies can be demonstrated in the next short activity.

TASK

Read the 'Post Office text' which follows. There are no right or wrong answers in this text. Try to find the best possible word for each deletion. The purpose is for you to become conscious of the strategies that you use to fill in the gaps. Forcing ourselves to 'read' mutilated texts highlights for us the reading strategies that we use as proficient readers.

At quarter past nine early in January, a woman entered the Post Office at Martin Place and inquired of one of the clerks if a letter was awaiting her. It was her third visit in as many days. On this _occassion_ the clerk was able to _help_ her.

He handed her a _letter_ which she opened immediately. Stepping back from the _counter_, she _quietly_ looked to see the name of the sender _as_ if to reassure herself, and then, c_rumplin_g the letter in her hand, hurried_ out _ with an air of strong nervous a_ttentio_n.

Although the day was warm and summery, she was _dress_ed entirely in

☞

black, _which_ served to set off the extreme pallor of her _complex_ ion
and the brilliancy of _her_ eyes. Her name was Petria Vassilova. She was
known as an _enemy_ of the country _and_ a grave risk to the security of the
State.

Carefully go back to each deletion that you have now tried to fill and consider
what you did as a reader (in other words, what strategies did you use as a
reader) in order to fill that deletion with a word that made sense to you, i.e.
made sense to the text.

What does this tell you about this aspect of reading and how it might be
effectively taught in classrooms?

Figure 3

Three Cueing Systems of Language

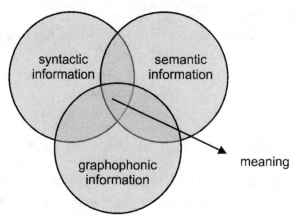

In order to complete this task you would have needed to access all three cueing
systems. When readers complete these types of tasks they usually discover similar
kinds of things about reading that they have never consciously thought about before.
What they discover (as we are sure you have also) can be expressed in the form of four
principles.

Four principles of reading:

1. Effective readers do a lot of predicting.
2. Effective readers use certain strategies to help them over difficulties and
    blockages.
3. Effective readers draw heavily on their background knowledge.
4. Effective readers are typically confident enough to read difficult texts.

Effective readers will always have their minds a little ahead of where their eyes are looking. They are anticipating or predicting what will be coming next. Predicting is just one of the strategies effective readers use all the time.

The range of strategies used by effective readers is made possible because of three sources of knowledge or information: the reader's background knowledge about the content of the subject, his or her knowledge of language itself as well as the reader's ability to work out the sound/symbol relationships of the letters in the text.

Everyone carries around in their heads a vast store of information about language and how it works. From this store comes information about the language patterns of a particular subject, the different letters, letter combinations and pronunciations as well as the kinds of words, phrases and sentence structures that are likely to occur in the text. This information is drawn on by the reader to make his or her predictions more accurate in the process of reading.

Effective reading strategies *— plan → outcome.*

If effective readers experience readers' block or loss of meaning they may employ any or all of the following strategies (did you also find that you used these strategies?):

1. Leave the problem and read on, hoping to find more information and clues to meaning in the rest of the text
2. Re-read the sentence in the hope that this will provide understanding once the words are more familiar
3. Leave a problematic word out or substitute a word that will fit the patterns of the text to see if meaning can be gained despite the word block.

Such strategies only become possible because the effective reader is confident enough and willing to take risks, to have a go at reading something that is unfamiliar or apparently too difficult.

On the other hand, ineffective readers are often unaware of or unable for particular reasons to use these strategies. They may experience difficulties in using these strategies perhaps because English is their second language. Ineffective readers remain reluctant to 'have-a-go', often because they lack relevant background information about the subject or alternatively relevant knowledge about the patterns of the language used in the text. Because of these reasons, ineffective readers are not confident that they can make sense of written text.

We have attempted to answer the question 'how does reading work' through examining our own reading process. Now let us explore this question by examining the theories of others.

making an attempt.

Reading Theories of Others

While we have attempted to develop insights in how reading works by examining our own reading practices, we must acknowledge that reading is a complex process. Research is constantly being carried out to unravel the complexities of reading. Many a teacher asks why is theory important, suggesting that all they need to know is how and what to do as teachers of reading without knowing why. However most reading experts will agree with Anstey and Bull (1996, p.28) who attest that '... theory is at the centre of the educational enterprise and plays a crucial role in delivering quality instruction'.

There are various reading theories that attempt to explain the reading process and the strategies involved in and related to the activities and operations that comprise the experience that we call reading. While we are not going to go into detailed analysis of the various reading theories proposed to explain how reading 'works' and how readers learn to read, we do want to outline the broad categories of reading theories (Sloan & Whitehead, 1986) and briefly explain these. We believe that understanding the range of reading theories is useful because it allows us to also understand the historical development of reading research and instruction.

Reading theories are also useful because they indicate the set of criteria or values used to create that theory. They also provide a basis for research that answers important questions about reading and reading behaviour. This research is used to redesign the theories. Often a theory of reading is able to be represented diagrammatically to explain how the theory works; this is called a model.

There are three broad categories into which most reading theories can be placed. These have an historical base related to the developments in psychology (the study of human behaviour) and linguistics (the study of language). The major theory groups are generally referred to as:

- The 'bottom-up' theory
- The 'top-down' theory
- The 'interactive' or 'transactive' theory

Let us briefly explore each of these.

Bottom-up theories

Bottom-up theories argue that meaning is embedded in the text and that meaning travels from the 'bottom' (the page) 'up' to the eyes. Thus bottom-up theorists define reading as beginning with the letters that form printed words, words then form sentences, sentences form texts and so on. From this building process of combining small parts to form the whole text it is argued meaning will emerge as the end result. Successful reading thus is the ability to perceive enough sequence of language from the page to allow the reader to understand what the writer intended the text to convey. If one subscribes to this theory of reading one would display certain beliefs about reading and how it 'works'.

Beliefs

The reading process consists of a number of skills. If these are taught from simple to more complex they combine to form the reading process. Reading is fundamentally visual. The visual stimulus on the page needs to be identified and matched with the corresponding sound. Thus children need to be taught how to make fine visual discriminations about text and to be able to match these with the sounds. The stress of this approach to reading is on accurate visual discrimination of letters and words and achieving an automatic phoneme-grapheme (sound/letter) correspondence.

Practice

Those who hold to bottom up theories of reading will argue that children need to be taught to discriminate letters, to recognise words in isolation quickly and to learn phonics systematically and hierarchically. Children who fail to learn using this approach tend to be given more visual discrimination and more phonic analysis training on the assumption that more intensive learning is required. This approach also believes that the written form of the language is more abstract than spoken language and requires a different set of skills in order to learn it.

This skills approach to reading dominated research prior to the 1970s and had its origins in behaviourist psychology (see Vialle, Lysaght & Verenikina 2000, p.7). It led to the development of commercially produced skills-based reading schemes for use in schools.

Top-down theories

'Top-down' theories emphasise that reading begins in the head of the reader; that is the reader moves from the' top' – the brain – 'down' to the text on the page. Readers use their background knowledge stored in their memories in the brain to unlock the text. Without this prior knowledge meaning cannot be made from text. The object of reading is making meaning of the text by using the reader's background knowledge. The top-down theories adopt a constructivist stance (see Vialle, Lysaght & Verenikina, 2000, pp.5,19) and link reading comprehension to factors both inside and outside the reader. This approach came to prominence in the 1970s. These theories link fluent reading with the ability of the reader to access the three cueing systems within written language, the semantic, syntactic and graphophonic systems simultaneously.

Beliefs

The reading process is complex and depends on factors both 'inside' and 'outside' the reader. Reading, it is argued, is only partially visual and that accurate phoneme/ grapheme response is peripheral to the reader gaining meaning from the words.

Successful reading depends on the interaction between the material selected, the context of the information and the reader's prior knowledge.

Sloan and Whitehead (1986, p.3) describe the bottom up theory thus:

'This view espouses that language (and in the case of reading, written language) contains three kinds of information (cues) :

- **Semantic** information, or meaning information, embodies word meanings and sentence meanings.
- **Syntactic**, or language structure information, is information about the order and structure of parts of language.
- **Graphophonic** information is information about the relationship of the graphemes(letters) and the sounds of the language (phonemes). This information embodies letter sequence information, or spelling information which signals meaning. For example, the letter sequences in the different spellings for an identically pronounced set of words show that letter sequences represent meaning as well as sound, e.g. *weigh*, *way*, *whey*.

Readers have semantic, syntactic and letter sequence information available as prior knowledge. Thus, when reading the semantic, syntactic and letter sequence cues available in the text trigger the semantic, syntactic and letter sequence information in the head of the reader. From this interaction between the print (visual information) and the prior knowledge (non-visual information) held by the reader, meaning is constructed. In bringing about this interaction, readers make use of prediction and exploit the redundancies which exist in written language.'

Practices

Emphasis in these classrooms is that reading is first and foremost a meaning-making process. Thus, children are encouraged to use all the information or cues provided to them from their background knowledge of the topic and their understanding about how the language functions and flows as well as the grapheme/phoneme relationships to predict, sample and confirm meanings that are being constructed in the reader's head. For example, in this type of classroom you may typically hear something like….

'You just read, "John lived in a brick horse with his mother and father". Does that make sense?'

Or when children encounter a word they don't recognise the advice might be…

'Read on and then come back and see if you can make sense of it.'

Interactive or transactive theories

Sloan and Whitehead (1986), Ruddell and Speaker (1985) and Rumelhart (1994) offer a third group of theories that they have labelled the interactive. They suggest that while that reading is predominately a meaning-making process and therefore incorporates all that is embedded in the 'top-down' view, it does require, on occasion, that readers focus on skills – a position more aligned to a 'bottom-up' view. In more recent times the interactive model of reading has taken on a more social view of reading.

This view reflects the current research perspective concerning the complexity of the reading process. Readers can be taught to adjust their reading strategies in a flexible manner in order to choose the best strategy that meets the purpose of the current text and their purpose for reading it.

Goodman and Watson (1999, p.114) propose that,

'reading is a meaning-making process. As readers, we consider the meaning the author is making, while at the same time, we build meaning for ourselves. We use our language, our thoughts, and our own view of the world to understand the author's meaning. The language, thoughts and worldviews of both the author and the reader are influenced by personal and social histories. Our interpretations are structured by what we know.'

Goodman and Watson suggest that reading is social in nature as readers 'transact' with the author's text and in doing so they argue, 'the author and reader are also powerfully influenced by views of literacy held by their cultural groups.'

Beliefs

Reading therefore is a social act. We read for many social purposes. The making of meaning is an active, constructive and cultural process (Reid, 1998). Reading is the transaction (Rosenblatt, 1978) that occurs between the cultural prior knowledge of the reader and the cultural meanings of the author. Children bring to the reading process all of their previous reading, writing, listening and speaking experiences which are cultural in nature. They use these previous experiences to assist them to 'make sense' of the reading task they are undertaking. So the text triggers a particular 'schema' (vision, viewpoint, experience) in the brain of the reader which is then matched against the specific text. This schema guides the reader to select from the text whatever relevant information assists in making meaning of that text. This particular model of reading sits well with the current focus on how specific text types are constructed (narratives, reports, recipes and so on) and how readers cope with reading these texts.

Practice

Supporters of this model of reading believe that skills are taught at 'the point of need' in the course of using reading and writing for 'real world' purposes. While it is believed that reading skills need to be taught explicitly, this theory also argues that these skills be contextualised, that is, be taught within the context of the whole text. This is often referred to as 'whole-to-part-to-whole instruction'.

Classroom teachers who adhere to this reading theory believe that:

- Reading teaching should focus on meaning-making
- Readers need to know their phonics and other word attack skills
- Readers need to know prediction strategies
- Reading can be improved by exposing children to games and other activities that develop their semantic background and teach basic syntactic structures
- Reading strategies should exploit prior knowledge

- Readers need to be exposed to a wide range of text types (this includes 'good' literature, magazines, factual texts, digital texts, media and other environmental texts)
- Readers need time to read
- Reading should be modelled by significant others
- Readers need to know the purpose for reading
- Readers need support when loss of meaning occurs
- Readers need to develop confidence in themselves as readers.

A Social Model of Reading

In the above discussion we have only been able to touch on some of the many theories of reading and how these relate to classroom practices. To do more in a book of this size and type is impossible. Debates over reading theories and their relevant practices have continued for decades. Whether to teach children using only a 'bottom-up' approach with a strong focus on teaching phonics or whether to teach a 'top-down' approach, we believe no longer are the relevant questions. Our view expands upon that discussed above and aligns with that of Allan Luke and Peter Freebody (Freebody & Luke, 1990; Freebody, 1992; Luke, 1993, 1994; Luke & Freebody, 1999a, 1999b; Luke, 2000) who have offered 'four components of success' (1990, p.7) for reading. They argue that,

'in drawing attention to these components we want to direct attention away from the question of "which method affords adequate literacy?" toward the larger and necessarily prior question of "which aspects of literacy or indeed which literacies are offered or emphasised by various programs?"'

Furthermore, they suggest that a successful reader in our society needs to develop and sustain the resources to adopt four related roles: code breaker ("how do I crack this?"), text participant ("what does this mean?"), text user ("what do I do within the here and now?") and text analyst ("what does all this do to me?") (p.7).

Freebody and Luke (1990) offered these categories for educators to 'consider what "literacies" are offered in various instructional programs'. We have taken up their challenge and used the categories as a framework for the rest of the content in this book. We believe that it is a framework that allows for, yet extends, the best of all the above models, particularly in that it can acknowledge the importance of the 'whole-to-part-to-whole process' and the role that the three subsystems of language - the semantic, syntactic and graphophonic systems – play in the reading process.

The following model adapted from the NSW Department of Education's Framework for Teaching Reading K-6 (1997, p.9) best depicts our views:

Figure 4

A Model of Reading as a Set of Social Practices

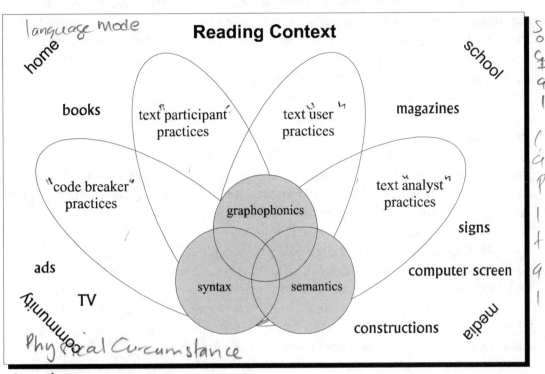

Handwritten annotations around the figure:

CULTURAL CAPITAL

language mode

SOCIAL CAPITAL

home

funds of knowl

Physical Circumstance

Community

This model demonstrates the complexities of the relationships between each of the components that need to be present in order that children become successful readers. We will briefly discuss the individual elements of this model. The remaining chapters will discuss these in more detail, relating them to classroom practice.

Reading context

Readers learn to read in social contexts. We use literacy to achieve a range of social purposes that are set within our cultural situations. The ways that we each use literacy reflects the social purposes that are valued by our differing cultural situations (Luke, 2000). These literacy practices are used and valued by different cultural groups in various ways.

As readers attempt to gain control of reading they will encounter a range of differing texts. These texts (that could also include illustrations, maps, diagrams, non-verbal communication, video, television and computer) will each be constructed in different ways in order that they achieve their social purpose. For example, the social purpose of a narrative is to entertain and instruct. This social purpose influences both the textual structure (orientation – a beginning, complication – a problem to be solved and resolution

– the solving of the problem) as well as the language features (use of past tense, word families, action verbs, particular nouns etc) common to the narrative text type or 'genre'.

At times it may appear that a particular range of text types are viewed as more legitimate, valuable or important than others. For example, the text types used within the school context, such as 'the essay' and 'the report', are often seen to have greater value (that is, more legitimate) than those texts used within the community or in the home environment, such as 'a birthday invitation', 'advertisements', 'signs', 'letter to Grandma', 'labels' and more recently the computer and internet.

In reality, children learn about the value of reading long before they begin their formal schooling through a variety of media in a myriad of situations. Many children come to their early school years with skills in the use of language and literacy knowledge that are based around those practices prevalent within their own unique home and community environment. These children are already aware of some of the ways that reading and writing are used within their own families and communities (Reid, 1998). They have been exposed to the ways that language is used to achieve a range of very individualised and perhaps culturally specific social purposes.

They see and use environmental print in their community as they use road signs and fast food symbols, recognise the title of a television program or a food label in the supermarket. At home they may be exposed to the reading of stories or in navigating a video game or to the power of advertising leaflets or in choosing food using a fast food outlets menu or in watching a television program chosen by using a TV guide.

Each of these reading experiences is valuable and important and capable of being used to create strong links between the community, family and the school. This could be promoted in the classroom by providing children with access to a wider range of text types that includes those found within the community and family situation, in addition to those considered to be more conventional or school-based text types.

Language information

Children learning to read must gain control of and integrate three language sources in order to become successful readers (NSW Department of Education, Teaching Reading: A K-6 Framework, 1997; English K-6 Syllabus, 1998).We have referred to these information sources as subsystems of language or 'the cueing systems of language'. See page 20.

In order to become successful readers children must learn to access and integrate all three sources of information. In addition, Freebody and Luke (1990) have proposed that to be successful readers in today's culture children must also learn and be able to use a range of other skills and practices that relate to what they originally termed 'the four reader roles'. In later writing Luke and Freebody (Luke & Freebody, 1999; Luke, 2000) suggest that each of these roles activate a particular 'family of practices', that is practices that are all highly related.

Freebody and Luke (1990) have labelled these sets of reader practices as code breaker, text participant, text user and text analyst. For the purposes of this book we will artificially separate each of these sets of practices and discuss them as disconnected entities. We will do this in order to highlight the practices involved in each. In no way do we mean to imply that these practices are separate entities or that they should be seen to be utilised by readers in a linear lock-step manner. In reality, successful readers utilise these practices according to the particular reading task. At times one particular set of practices will feature more prominently in a reading encounter while the others assume more minor roles. In a different reading situation another set of practices may need to be utilised to a greater degree depending on the text and the purposes for reading the text. As Luke and Freebody (1999, p.7) point out,

'... all of these repertoires are variously mixed and orchestrated in proficient reading and writing. The key concept in the model is necessity and not sufficiency – each is necessary for literacy in new conditions, but in and of themselves, none of the four families of practice is sufficient for literate citizens/subjects.'

Code breaker practices

To be a successful reader one needs to successfully engage in the written script of the culture. This includes the alphabetic script of written English, but also the logos, media signs, layout and format that are all used to convey meaning in some way. A reader takes on code breaker practices to decode the visual information in the text, to work out what the text says. Readers will ask questions of themselves such as 'how do I crack this text?' or 'what are the patterns and conventions of this particular text?'

Readers activate code breaker practices when they focus on the sounds in words, whole words, sound/letter correspondences, sentences and paragraphs, punctuation conventions, left to right directionality, book conventions, grammatical information, word meanings. Code breaker practices are a major focus for early readers as they struggle to make sense of unknown words in the context of what looks and sounds right. Older readers use code breaker practices but they only become conscious of them when they monitor their own reading and self correct when meaning is lost.

Text participant practices

A reader uses text participant practices when activating prior knowledge about a text in order to understand the meaning of that text. Readers will ask questions like 'what is this text trying to say?' or 'what are the possible meanings of this text?' or 'what do I already know about this topic?'.

Readers activate text participant practices when they focus on the way the text is constructed to make meaning, the literal and figurative meanings of words and expressions and how this text relates to their prior knowledge. This is a role that parents and teachers often perform for beginning readers as they attempt to engage the reader by personalising the text for early readers. Early readers often use the illustrations to gain an understanding of the text. Older readers use text participant practices when they explore the variety of meanings in a text.

Text user practices

A reader draws on text user practices to understand the way in which the particular text urges them to take some action. They will ask questions like 'what do I do with this text, here and now?' or 'what are my options and alternatives?' or 'why am I reading this text?'

Readers activate text user practices when they use the text in social situations to achieve social purposes, interact with others in the classroom around the text or participate in events in which the text plays a part. Early readers could be using a recipe to make pancakes or a procedure to construct an ant farm. Older readers may respond to a text and justify that response. They are also aware of their ability to use a text in order to select from an array of products or services.

Text analyst practices

A reader uses text analyst practices to understand the underlying and unstated assumptions in the text and the way the text attempts to position them as a reader. They will ask questions like 'what is this text trying to do to me?' or 'whose interests are being served by this text?' or 'which views or points of view are silent?'

Readers activate text analyst practices when they talk about an opinion, bias and point of view in a text, present an alternative position to the one taken by the text or decide to endorse the position taken by the text or perhaps think about what the writer of the text believes. Early readers may consider that texts are written from a particular point of view. Older readers are able to recognise that no text is neutral and the information is presented by the author to influence a reader in some way.

Summary

In this chapter we have examined how we go about the process of reading. We have briefly explored the broad categories of reading theories that others have proposed and we have offered a model of reading that we feel best suits our current philosophy and practices as teachers of reading.

In summary, we believe that effective readers display and use the following skills, strategies and knowledge:

- have knowledge about the sources of information (semantic, syntactic, graphophonic)
- have strategies for accessing and integrating information from these three sources

- have knowledge of texts and how these are structured within different contexts
- have strategies for activating the four 'families of practices' of the reader

Reading is a complex process and the range of definitions used to describe this process reflects the diverse viewpoints of the many differing theorists that have contributed to reading research. As children grow and develop as readers they demonstrate growing skills, knowledge and understanding of reading. It is important to realise that not all children will develop in the same way or at the same time. And teachers must plan for the diversity of skills, understandings and knowledge that children bring to the reading context.

Therefore children need a balanced school reading program to develop a range of essential skills in order that they develop:

- contextual knowledge
- knowledge about the sources of available information
- skills and practices in reading as code breakers, text participants, text users and text analysts.

The remaining chapters in this book will examine these areas in more detail.

Key Concepts

- 'bottom-up' theories of reading
- interactive theories of reading
- code breaker practices
- text user practices
- 'top-down' theories of reading
- reading as social practices
- text participant practices
- text analyst practices

Tutorial Activities

As we have already discussed there is a strong relationship between people's view of reading theory and how they believe reading should be taught (what we call the pedagogy of reading). It is interesting to gauge how people in the community perceive reading and reading instruction. In order to do so we suggest you ask these questions of at least two people.

Choose two people who are quite different (for example, a school aged person and an older person; a professional person and a skilled worker; a male and female)

Record the responses to the questions and then write a brief account of what these responses tell you about your interviewees' views of reading:

Begin by asking yourself these questions:

1.   What do you think 'reading' is?

2.   Why do you read?

3.   What do you read?

4.   How do you think reading is best learned?

Further Readings

Lowe, K. (ed), 1994, *Growing into Readers,* Primary English Teaching Association, Sydney.

Hancock, J. (ed), 1999, *The Explicit Teaching of Reading*, International Reading Association, Newark, Delaware.

NSW Board of Studies, 1998, English K-6 Syllabus and Support Materials, NSW Board of Studies

NSW Department of Education and Training, 1997, Teaching Reading: A K-6 Framework, NSW Department of Education and Training, Sydney.

Chapter 3

THE READING CONTEXT

*'All reading has to happen somewhere. And every reader
knows that where we read affects how we read.'*
(Chambers, 1991, p.7)

Chapter Preview

This chapter focuses on the reading context in the school setting. It will
revisit the Conditions of Learning outlined in Chapter 1 and explore how
these are reflected in the reading context of the classroom. It will also
briefly examine the organisational strategies that best support the teaching
and learning of reading.

Focal Questions

- What factors constitute the reading context of a classroom?
- How do the Conditions of Learning translate into an effective
  reading context?
- What are the organisational strategies of modelled reading, guided
  reading and independent reading?

Introduction

In the last chapter we introduced a model of reading that we believe best depicts our
view of the reading process and how it is best learned. We pointed out that reading is
both a social and functional process. Just how and why we read therefore is dependent
upon the context in which we find ourselves. Classrooms are such contexts as are
reading on a train, at work, in bed and so on. We also introduced the framework of
Freebody and Luke's 'four reader roles'. However before we explore each of these
roles and the practices they entail in detail, we believe that it would be helpful for us to
provide a brief overview of the ideal reading context in the classroom.

The Conditions of Learning in the Reading Context

In chapter 1 we shared with you Cambourne's Conditions of Learning. Cambourne argues that his research has demonstrated that when these conditions are operating in a setting at an optimal level learning is both powerful and durable (1988, 1995). So just how do these conditions translate into classroom practice for the teaching and learning of reading? The following framework demonstrates the general principles for each condition and some key classroom practices. We refer you to the References for Further Reading at the end of this chapter for a more detailed description.

Figure 1

A Framework For Turning A Theory Of Learning Into Classroom Reading Instruction

CONDITION	GENERAL PRINCIPLE	SOME POSSIBLE CLASSROOM STRATEGIES
Immersion	• Visual saturation with print/text • Aural saturation of sounds of written texts	Wall Print, Print Walks, SSR, Shared Book (Big Books) Teacher Read-Aloud, Shared Reading, Taped Books, Chanting, Choral Reading
Demonstration	• Model the process, make explicit the invisible processes that make critical literacy possible • Collect and display models (examples) of different kinds of texts	Teacher Read-Aloud, Shared Reading accompanied by 'think-alouds' Joint construction of texts accompanied by 'think-alouds'. Focus can be on processes, knowledge and understandings that make effective spelling, reading, writing, and critical literacy possible.
Engagement	• Communicate a set of reasons for becoming highly productive, critically literate learners. These reasons must be relevant to the students you teach.	Propagandise the value of literacy through constant messages, explicit reasons, personal stories, 'nagging', posters, models, demonstrations of power and value of literacy in this culture
Expectations	• Communicate message through language and behaviour that every student is capable of acquiring literacy, and that you expect every child to become a critically literate persons	Avoid ability grouping, 'put down' language. Use flexible, mixed ability groups which continually change. Make explicit the processes, knowledge, understanding that effective users of literacy have under control. Constantly remind them that they all learned to talk -a much harder task.
Responsibility	• Encourage students to make some decisions about what/how they learn. Make explicit the idea that good learners know how to make learning decisions. Model and demonstrate examples of 'taking responsibility' or 'ownership' of learning.	Devise activities which don't have simple 'right-wrong' answers. Insist that comments and judgments are justified wherever possible. Set up support structures, processes that allow students to 'take responsibility' for learning. Use language of speculation, e.g. 'What else could you do? Why would you do that?'
Employment	Opportunities to use and practice developing spelling skills and know-how	Lots of activities which can only be successfully completed through reading, writing, talking, listening, discussing, sharing, reflecting, for authentic and meaningful purposes.

☞

Approximation	• Communicate that: – 'having-a-go' i.e. making an attempt and not getting it perfect first go is fundamental to learning. – 'mistakes' are our friends in that they help us adjust and refine our knowledge, understandings and skills so that next time we do better. – ultimately our approximations must become conventional (Expectations)	Share stories of how we learn to do things outside of school – like learning to talk, learning to skate, play tennis etc. Highlight the role that approximations and responses play. Model and demonstrate good/bad miscues as approximations that help/hinder readers writers, spellers etc. Discuss spelling approximations as 'temporary spellings' (not 'invented') and study similarities/differences to conventional spelling. Model/demonstrate how effective readers/ writers deal with approximations.
Response	Pay close attention to learners' approximations and re-cycle demonstrations, models which contain information, knowledge they've not got under control. Draw explicit attention to salient features of demonstrations/models that will help learner modify approximation.	Set up structures/processes which make it possible for learners to receive feedback (responses) from multiple sources, e.g. other students as well as teacher. Constantly model how effective readers use various cues available to create/understand meaning.

TASK

Try using these conditions as a framework for observing classroom teaching, particularly during the reading block. What type of immersion in written language exists? What demonstrations of reading and written texts are the students receiving? What expectations does the teacher and the classroom context give to students about reading? Who is taking responsibility for the learning of reading? How are approximations accepted? In what way? What opportunities do students have for reading? What type of response or feedback do students get to their reading? What purpose does this serve?

Teaching/Learning Strategies in the Reading Context

The above conditions and the various classroom practices that are provided and that you may have seen can be organised into three broad teaching/learning organisational strategies. These strategies are periods of time set aside each day for the teaching and learning of reading (and writing, spelling and all aspects of language). Each has a specific purpose and structure in which both teacher and students play certain roles.

The following model adapted from the work of Margaret Mooney (1990, p.12) clearly shows the teacher/student relationship. Mooney talks about the importance of providing time for 'reading to' children, time for 'reading with' children and time for 'reading by' children (i.e. time when children read by themselves). In the reading context of the classroom these opportunities of time can be translated into Modelled Reading, Guided Reading and Independent Reading times.

Modelled Reading	Guided Reading	Independent Reading
Child control Teacher support	Child control Teacher support	Child control Teacher support
Reading to children	**Reading with children**	**Reading by children**

Modelled Reading

Modelled reading is a time when the teacher reads to children, immersing them in the language of written texts. These texts may include brochures, science books, poetry, narratives and much more. The material chosen to be read may take the form of a 'big book' – books that have been enlarged so that students can see and even 'read along' with the text as the teacher reads it; texts that have been enlarged and placed on overhead projectors or children may simply listen as the teacher reads from a conventional book. The purpose of this reading is to firstly demonstrate how a proficient reader reads. However, the teacher also may choose to demonstrate any one of the many skills and knowledge that a reader needs to understand and use. Modelled reading (sometimes called Shared Reading, or Shared Book Experience) is high on teacher support and guidance. Teachers use this time to teach certain skills or knowledge that they have assessed their students need to learn. Modelled reading can be carried out with the whole class or with a smaller group of children.

In modelled reading:

- teachers – read to, show, demonstrate, explain, instruct, interpret student responses
- students – watch, engage, listen, follow, share, question, participate.

Guided Reading

Guided reading is a time when the teacher works with a small group of children who have been assessed by the teacher to have similar reading needs. It is an instructional time when the children read and the teacher guides or 'scaffolds' the reading. The purpose of the guided reading session is to enable students to practise effective skills and strategies which have been taught in modelled reading sessions.

Guided reading is a context in which the teacher supports each reader's development of effective skills and strategies for processing new texts at increasingly challenging levels of difficulty. It:

- gives children the opportunity to develop as individual readers while participating in a socially supported activity
- gives teachers the opportunity to observe individuals as they process new texts
- gives individual readers the opportunity to develop reading strategies so that they can read increasingly difficult texts independently
- gives children enjoyable, successful experiences in reading for meaning
- develops the abilities needed for independent reading
- helps children learn how to introduce texts to themselves.

Two important factors in organising guided reading groups are that teachers constantly assess their students' reading needs so that they can be grouped in 'like groups' and secondly that teachers choose reading books that challenge yet will support the readers in the group. *How does G.R. actually wks.*

In guided reading:

- teachers – support, prompt, guide, question, scaffold, observe, instruct, make inferences about further reading, assess and record
- students – try, explore, problem-solve, experiment, take risks, approximate, predict, self-correct, practise.

E.g. Dem skil ⇒ Bloom's Taxanomy activities, were allocated for readers of all reading levels + G.R. level had activities to do from..

Independent Reading

Independent reading is a time when children read by themselves. Books that they *Synthesis* read need to be familiar and at a level that children can read with ease. In independent reading situations teachers construct conditions for children to read, explore and respond to texts independently. This may include working through activities such as sequencing texts, researching information, and many other reading activities that children can carry out independently. In independent reading:

- teachers – construct, encourage, respond, question, observe, record
- students – initiate, select, use, control, practise, consider, discuss, evaluate, justify, record.

A key to the success of these organisational strategies is being able to assess the children's reading needs and to group them accordingly so that the children can work in small guided reading sessions with the teacher. However, Mooney reminds us that equally important is that the book that the teacher chooses for the students to read needs to support the reader yet has sufficient challenges in it to 'stretch' the reader (or as Vygotskians would say – draw the reading into their 'zone of proximal development'. See Vialle, Lysaght & Verenikina, 2000, p.33).

Assessment and Evaluation

Assessment is the process of the collection of data that provides the means to evaluate a learning act, in this case, reading. Assessment and evaluation are a vital part of the teaching and learning cycle that forms the basis for a range of decisions that impact within the learning culture. They provide information about the learner and also about the learning culture. The NSW English K-6 Syllabus (1998) suggests that there are three forms of assessment. These are formative, summative and diagnostic. Formative assessment is based upon day-to-day classroom activities and involves informal interaction and systematic observation of the student. Formative assessment provides an on-going profile of the student.

Summative assessment is the practice of making more formal judgements about student achievements and usually occurs towards the end of a unit of work or a term. It involves a more systematic analysis of the information that has been collected on students' learning. The results of summative assessment are some form of record or report or profile of the students' achievements. Formative and summative assessment work hand-in-hand as one cannot make judgements about students achievements if one has not collected sufficient information about the students from the day to day teaching learning activities.

A third form of assessment suggested by the Syllabus is diagnostic assessment. This is the process of using the information gathered to determine the each student's future needs.

Teachers implement a range of assessment strategies in order to observe the range of reading behaviours that students are using in the reading context. These include:

- Observation. Teachers are constantly observing what their students are doing. These observations form the basis of teacher judgements as to how students are progressing, if an activity is working or not and so on.
- Checklists. Teachers develop lists of 'things' – skills, strategies, books read – that they want their children to achieve. They then can use strategies such as observation to check whether their students are achieving these or not. Sometimes checklists are commercially produced, however the most useful checklist is one that the teacher has developed to best suit the reading context.
- Teacher-made tests. A teacher-made test can be something as simple as a series of words on cards and used to see if children can read the words automatically,

A Process for Assessing Reading Development

Collecting Evidence	• Teachers collect information about students' reading using a variety of strategies, multiple opportunities and varying contexts, for example: – observing reading behaviours in modelled, guided and independent reading situations, – observing young students' early 'reading' behaviours – using oral and written retellings of text read, – taking running records, – keeping records of student progress in guided reading, – using comprehension responses during and after reading, – analysing the reading strategies the student uses in guided reading, using student self-assessment, such as independent reading records, – using work samples, such as student's writing to check sound/letter correspondence, – analysing student's incorrect responses to a cloze procedure to determine the type of error the student is making, – analysing student's standardised test results.
Making Judgements	Teachers analyse the evidence collected to identify what students can do, and match this against the K-6 English syllabus outcomes and their knowledge of students reading behaviours.
Planning learning experiences	Teachers plan ways to meet students' needs through grouping for whole-class, small group and individualised instruction.
Teaching	Teachers use teaching and learning experiences that develop the skills and knowledge needed to achieve the reading outcomes towards which students are moving.
Monitoring, recording student progress	Teachers continually look for evidence of development in students' reading over time, and design specific opportunities for students to demonstrate reading achievement.
Reviewing, replanning teaching/learning programs	Teachers monitor reading development and record students' progress. Effective methods that operate as part of teaching and learning and that are manageable, not overly detailed or time consuming are best. Teachers constantly review, adjust and re-plan teaching and learning activities to support the reading needs of the whole class and of individuals or groups of students in order to facilitate progress along the reading pathway.

(Department of Education 1997, Teaching Reading K-6 Framework, pp.8-9)

to a cloze passage with specific deletions chosen in order to check students' skills and knowledge.

- Observation Survey. An observation survey is a type of checklist of reading skills and behaviours that teachers can use as they observe students read. (See Clay 1993, *An Observation Survey of Early Literacy Achievement*, Heinemann, Auckland.)
- Standardised Tests. These are tests that have been standardised. That is, they are created in such a way that the test if given the same way to all children. The children's scores can then be judged against the standard of other students. The NSW Basic Skills Test is a form of standardised testing.
- Portfolios. Portfolios are a collection of students' work that has been collected for the purpose of demonstrating progress over time.

The NSW Department of Education's Framework for Teaching Reading K-6 (1997) has provided a useful overview of the process for assessing reading. A similar assessment and teaching cycle is advocated by Cambourne and Turbill (1994).

Catering for Students from Diverse Cultural and Linguistic Backgrounds

Australia is a multicultural, multiracial and multiclass society and thus there is a great deal diversity in the cultural and linguistic backgrounds of children as they enter our schools and classrooms. School cultures represent the dominant middle class culture of our society so for the children from diverse backgrounds the culture of school is likely to be a very different one. Children's language and culture are inextricably linked; thus it is important for teachers to understand that students from diverse linguistic and cultural backgrounds may find the language used in the school culture rather strange and confusing and thus as a result be at a disadvantage to their peers whose home culture and language is more likely to match that used in the school. Such an understanding has implications for the reading context that will be set up by the teacher.

Some children such as Aboriginal and Torres Strait Islanders come from cultures that have existed in Australia for thousands of years. Other children have been born in Australia yet grow up in cultural groups where English may not be the first language. Others experience poverty and family crisis and others are born in various countries of the world and come to Australia as immigrants. All these children have a language that serves them well in their cultural group. It simply is not the language of school or the dominant culture of Australia. Thus teachers need to be very conscious of the differing language and reading needs of these students when planning the reading context.

For these students the semantic, syntactic and graphophonic systems used in their first language (whether this be Aboriginal English, 'working class' English, Chinese,

Arabic, Italian and any one of the many languages other than English spoken in Australia) will be markedly different from that used in Standard English of the classroom.

These students will enter school displaying a wide range of proficiency even in their first language. Some children will come from homes where English is not spoken at all, some perhaps from bilingual households where English and a language other than English is spoken. While some children may have excellent literacy skills in their first language others will arrive at school with limited first language literacy (Gibbons, 1991). Some, or a combination of all these scenarios are possible (and probable) in a classroom.

Gibbons (1991, p.3) reminds us that it would be foolish to assume that because children so readily acquire a 'playground language' at school they will also readily acquire the more formal type of language associated with learning.

'... the language associated with school learning takes a long time to develop: it is frequently quite abstract, and there may be fewer concrete visual clues to support meaning'.

As previously discussed reading is the process of gaining meaning from text. This active, dynamic process requires that readers select from a range of strategies to 'make sense' of a text. In order to gain meaning readers rely on the interplay of their semantic, syntactic and graphophonic systems of the language in which they are operating. They also call upon various combinations of the code breaker, text user, text participant and text analyst practices to assist their comprehension. However, readers from the diverse groups discussed above will bring varying degrees of semantic, syntactic and graphophonic knowledge to the reading context.

In order to assist these readers to gain greater understanding when reading there are a range of teaching strategies that can be integrated into a classroom literacy program. It is important to realise that many of these strategies not only assist readers from diverse cultural and linguistic background but also the majority of developing readers in our classrooms.

These strategies will be briefly mentioned here and expanded upon in later chapters. These include:

- Modelled reading using a range of literature. In particular this should include text with predictable and repetitive English language structures, books with illustrations that support the text and thus help build the children's semantic knowledge. During modelled reading build links between children's background knowledge and the meanings embedded in the text. Encourage children to predict the story line using the cover of the book, the illustrations and so on. Discuss the language structures used or vocabulary that may be unknown. Reread known books using a great deal of expression. Often these books can also be used for role play by the children, or Readers' Theatre with older children (Hill, 1990).

- Guided reading is a powerful activity where an individual child or a small group of children of like ability work with the teacher who guides and scaffolds their understanding. The children all have access to a copy of the same text and the teacher performs the role of a supporter and 'reminder of strategies'. During guided reading the teacher can check the children's semantic, syntactic and graphophonic knowledge and be in a position to teach 'gaps' in the children's knowledge quite explicitly.

- Fill the classroom with print. Label various objects in the room. Create class 'Big Books' for children to use. Draw children's attention to the environmental print by taking them around the room to read it (often called 'Print Walks'). Encourage children to use the print in the room when they write. Develop word banks of words that have the same ending (for example, 'cat', 'hat', 'mat'; 'skip – skipping', 'run – running'…. Create flow charts or diagrams or story boards about a text. For instance, 'The Three Little Pigs' can be told using pictures of their houses of sticks, straw and bricks and so on.

- Create posters as a class. List strategies that may assist when readers are unable to read a word.

- The use of teacher-made 'cloze activities' reveal a great deal about the types of reading strategies that children are presently using. (The task we did on page 23, The Post Office task, is an example of cloze. The first few lines are usually kept in tact in order for the reader to begin to develop some meaning. Then the text is 'mutilated' by removing some words, called deletions. As you found you needed to draw on all cueing systems to predict an appropriate word for the deletion. The choice of the deletions can vary so that the reader is forced to use only syntactic knowledge or only semantic knowledge or a mix as we did.) Cloze can be either small group or individual activities. They can be designed to be completed either as an oral cloze, on an overhead projector or as an activity sheet.

- A range of speaking and listening activities can be used to scaffold the acquisition of English structures and meanings. Students from diverse backgrounds also need to be made aware of the differences between spoken and written text.

- A set of guidelines that provide a structure for reading. These would include stressing aspects of directionality, sound and letter correspondence and punctuation.

- An understanding that various texts are read in different ways and for a variety of purposes.

- The knowledge that the purpose of all reading acts is to gain meaning from the text.

Summary

In this chapter, we have looked at how teachers might implement the Conditions of Learning to provide optimal classroom reading environments. In classrooms, teachers need to cater to children from diverse cultural and linguistic backgrounds. Strategies for catering to diversity draw on principles of effective language teaching, and are applicable to all children. Modelled, guided and independent reading provide scaffolding for developing readers, and emphasise the importance of interactions in learning to read. Classroom assessment should strike a balance between formative and summative assessment, and follow a cycle which integrates teaching and learning experiences.

Key Concepts

- modelled reading
- independent reading
- summative assessment
- cultural backgrounds

- guided reading
- formative assessment
- diversity
- linguistic backgrounds

Tutorial Activities

1. Visit a classroom, several if you can. Observe the reading context that is set up. Is there 'wall print'? What type of wall print is it? How do the students use it? What other reading materials are available to the students.

2. Talk to some children (seek permission from both the teacher and the children) about the books they like to read. Ask them to show you the books if they can. Ask them questions such as:

   - Why do you like these books?

   - How would you describe the book to someone else?

   - Do you read at home? When do you do that?

   - Do you read at school? When do you do that?

Further Readings

Cambourne, B. & Turbill, J. 1994, *Responsive Evaluation: Making Judgments about Student Literacy*, Eleanor Curtain Publishing, Melbourne.

Chambers, A. 1991, *The Reading Environment: How Adults Help Children Enjoy Books*, Primary English Teaching Association, Sydney.

Clay, M. 1993, *An Observation Survey of Early Literacy Achievement*, Heinemann, Auckland.

Gibbons, P. 1995, *Learning to Learn in a Second Language*, Primary English Teaching Association: Newtown, Australia

Hill, S. 1990, *Readers Theatre: Performing the Text*, Eleanor Curtain Publishing, Melbourne.

Mooney, M. 1990, *Reading to, with and by Children*, Richard C Owens Publishers, New York

Nicoll-Hatton, V. 1998, *Getting Started. Ideas for the Literacy Teacher*, Primary English Teaching Association, Sydney.

Chapter 4

READERS AS TEXT CODE BREAKERS

*'Pooh plunged into the water, seized the bottle, and
struggled back to his tree again. "Bother!" said Pooh, as he
opened it. All that wet for nothing. What's that bit of paper
doing?' He took it out and looked at it. "It's a message," he
said to himself, "that's what it is. And that letter is a 'P', so
it's a very important Message to me, and I can't read it. I
must find Christopher Robin or Owl or Piglet, one of those
Clever Readers who can read things, and they will tell me
what this Message means. Only I can't swim. Bother!"'*
(A.A. Milne, *Winnie-the-Pooh*, 1927, p.123)

Chapter Preview

This chapter focuses on the reader as text code breaker. It explores what
code breakers do, and related knowledge and skills. It examines aspects of
phonological awareness and development, as well as concepts about print
and word awareness. We consider how non-visual information comes into
play when breaking the code of written texts. We also look at the code
breaking of illustrations in children's picture books. Developmental trends
in growth as code breakers are identified, and related classroom practices
are described. Procedures and criteria for assessing development of readers
as code breakers are described.

Focal Questions

- What are text code breaker practices?
- What does a text code breaker know and do?
- What are patterns in readers' growth as code breakers?
- How might teachers support and assess the development of code
  breakers?
- How might readers from diverse cultural and linguistic
  backgrounds be best supported as code breakers?

Introduction

In Chapter Two, we explored reading as a set of inter-related social and cultural practices. Specifically, we identified four sets of practices, which are derived from the work of Luke and Freebody (Freebody, 1992; Luke & Freebody, 2000). These practices are:

- code breaking practices – working out what the text says;
- text participant practices – making sense of texts;
- text user practices – identifying and using social purposes of texts; and
- text analyst practices – identifying what a text wants a reader to believe.

Over the next four chapters, we will be examining in detail each of these reading practices, in terms of what the reader does, how the reader develops, and what we might do as teachers to nurture these reading practices.

This chapter examines readers as code breakers, as highlighted in Figure 1.

Figure 1

Model of Reading as Social Practices, with Code Breaking Practices Highlighted

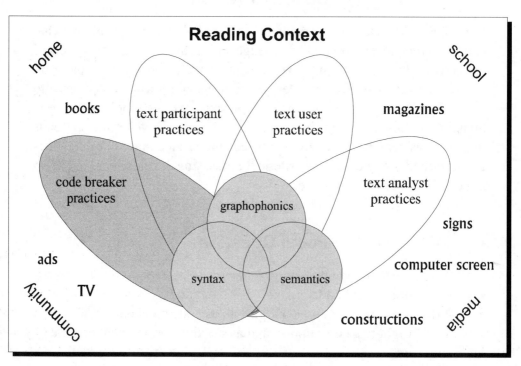

We begin by asking you to complete the following task.

TASK

I.   Read this paragraph, then answer the questions which follow.

'Eth exten four pacherts will manimex three spectas of dinger crapites. The three spectas of dinger crapites which will be manimexed are:

1.   thaw eth ding esod;

2.   who eth ding spoleved; and

3.   thaw cheaters od ot tureen sheet dinger crapites.

Sith pachert manimexes dings sa edoc-karebers.'

a)   How many pacherts are there?

b)   How many spectas of dingers are there?

c)   What spectas of dingers will be manimexed?

d)   What does sith pachert manimex?

e)   What are dinger crapites?

II.   Now think about how you deciphered this text. What knowledge did you use? (For example, where did you begin reading the text, and how did you know?) Were you able to answer all the questions about the text? What helped you answer these questions? What questions could you not answer, and why not?

What does this tell you about this aspect of reading and how it might be effectively taught in classrooms?

Functioning as a code breaker involves focusing on both visual information and non-visual information in a text to work out what it says: How do I crack this text? What are its patterns and conventions? How might I access what the text says?

Code breakers attend to visual information, such as letters and their relationships to sounds, words, chunks of words, punctuation marks, layout and directionality of text (which vary not only across different language systems but also across print and computer media) and conventions of text across different media (print texts, computer texts, and so on).

As code breakers, readers also draw on non-visual information, bringing together their grammatical and semantic knowledge to predict and to confirm or modify the meanings they are beginning to construct. Such questions as 'Does this make sense?' are relevant questions to confirm or to change their meaning construction.

Knowledge and Skills of a Text Code Breaker

Figure 2 overviews the kinds of knowledge and skills involved in being an effective text code breaker.

Figure 2

Overview of Text Code Breaker

Definition	*Knowledge*	*Skills*
Text code breakers attend to visual information and to non-visual information to decipher text:	Written language systems are governed by particular conventions	Word attack skills: sounding out, blending, segmentation, syllabification
how do I crack this text?	Conventions which govern written language systems, such as directionality, grammar, punctuation, capitalisation, word boundaries	Phonological perceptions and discriminations: hearing words in sentences, and sound units in words
	Word recognition skills	
what are its patterns and conventions?	Concepts of print: letter, word, sentence, punctuation symbols and their labels & functions, distinctions and relationships between words and pictures	Sampling text
	Concepts of IT texts (as described in this chapter)	Making predictions about text
	Phonological knowledge: awareness of words in sentences; syllables, segments, onset and rime, and phonemes in words	Checking and monitoring predictions
	Alphabetic (or graphological) knowledge: letters and how they are formed	Using decoding skills to confirm or change predictions of words
	Relationships between letters and sounds (between graphological and phonological features of language)	Using context, grammar and meaning to confirm or change outcomes of word attack and word recognition skills
	Sight vocabulary	Deciphering pictorial/visual symbols
	Pictorial and other forms of visual symbols	Using IT skills (as described in this chapter)

Based on Freebody (1992), Luke (2000), Luke & Freebody (1999) and NSW Department of Education and Training's *Reading Framework K-6* (1997).

Phonological awareness is an important aspect of being a text code breaker. It refers to the ability to hear the sounds in spoken language. This includes the ability to hear:

- individual words in phrases and sentences (such as the individual words in sentence, 'The cow jumped over the moon')
- syllables within words, such as in 'o-ver'
- beginning sound unit of a word, which is called onset, such as /m/ in the word 'moon'
- the rest of the word which follows onset and is called rime, such as /oon/ in the word 'moon' and
- individual phonemes in words, which are the minimal sound units in words, for example, 'moon' consists of three phonemes, /m/-/oo/-/n/'.

Phonological awareness is not the same as 'phonics', which refers to the system by which letters represent sounds in an alphabetic writing system such as written English. For example, the letter combination 'th' in many words takes the sound /th/. When learning phonics, then, we are referring to learning about the relationship between sounds in spoken language and the way they are represented by letters in written language.

As code breakers, readers need to understand that those sounds which are paired with the letters are the same as the sounds of speech. The small units of speech which correspond to letters of an alphabetic writing system are called 'phonemes'. They are 'the minimal units of sound that make a difference to meaning' (Adams, Foorman, Lundberg & Beeler, 1998, p.3). Differences can be subtle – such as the difference between /t/ and /d/ in 'tug' and 'dug'. Phonemes are not spoken as separate units – rather they are blended – as in 'park' – not /p/ /a/ /r/ /k/. The awareness that language is composed of these small sounds is called 'phonemic awareness'.

Phonemes 'are also the units of speech that are represented by the letters of an alphabetic language [such as English].Thus developing readers must learn to separate these sounds, one from another, and categorise them in a way that permits understanding of how words are spelled (and therefore may be recognised]. It is this sort of explicit...knowledge that [falls under the term] *phonemic awareness*' (Adams *et al,* 1998, p.3).

Research cited by Adams *et al* (1998) indicates that without direct instructional support, this awareness eludes roughly 25% of middle-class first graders and substantially more of those who come from less literacy-rich backgrounds. Review of research by Adams *et al* (1998) indicates that these children are most likely to have serious difficulty in learning to read and write.

Why is awareness of phonemes difficult? Because we don't tend to pay conscious attention to sounds or phonemes as they are uttered as we talk or listen. Rather, we tend to process them automatically as we instead focus on the meaning of the utterance as a whole.

Development of phonological awareness

Let's now take a brief look at some developmental trends regarding the growth of phonological awareness over the first four years or so of an child's life. We need to caution that ages are not necessarily attached to these 'stages'; they are useful insofar as they indicate patterns in growth and assist teachers in knowing what they might expect in children's development, and thus plan accordingly. As always, however, it is important that teachers tune into individual patterns of growth, so as to ensure their instruction will be individually appropriate for each reader in their classroom.

According to Treiman & Zukowski (1991, cited in Soderman *et al*, 1999), the development of phonological awareness begins with hearing individual words in sentences. For example, individuals can detect the seven individual words which make up the sentence,

'Little Jack Horner sat in a corner'.

Have you ever noticed how children sometimes play clapping games which accentuate words in sentences? We can recall a clapping game from our childhood days, called 'Eeny meeny macca racca'. Each word in this sentence was accompanied by a unique clap or other hand action with a partner. For example,

word	*hand action*
ee/ny	clap partner's hands with left hand up and right hand down
mee/ny	clap partner's hands with right hand up and left hand down
mac/ca	cross your own hands over and clap them against your shoulders
rac/ca	cross your own hands over and clap them against your knees

And so it went on. Sounds complicated, doesn't it? Yet games like this are played by children with great gusto (watch out for sore red palms!) and expertise, based on this kind of phonological awareness.

After the discovery of words as separate entities, children begin to recognise that words are made up of syllables. For example, the words in our previous 'Little Jack Horner' sentence may be further broken down into syllables thus:

'Lit-tle Jack Horn-er sat in a corn-er'

Again, we might notice children playing clapping games which accentuate syllables in words. Can you think of any?

The next step in this progression of phonological awareness is the awareness of onsets in words – that is, the beginning sound of any word, for example:

'**L**itt-le **J**ack **H**orn-er **s**at **in** a **c**orn-er'

The fourth piece in the progression of phonological awareness is rime (not to be confused with rhymes), which refers to that part of a word which follows the onset, as in:

'**Little Jack Horner** sat **in** a **corner**'

Phonemes are the final piece of the code that young children develop in this progression. Children at this point can take a word like 'Jack' and break it into its components of:

/J/ – /a/ – /ck/.

There is a good deal of research which supports and advocates the direct and explicit instruction of phonological and phonemic awareness in young children. Ball & Blachman (1988, cited in Soderman, Gregory & O'Neill, 1999, p.32) found that kindergarten children who were trained in phonological awareness and knowledge about letters and sounds could figure out new words more often and successfully than children without training. However, Soderman *et al* (1999, p.33) argue that training in phonological awareness is not enough – this must be directly linked to a working knowledge of the alphabet as well as an accurate understanding of letter/sound relationships.

Print awareness

Along with awareness of individual words and sounds in spoken language, children also need to develop an awareness of words and letters in written language. Children must learn that print symbolises spoken language and holds information (Adams, 1990, cited in Soderman *et al*, 1999, p.33).

According to Adams (1990), print awareness includes five important pieces of information:

- Print is categorically different from other kinds of visual patterns in the environment. That is, print is governed by a particular set of rules and conventions which sets it apart form other visual displays such as pictures, logos and abstract patterns.
- Print remains constant across any variety of physical media. For example, the words, 'I can read', will remain the same whether written in ink, painted on a wall, inscribed in stone or written in chalk on a blackboard.
- Print seems to be everywhere in a literate society. Print performs many different functions and is integral to the way people in literate societies live their lives. At the same time, we must recognise that the functions of literacy vary across different sociocultural contexts.
- Print is used in many different ways and occurs in many different forms. Print serves different purposes, and these purposes will have different priorities across different contexts.
- Anyone can produce print. The ability to produce print is not the domain of commercial authors and publishers.

In addition to these, Marie Clay (1991) refers to specific concepts about print:

- recognising a letter and a word;
- understanding that words are made up of letters and sentences are made up of words;

- knowledge that the words are the part we read;
- knowing where to begin reading a book and how the text progresses left/right and top/bottom, and front/back).

Clay (1979) has developed a detailed assessment tool for determining children's concepts about print. We recommend that you take a look at this and consider its usefulness in classrooms. It calls children's attention to such features as words, letters, sentences, directionality of print, and distinctions between words and pictures. It asks children to point out where a reader starts reading on a page (directionality); what is actually read (words), and to point out a word, a letter, particular punctuation marks; and so on.

Whether with formal instruments such as this, or with more informal procedures such as talking about words, letters, sentences and such in texts with children, it is important to assess their understanding of such terminology, for it will influence how teachers will develop their language of instruction (such as 'word', 'letter', 'sound', 'sentence') to ensure that all children understand both the terms and the concepts behind them.

Knowledge about words

Another important set of understandings behind code breaking practices concerns knowledge about words. Frith (1985) suggests that children go through three stages as they learn about words.

The first stage is *logographic*, when children give meaning to logos and pictures they see in familiar settings. For example, as early as 10-12 months many children can begin to associate the golden arches of MacDonalds with french fries and hamburgers. Later they will refer to the sign as 'MacDonalds', not because they are directly reading it but because they are relating the sign to the context (that is, hamburgers and french fries). If the McDonalds sign were to appear in blue and green on a piece of paper, children at this stage probably would not recognise it.

Logographic reading is commonly seen in young children's interactions with their favourite story books, which they have heard so often before they know them off by heart. By looking at what's on the pages (context), they are able to associate the illustrations with the words they have heard read to them, before they can read the actual words. This is illustrated below in the extract below which comes from Holdaway (1979, p.41), where a child, Leslie, is reading 'Where the Wild Things Are', a picture book narrative by Maurice Sendak (1968):

Original text	**Child's version**
and an ocean tumbled by with a private boat for Max and he sailed off through night and day	Max stepped into his private boat and sailed off one day and one night

Leslie is in tune with the way the book generally sounds, and has picked up on many of its words and turns of phrase. As she turned each page, the illustrations cued her in to what the words said. It is likely that as Leslie develops and becomes more aware of words and their function in print, her fluency may slow down as she attends to the more difficult and technical aspects of written script.

Alphabetic is the second stage in the development of word knowledge. As this stage unfolds, children with some knowledge of letters in the alphabet begin to recognise that letters are associated with sounds. Early in this stage children may view the names 'Max' and 'Mike' and read them both as 'Max' because they know the letter 'M'. They cannot yet separate each letter and pair it with a single sound. Nor can they sound out words one phoneme at a time, or blend them.

Later in this stage children can do these things, to the extent of being able to read and figure out nonsense words by associating sounds with individual letters.

At the *orthographic* stage, children can associate familiar letter patterns with sound segments. Children notice familiar patterns and strive to recognise these automatically. When this happens, children spend more time reading for understanding and less time decoding words. Their reading fluency as well as accuracy consequently develops.

Influence of Text Genres on Code Breaking Practices

In literate societies, different kinds of written texts exist to serve different purposes. For example, narratives form a particular kind of text whose purpose it is to entertain the reader. Instructional texts, such as recipes, car manuals and computer manuals, serve the purpose of telling how to perform particular procedures. Information reports serve to provide factual information about a topic, and explanations detail how something works. Recounts describe events which have occurred in the past, and arguments serve to put forward a point of view about an issue. All these kinds of texts may be called text genres.

Text genres influence code breaking practices in at least two ways which we now explore briefly. One way is concerned with the particular kinds of language features which are associated with particular genres. Another way is concerned with how particular genres set up particular strategies for tackling a text at hand.

Let's first consider language features in text genres. By language features we mean the kinds of words and grammar in texts. Code breaking practices are based in part on knowledge about words and grammar (as we saw in Chapter Two, when we wrote about the cueing systems). By way of exploring this, we ask you to complete the following sentences:

'George Hewitt is an Olympian swimmer. He _swims_ every day.'

'George Hewitt is an Olympian swimmer. Right now, he is _____ a 1500 metre race.'

'George Hewitt is an Olympian swimmer. In the Sydney 2000 Olympics last month, he _____ 1500 metres in less than 15seconds.'

'George Hewitt is an Olympian swimmer. He will _____ in the next Commonwealth Games'

In each case, you probably used a verb, for that is the only form of word that would complete each sentence and sound 'right'. You probably chose the verb 'to swim' in each gap, but you probably didn't use the same form of this verb in each case. In the first sentence, you probably put 'swims', adding an 's' to 'swim' to again make it sound right. Do you know why?

In the second sentence, you probably put 'swimming', to make it join with the auxiliary verb 'is' and make it fit the present tense which is suggested by 'is' and the words 'right now'.

In the third sentence, you probably put 'swam', which is the past tense version of 'to swim', which would have been cued by the words 'last month'. In the last sentence, you probably put 'swim', to join it appropriately with 'will' and complete its future tense form, cued by 'the next Commonwealth Games'.

To quite a large extent, the occurrence of particular language features is influenced by the different types of texts in which they are found. Using six text genres, we have shown in Figure 3 what kinds of language features may be predictably found in these genres.

From this, we hope you can see patterns which emerge across different genres and their impact on code breakers. For example, narratives are typically written in past tense. Therefore a reader may expect to decipher verbs in the past tense in such texts. A reader may also expect to find dialogue in many narratives, and so will need to decipher conventions such as quotation marks (' '), question marks (?) and exclamation marks (!). For more information about language features and text genres, we refer you to 'Exploring How Texts Work' by Derewianka (1990).

Figure 3

An Overview of Language Features Found in Six Text Genres

Recount genre — *factual* [handwritten]

Purpose: to tell what happened

specific participants, e.g., the dog, the chair
simple past tense, e.g., ran, walked
action verbs mainly, e.g., jumped, threw
linking words for time, e.g., then, next
 personal recounts:
 first person pronouns, e.g., I, me, us, we
 factual recounts :
 usually third person pronouns, e.g., they, her,
he, she .

[handwritten: Historical, Imaginary / literary]
[handwritten: STRUCTURE:]
[handwritten: oOrientat¹ c.events]

Instructional genre [handwritten:] Procedural]

Purpose: to tell how to do or make something
[handwritten: explain how to do a procedure]

generalised participants, e.g., tools, materials
specific participants, e.g., the milk
linking words for time, e.g., first, then, next, last
action verbs mainly, e.g., cut, stir, take, fit
simple present tense, e.g., pour, join, paste
descriptive words for shape, size, colour, quantity, etc
descriptive words for how, where and when to do
 things [handwritten: Goal, materials, steps,]
[handwritten: STRUCTURE:]
[handwritten: Optional steps]

Narrative genre

Purpose: to entertain, teach and inform

specific participants, e.g., Rosie the hen
action verbs mainly, e.g., pounced
verbs for saying, thinking and feeling
usually past tense, e.g., laughed, said, thought
linking words to time, e.g., afterwards
dialogue
descriptive words
first or third person pronouns, also second person
pronouns (e.g., you, your, yours)

Information report genre [handwritten: abt a]

Purpose: to provide factual information on a topic
[handwritten: phenomenon or a phenomena.]

some action verbs
many linking verbs, e.g., are, were, have, has
timeless present tense, e.g., are, is
descriptive words for appearance, habits and parts
words for defining (e.g., is known as), classifying
 (e.g., belong to), comparing (e.g. is the same
 as),contrasting (e.g., is different from), and
 generalising
technical words specific to the subject matter, eg,
 'stegosaurus' in a text about dinosaurs

Explanation genre

Purpose: to tell how something works

generalised participants, e.g., computers, keyboards
linking words for time, e.g., first, then, finally
cause and effect relationships, because, as a result
mainly action verbs, e.g., crash, restart
timeless present tense, e.g., save, shutdown

[handwritten: Exposition - argument .]

Argument genre

Purpose: to put forward a point of view

generalised participants, e.g., the environment, trees
variety of verbs for action (e.g., cut down), linking
(e.g., are), saying and thinking
mainly timeless present tense
linking words for giving reasons, e.g., because, so,
 therefore, however
nominalisation (verbs being turned into nouns, e.g.,
 'the destruction' from the verb 'to destroy'

Derived from Derewianka, B. 1990, *Exploring How Texts Work,* Primary English Teaching
Association (PETA), Sydney.

TASK

Locate a magazine article, a recipe or a manual, and a University reading. Explore the word structures in each text. How are they the same and different from one kind of text to another?

What does this tell you about this aspect of reading and how it might be effectively taught in classrooms?

Knowledge about different text genres not only can serve to activate particular expectations about the coding of texts. It also provides code breakers with a basis for recognising the kind of text at hand and so being able to adjust reading strategies accordingly. For example, a reader might choose to read a narrative from beginning to end (skipping ahead to the end notwithstanding!). This may be different from skimming and scanning strategies which you might use with your assigned University texts. Contrast these strategies to reading a recipe, where you might first overview a recipe, then get organised with the necessary ingredients, then read one part of the recipe before you carry out a particular step, then read the next step, and so on.

TASK

Using the same three texts as in your previous task (i.e., a magazine article, a recipe or a manual, and a University reading), reflect on how to approach each text as a code breaker. Write down the strategies you use as a code breaker for each kind of text. Make note of any difficulties you might associate with each text, and how typically you resolve these as a code breaker.

What does this tell you about this aspect of reading and how it might be effectively taught in classrooms?

In considering how we might use different reading strategies across different texts, we see important links among text code breaker, text participant, and text user practices. These links come together in terms of selecting specific reading strategies as code breakers; using knowledge about how texts are organised as text participants (see Chapter 5); and using knowledge about purposes served by texts, as text users (see Chapter 6).

The Internet and Code Breaking Practices

While we have examined how different text genres emphasise particular coding conventions and features, it is also true to say that these conventions vary across media. Say, for example, you are researching a topic on whales. If you are researching this topic in books, then you may draw on a particular set of coding orientations to libraries and information books. You might begin with a library catalogue search, by broad subject, exact title, author or key words. Having obtained results, you probably would make note of relevant call numbers and go to the library's shelves to locate these materials. This in itself is a code breaking exercise of navigating library shelves and matching your specific call numbers to classification labels on shelves.

Finding the relevant section, you might then skim call numbers on the materials to match those in your notes. You might then pick these out and perhaps look at them to assess their relevance to your needs. This could involve reading the title, author and source of the material, summary blurbs and table of contents. You might eliminate some materials and focus on others. You might skim and scan remaining materials more carefully, perhaps chapters which seem especially relevant, perhaps by key headings, perhaps by samples of text, and perhaps by index.

But what if you were researching the topic on the internet? Then, a different set of coding orientations come into play – including those related to codes of print materials and library use, but also those related to codes of internet use.

TASK

Go to the World Wide Web and choose a topic of interest which you would like to research. As you begin, keep a note pad by your side, to write down each step you took (e.g., conduct a key word search) and what kind of coding knowledge you needed to be able to perform that step. You may want to consider orientation to things like the keyboard; the WWW menus; tool bar buttons; search engines; web pages; links within and beyond web sites; differences between hot links and other kinds of links; the use of keywords and phrases to conduct a search; the forms that web addresses take (and how their conventions differ from what we might expect in print).

What does this tell you about this aspect of reading and how it might be effectively taught in classrooms?

For children to learn how to crack the code of the internet, we advocate the same approach used for code breaking skills generally – children need to learn such skills in the context of their curriculum rather than as isolated lessons (as shown by Snyder,

1999). Moreover, we argue that becoming oriented to computers and computer-generated texts includes on screen, off screen and keyboard orientation – and certainly not just word processing alone.

When talking about the internet, we include email, the World Wide Web, and Newsgroups. We are not including comments about other Information Technology (IT) texts such as computer games and software programs. For information about these as they relate to reading, we refer you to our Further Readings list at the end of this chapter.

World Wide Web

Reading a World Wide Web text has been likened to 'a frog jumping around a three dimensional lily pond. It can be difficult to stand back from the text to see where you are in relation to its whole' (Moore, 1999, p.54). The World Wide Web (WWW) provides what seems to be an infinite array of information represented as texts, images, animation, audio clips, and videos. Its strengths can sometimes be its drawbacks – such as the overwhelming amount of information it provides; the questionable reliability of unnamed sources because anyone can publish material on the web; and the addictiveness of browsing or 'surfing the net'.

Knowledge and skills children need to learn as code breakers of texts on the World Wide Web include:

- knowing that 'home page' is an entry point into the WWW and to particular web sites
- knowing that the WWW consists of a series of screens containing words and images
- understanding the multidimensional, parallel, interactive nature of web-based texts
- knowing the generic form of WWW addresses, for example

$$\mathtt{http://www.uow.edu.au}$$

whose code can be cracked as follows:

http	stands for 'HyperText Transfer Protocol', the language of the WWW
://	must always be included
www	shows location on the World Wide Web
uow	is the domain name for the address, in this case University of Wollongong
edu	shows this is an <u>edu</u>cational site; others are <u>com</u>mercial, <u>gov</u>ernment, <u>org</u>anisation (non-profit), and <u>net</u>work (as designated by Australia, U.S.A. and many other countries, but not by others such as New Zealand and United Kingdom)

> au   is the country, in this case Australia
>
> .   must be included after location, domain, site type and country, *without*
>
> spaces and *not* at the end of the address

- watching out for tilde ~ and under_score in WWW addresses
- appreciating the need for 100% accuracy in WWW addresses, right down to use of upper and lower case letters and punctuation marks which serve a different function than in non-IT media such as print
- understanding that WWW screens are sometimes separated into frames, each one independent of the others, containing different kinds of information, and updated individually
- knowing the forms and functions of buttons on tool bars in web browsers
- knowing the forms and functions of menus in web browsers – e.g., 'bookmark' (Netscape Navigator browser term) or 'favorites' (Microsoft Outlook Express browser term) for earmarking WWW pages of special interest and relevance
- knowing and being able to use conventions of search engines, including forms that a search may take (e.g., exact phrase, all the words, some of the words); where to enter the search; typing in key words; importance of spelling words accurately; and understanding variations in spelling such as across Australian and U.S. searches and the implications of these differences for search results
- identifying and clicking on the web browser icon on the computer screen
- skills for viewing WWW videos, listening to WWW audio clips, and viewing WWW animated images
- navigating texts by clicking on an underlined text or image which is a link to move to another text
- distinguishing between words/images which make up the main text on a WWW page, and words/images which act as links to other screens containing information
- noticing change in colour that sometimes occurs with a link once it is used
- using the mouse to point to links, watching the cursor turn into a hand once on a link, and then clicking on that link
- maintaining a sense of direction as a reader moves across pages (screens), frames and sites
- turning pages on a multi-page text posted on the world wide web, such as by clicking buttons at the end of each page on the screen
- locating information about author, copyright, source and date when a site was last updated (usually at the bottom of the page)
- recognising WWW terms such as 'frames', 'links', 'hyperlinks', 'hot links', 'search', 'web', and 'surfing', and the very different meanings of some of these words when used in other contexts away from Information Technology contexts

- recognising abbreviated forms and acronyms such as 'www', 'http', 'htm', 'html' and 'URL'
- distinguishing between functions of the same forms as they appear in print-based texts and Information Technology texts – such as underlining, upper and lower case letters, and full stops ('dots' as they're called in IT texts)

Email

Email stands for 'electronic mail' and involves the use of the internet to digitally transmit messages around the world. Its advantages include speed of delivery (all going well with the technology), ability to simultaneously send a message to a number of different recipients near and far, saving paper otherwise used in letters and memos, and freedom from time constraints associated with telephone calls and forms of postal delivery such as Express Post. Electronic mailing lists also expedites correspondence by allowing a sender to send a message to a number of individuals by incorporating into a group listing.

As noted by Ingvarson (1997), email can have a valuable place in classrooms as it allows children to exchange ideas and experiences across the world:

'The reason for the contact might be a discussion of cultural values, a comparison of living conditions or recreational activities, or almost any other subject of common interest. It might also be to engage in quite sophisticated projects in collaboration with distant schools.' (Ingvarson, 1997, p.3)

Becoming oriented to the code of email texts is an undertaking different from WWW and print codes, although there are similarities, too. On the screen, email readers need to become oriented not only to the forms that email messages may take, but also to email menus and the forms of email addresses. Ingvarson (1997, p.24) noted children can find 'it difficult to understand the importance of that full stop in the address, or how capital letters can sometimes affect things.'

Children need to appreciate the importance of accuracy in email addresses, and understand that where a reader might expect word spaces and full stops at the end of sentences in print-based texts, these same conventions definitely do not apply to email addresses (or to WWW addresses for that matter, as we saw above).

In addition to practices for decoding print which apply to reading email messages as they appear on the screen or in a printout, other code breaking skills involve opening email, and distinguishing between read and unread messages (such as new messages being coded in bold face type or bulletpoints).

For each email message received, a reader needs to know where to locate its sender, the sender's email address, date the message was sent, and the subject of the particular message. Other code breaking skills relate to printing a message, filing it and down loading it.

Other distinctions involve email menus – such as the difference between replying to a read message, sending a new message, and forwarding on a message to a third party.

When reading a reply to an email message, the arrow symbol > indicates the original message. Often respondents weave their replies into the original message, so as to address each main point in that message. When sent back, the message will include text chunks designated by an arrow > at the beginning of each line, to indicate that chunk was part of the original message; if not designated as such, this indicates the reply which is new text.

Newsgroups

Newsgroups are discussion forums. A Newsgroup user may choose a subject of interest from an existing list of around 5000 or so subjects (and growing), or else create their own special interest Newsgroup. Users post their comments and questions about that subject, for others in the particular Newsgroup to read as an offline activity. A common feature of Newsgroups is a list of Frequently Asked Questions (FAQs), which allows readers to visit questions which repeatedly arise, without bogging the group communication down by asking and addressing the same questions over and over again.

Code breaking practices related to Newsgroups include:

- reading and choosing a subject of interest from the very long list of subjects
- knowing the form that subject titles of Newsgroups generally take, for example,

  `alt.comedy.marx-bros`

  which follows a pattern of generic descriptor ('alt' for 'alternative'), followed by another generic descriptor ('comedy'), followed by a specific descriptor ('marx-bros' for 'Marx Brothers')
- knowing forms and conventions for subscribing to Newsgroups
- knowing and using conventions for logging on to a Newsgroup discussion
- understanding that once logged on, discussion which is downloaded is the discussion which has occurred since the user last logged on
- knowing and using various conventions for grouping discussions, such as by date, sender of message, or subject of message
- as in email too, knowing and using conventions for injecting emotion and other paralinguistic devices, where we might otherwise use facial expression, tone of voice and gesture in face-to-face conversations – for example,

  :-)   to indicate a smile or happy feeling

  :-   to indicate an unhappy feeling

  ):<   to indicate anger

Newsgroups are different from Chat Rooms, which involve online communication in real time, and where the screen shows dialogue as it is being entered and transmitted through cyber space. An issue for code breakers here is to keep track of threads of continuity. A user for example may enter a response to an earlier question at the same time that several others are posting their comments to that or some other comment made earlier. Synchronicity can be a challenge in this context, and requires quite a complicated visual mapping of who has written what in response to whom.

CD-Roms and the Internet

CD-Roms are not part of the internet, although a user can often hook up with the internet by clicking appropriate links on the CD-Rom to move to a specific web site (if they are connected to an internet service provider). A computer compact disc, CD-Roms can show images, display short animations and videos, and play audio clips. As well, they display large amounts of text in vast but not infinite quantities. Unlike the WWW, pages don't change.

Codes for using CD-Roms are similar to those used for the WWW, in their use of hyperlinks, tool bars, buttons whose functions are designated by images as well as words, home pages, search functions and so on.

Educational CD-Roms are used in many classrooms. While some children may find their own way in cracking their codes, teachers should not assume these skills and provide explicit orientation to the features of these IT materials.

And what about the computer keyboard?

It is all well and good to note here some of the conventions which readers need to learn if they are to use these various forms of internet texts. But perhaps most fundamental of all in this discussion should be the ubiquitous keyboard – its use essential in all these forms and more. Children need to be oriented to the layout of a key board, the functions served by each key and how these functions change with the press of other keys – such as changing a lower case letter to upper case by pressing the shift key; or using various combinations of option, control, shift and icon keys to perform equivalent mouse functions.

Developing Readers from Diverse Cultural and Linguistic Backgrounds as Text Code Breakers

In Chapter Three, we identified a number of principles and practices for supporting readers from diverse backgrounds. Using these as a framework, we describe below how teachers might support the development of code breaking practices among readers from diverse backgrounds. These practices, however, are equally applicable to all children.

Reid (1998) reports on a highly significant and innovative study of 100 diverse families in Australian contexts. Outcomes highlight diverse ways of being literate and factors which impact on children's literacy learning generally. They serve to challenge any fixed and mono-cultural views we may have of the world and what we <u>assume</u> children experience as readers in their homes and communities.

One key finding is that similarity across literacy experiences which schools provide stands in sharp contrast to the many differences found across different homes and communities. In part, this is due to the standardisation of curriculum through mandatory syllabus documents, and in part to the many different functions which literacy serves at home versus perhaps a more limited range at school. Thus children learn to read – and for the purposes of this chapter, learn to be code breakers – in various contexts, with various texts and purposes. From this, we can further deduce that what code breaking skills children specifically learn will vary, according to the kinds of texts to which they are exposed (e.g., cracking the code of comics is different to cracking the code of picture book narratives, or food labels, or television guides). How explicit these skills are will also vary across homes and communities.

A second key finding from Reid's report (1998) is that it is extremely difficult to characterise the range of home literacy experiences of the 100 children in the study. These differences arose from:

- the initiatives which children take as active learners – for example, Erin had a collection of 50 Little Golden Books, neatly categorised on her shelf and shared with her older brothers and sisters. This was not something pushed by her parents, yet the ways in which she and her older, school-going siblings read these books very much mimicked what was used at school to develop code breaking as well as meaning making skills (known from her older siblings).

- families' beliefs about their roles in their children's literacy development – for example, Freya's family emphasised explicit talk about their literacy practices, of which there were many (phone messages, home renovation magazines, computer, newspapers, calendar). Thus in such contexts, children could see not only the functions of a range of different texts in their lives, but also become oriented to their respective codes.

- family circumstances – for example, in an extended family, there were lots of sharing time, with Christianne sharing stories with her Yaya. This may contrast with families with single parents, or families dealing with chronic illness, or other extreme circumstances like poverty or alcoholism.

- children's individual differences – for example, Alan had a history of illness, which explained his lack of engagement with the many literacy experiences which his family provided. Thus while teacher might look at home contexts in terms of how they orient children to the codes of written texts, children's actual engagement presents another important consideration.

- beyond this article, of course, cultural and class differences also come into play in a significant way. Different cultural communities use texts in different ways, for different purposes and to different degrees of explicitness which influence, among other things, ways in which children are oriented to codes of written texts. We explore these differences further in our next chapter.

Finally, another key finding was that differences in home experiences mean that children bring different amounts and kinds of 'capital' to school. Those children who have experienced and engaged with literacy activities, texts and talk that are all very similar to the activities, texts and talk at school, will be able to tune in to how texts are used and how their codes are cracked in ways that are taught at school. These children will have a leading edge, possibly, over those children who have had different (not inferior) experiences which are not found at school. These children experience a double jeopardy in relation to code breaking practices: they need to work harder at figuring out the kinds of code breaking skills which are emphasised at school; and their own reading experiences from their homes are not seemingly valued and taken up at school.

These differences highlight the importance of close partnerships among teachers, children and their families, as argued by Reid (1998, p.246):

'[There is] a need for close contact and sharing between an informed teaching service in the local school and the home cultures and environments of the children they serve'

Reid immediately goes on to emphasise, 'but this is not to mould the differences in children's home backgrounds' so as to produce a homogeneous group of learners. Rather, the challenge is one of 'working with, rather than against' these differences.

Applying these findings to the development of code breakers from diverse backgrounds, teachers need to provide contexts where code breaking as a set of reading practices is valued, used and made explicit.

In order to effectively promote the development of code breaking practices in readers from diverse linguistic backgrounds, teachers need to assess if children from non-English speaking backgrounds (NESB) have concepts about reading and what they are, and to find out about their reading experiences in their first language.

Below, we have charted a comparison of what readers fluent in English may know and the skills they may have, with readers from non-English speaking backgrounds (NESB). This is not to suggest that NESB learners are inadequate readers. Indeed, teachers, with the help of expert ESL teachers working in their schools, must recognise the knowledge and skills which NESB readers possess in their first and other languages. At the same time, it is necessary to determine where reading may be breaking down as an outcome of differences between reading in English and other languages.

A reader fluent in English	*An NESB reader working with an English text*
Knows that written language systems are governed by particular conventions	May have this same understanding
Knows conventions which govern written language systems, such as directionality, grammar, punctuation, capitalisation, word boundaries, and book conventions	May not know the conventions which govern written English. May have experienced different conventions such as directionality, different alphabets, or idiographic systems unlike English
Knows concepts of print: letter, word, sentence, punctuation symbols and their labels & functions, and distinctions and relationships between words and pictures	May have experienced different forms of print which involve different print-related concepts
Has phonological knowledge: awareness of words in sentences, syllables, segments, onset and rime, and phonemes in words	May be unfamiliar with phonological system of English
Has alphabetic (or graphological) knowledge: letters and how they are formed	May not be familiar with the English alphabet or with written languages based on an alphabetic system
Knows relationships between letters and sounds (between graphological and phonological features of language)	May be unfamiliar with graphological and phonological features of English
Has an extensive sight vocabulary	May have a sight vocabulary in their native tongue and other languages, but not English
Recognises pictorial and other forms of visual symbols	May associate different meanings and cultural values to visual symbols
Uses word attack skills such as sounding out, blending, segmentation, syllabification	May not be familiar with graphological and phonological features of English
Samples text	May not recognise visual information to decipher text or recognise key words
Makes predictions about text	May not have knowledge about written English, and/or background and cultural knowledge, relevant to the text
Checks and monitors predictions	May not have sufficient grasp of context to check predictions, and/or may not be able to tell whether a prediction fits in the flow of a sentence or makes sense
Uses decoding skills to confirm or change predictions of words	May be unable to confirm or wrongly confirm, for above reasons
Uses context, grammar and meaning to confirm or change outcomes of word attack and word recognition skills	May not have sufficient grasp of context to check predictions, and/or may not be able to tell whether a prediction fits in the flow of a sentence or makes sense ☞

May draw on cultural knowledge to recognise words and phrases in written texts	May not have cultural knowledge relevant to deciphering words and phrases like 'as long as a cricket pitch' or 'as far as the crow flies' in written texts
Draws on knowledge of spoken English to decipher written English	May be unfamiliar with or have had little experience with spoken English, such as with informal phrases they might find in written texts
Sounds out unfamiliar words in written English	May not have a concept of letter/sound relationships and sounding out words, especially if first language is non-alphabetic (such as Chinese)

Gibbons (1991, pp.75-80) has suggested a range of strategies which specifically address these differences and so support readers from diverse backgrounds in gaining competence as code breakers in written English. These strategies include:

- Choose books which use real-to-life language rather than stilted and controlled language. Gibbons (1991, p.76) argues that 'language is likely to be distorted and actually be *more* difficult for second language learners to understand if the choice of words has been governed mainly by an attempt to teach particular phonic skills or use only short, "simple" words.'

- Choose books which are both personally and culturally relevant to readers from diverse backgrounds. This means teachers need to tune into and understand their children's cultural backgrounds, and select texts accordingly. This will allow readers to draw on their background knowledge to decipher texts.

- Choose books for beginning NESB readers which use patterned texts. This may include repetition, such as in 'The Gingerbread Man', 'The Three Little Pigs', or 'The Bad Tempered Ladybird'; predictable sequences such as numbers or days of the week (although, these too, are culturally influenced), such as in 'The Very Hungry Caterpillar', and cumulative texts where the story builds upon itself, such as in 'The House that Jack Built'. Readers familiar with these patterns will find their potential to crack the codes of such texts to be much enhanced. Their confidence, too, will grow as they find themselves able to join in with these patterned texts.

- Choose texts where the words are written clearly, and not in a font style which might hinder word and letter recognition for NESB readers.

- Use 'shadowed reading' (Gibbons, 1991, p.80), which involves a teacher slightly behind the reader, with the book in front of the child. The teacher reads the text to the child, and as the teacher re-reads it a number of times, encourages the child to join in. This allows the child to build familiarity and confidence with the text, until comes a time they are able to 'have a go' with the text on their own.

- As for all readers, develop knowledge of letter/sound relationships in meaningful contexts, and not in exercises separate from reading real books. Gibbons (1991, p.78) states that 'children who speak another language may not "hear" or recognise some of the sounds in English, or may confuse similar sounds'. Developing phonological awareness in the context of real books will assist NESB readers in hearing different sounds, making sense of them, and recognising them in other contexts. Strategies for doing this are further explored in our later section on 'Scaffolding text code breakers', which apply to English-speaking and NESB readers alike.

- Use cloze activities (Gibbons, 1991, p.82), to aid and encourage children's strategies for predicting, confirming predictions and changing predictions. For example, post-it notes can be placed on a selection of words in a big book used in modelled reading to demonstrate how a reader predicts. Likewise, words in texts for guided reading can be masked and children guided through the process of predicting – such as from the context of what has been read so far, reading on, looking at images and confirming these predictions by viewing the word in its entirety or in its smaller sound units one by one. These can involve 'fill-in-the-blank' texts. There are several kinds of cloze activities:

  – *traditional or random cloze*, where words are deleted on the basis of frequency, such as every fifth word is deleted.

  – *grammatical or syntactic cloze*, where structure words which have a common grammatical function are deleted, to focus readers' code breaking strategies on syntactic information. Deleted words may include pronouns such as 'we', 'he', 'she', and 'it'; linking words such as 'and', 'but', 'because' and 'therefore'; articles such as 'the', 'a' and 'an'; auxiliary verbs such as 'have' in 'have finished', or 'has', 'can', 'may', 'will', 'shall', 'could' and so on; and word endings such as '_ing', '_ed' and '_s' at the end of verbs, or other suffixes such as '-less' or '-ness'; and prefixes such as 'un_', 'in_', and 'pre_'.

  – *semantic or content word cloze*, where content words such as verbs (e.g., 'galloped'), nouns(e.g., 'horse'), adverbs (e.g., 'quickly') and adjectives (e.g., 'black'), thus focusing code breakers' attention on the semantic cueing system of language.

  – *graphological/phonological cloze*, where single letters or clusters of letters are deleted within words, or syllables are deleted, or onsets or rimes are deleted. These kinds of cloze may also indicate how many letters in a deleted word, and show the actual outlines of deleted words.

Contextualising the development of code breaking skills is important for <u>all</u> readers. Texts growing out of children's personal experiences and experiences shared with teacher and peers most certainly will be relevant. Shared experience enhances mutual understanding of what is to be recounted, and enables the teacher to ask pertinent questions by way of guiding the construction of recounts of these experiences. Once written, these recounts may be collated in individual or class books for children to read and develop word recognition skills and build vocabulary. These recounts may be dictated by the children and scribed by the teacher, and illustrated by the children, to further develop familiarity with written English and the relationship between words and pictures.

Children's own recounts, as well as recounts with which they are familiar, may be jumbled for children to re-order. This directs children's attention to text coherence and structures and their relationship to meaning. Teachers can discuss with children words that give clues to how the text was re-ordered – words such as pronouns (e.g., 'she', 'he', 'it') and connecting or linking words (e.g., 'and', 'but', 'so', 'because'). Another activity is based on recounts focusing on past events – word banks can be built with children which are made up of past tense verbs. These banks can be further developed to show how the form and function of past tense verbs relate to present and future tense.

Recounts may be used as springboards to another text genre – procedural texts, designed to instruct a reader how to perform a particular procedure (after Derewianka, 1990). Procedural texts such as recipes may be built from children's recounts of procedures they've actually carried out as a classroom shared experience like cooking. Children then may be involved in identifying key words in these as well as other familiar procedural texts. Teachers may develop cloze and sequencing activities which focus on the appearance and meaning of content words – that is, nouns and verbs.

Working with narratives (stories) shared in shared and guided reading, children may be asked to locate key words and to identify and label the narrative's title, as well as particular words, sentences, punctuation. Speech bubbles drawn next to characters serves the purpose of highlighting the function of dialogue in the main text, as well as to recycle vocabulary. Retelling and re-enacting familiar narratives enables children to become more familiar with the forms and structures of narrative texts as well as words and what they look and sound like.

NESB readers' re-tellings may be transcribed and collated as big books for shared reading and for specific code breaking instruction. Word banks of common action verbs can be built, acted out and linked to particular narratives.

Tuning into descriptive words in narratives, word banks of synonyms may be developed, which will expand children's vocabulary.

Scaffolding Children as Text Code Breakers

Figure 4 overviews developmental patterns in children's growth as code breakers, along with some suggestions for classroom practices. This is intended to be used as a guide only, and the practices described are by no means exhaustive. We encourage you to find out more about and even generate your own specific practices which appropriately nurture children's development as code breakers. In whatever you do, remember that children's development and backgrounds should be your guide to selecting experiences and strategies which are appropriate to individual children.

As teachers go about the business of supporting and promoting readers' development as code breakers, a number of principles are important to keep in mind:

- foster children's enjoyment of reading
- read to children daily and share your own enjoyment of reading
- model code breaking skills
- engender a sense of purpose for using code breaking skills
- talk to children about their code breaking skills and strategies
- explicitly scaffold children's code breaking of texts by drawing their attention to visual and non-visual features of texts
- encourage children to take risks with confidence
- develop a metalanguage – a language for talking about how we read and for talking about graphological and phonological features of texts
- develop code breaking skills in meaningful contexts; reading is about meaning and so its skills need to always be in meaningful contexts and not in isolation from real texts and the act of reading
- remember children also need to learn to read diagrams, graphs, flow charts, and so on.
- facilitate application and transfer of code breaking skills though a systematically orchestrated teaching and learning cycle. Use big books to develop code breaking skills in meaningful contexts. Reading experiences in effective classrooms do not occur in isolation. They build on previous learning and experiences, and foreshadow those to come. To ensure this, during and across reading experiences, teachers move through the following cycle.

Modelled reading

Modelled reading provides opportunities for teachers to explicitly demonstrate how a reader cracks the code of written texts – focusing on strategies for decoding visual features of print; making predictions; confirming predictions; changing predictions; and making self-corrections.

Texts used in modelled reading should be relevant to children's homes and communities, and include texts brought in by the children. Other suitable texts include

Figure 4

Developmental Trends of Text Code Breakers and Related Pedagogic Practices

Indicators

Emergent Phase (*includes Role-Play & Experimental Reading; approximately links to Early Stage 1*)*

- Display book-handling skills, e.g., holding a book appropriately and turning pages
- Display reading like-behaviours such as looking at words and pictures, using memory and pictures to "read"
- Recognise own name & personally significant words in context match
- Come to some written words in environmental print

Early Phase (*includes Early and Transitional Reading; approximately links to Stage 1 and into Stage 2*)*

- May read unfamiliar texts slowly and deliberately, with a focus on print
- Has a sight vocabulary of words which they recognise in different contexts
- Relies heavily on beginning letters and sounding out words to unlock words

Pedagogic Practices

- Re-read favourite texts and encourage children to participate in reading with you
- Establish a print-rich environment which incorporates a variety of forms and functions which are relevant to children's lives
- When reading big books, skim the print with a pointer to allow children to see directionality, spoken/written correspondences, and talk about word boundaries
- Demonstrate through self-directed commentary and questions how you
- Use context clues (e.g., what you know about a topic, what's shown in pictures) to make meaning
- Develop phonological awareness through games such as 'I spy' and activities such as clapping syllables in words, oral cloze with familiar rhymes; segmentation activities where words are broken into onset and rime
- Develop word recognition skills through labels, captions, word displays, displays of real texts in different forms and for real purposes
- Develop knowledge about letter/sound relationships
- Trace around words to highlight their distinctive shapes and explore similarities and differences in word shapes
- Read to children and demonstrate book-handling skills
- Discuss relationships between words and pictures
- Model how words may be sounded out, with support of masking devices which reveal sound units one at a time in words
- Highlight similarities among words, such as common word beginnings
- Provide opportunitie s for children to select letters to match letter sequences in print
- Practise using graphological and phonological cues to unlock words in texts
- Sound out consonant-vowel-vowel-consonant patterns, vowel digraphs and double vowel sounds
- Identify blends, syllables, onsets and rimes in modelled and guided reading

- Manipulate letter sequences to create new words
- Engage children in word play such as rhymes, tongue twisters and songs
- Build onto known words with affixes and prefixes
- Conference with individual children and encourage them to talk about their decoding strategies
- Model and talk about sampling, predicting, monitoring and confirming strategies
- Model and build activities around word patterns
- Model and develop reading strategies specific to different texts and purposes
- Model and build activities around structural word analysis (e.g., root words)
- Create word banks from familiar texts and children's writing
- Provide personal dictionaries for each child
- Use a variety of graphological and phonological strategies, e.g., use knowledge of syllables, word families and common prefixes and suffixes
- On further development, use knowledge of homonyms, contractions and irregular multisyllabic words
- Model strategies of re-reading, reading on, slowing down and sub-vocalising

- Encourage and guide children to articulate their reading difficulties [in addition to those strategies identified for emergent and early readers]

- May ask others for help with unknown words
- May skip words as they read
- May self-correct
- Uses pictures and knowledge of context to check their understanding of a text's meaning
- Comes to integrate knowledge about text structures, language features, and subject-specific language
- Comes to predict, confirm, re-read, read on and make meaningful substitutions for words they do not recognise
- Becomes efficient in: predicting and substantiating; self-correcting; re-reading to clarify meaning; reading on when facing difficulty; slowing down when in difficulty; substituting familiar words; using knowledge of print conventions
- Makes meaningful substitutions

Fluent Phase (includes *Independent and Advanced Independent Reading; approximately links to Stage 3)**

- Uses word identification strategies appropriately and automatically with unknown words
- Knows and uses word patterns, word derivations, prefixes, suffixes and syllables
- Integrates the use of semantic, syntactic and graphophonic information
- Adjusts strategies for different text types (genres) and purposes
- Has metacognitive awareness of meaning and when meaning breaks down
- Slows down and sub-vocalise when meaning breaks down
- Self-corrects, re-reads and reads on.

* Emergent, early and fluent labels are derived from Mooney (1990). Role Play, Experimental, Early, Independent and Advanced labels are derived from the Western Australian Department of Education's *First Steps – A Reading Developmental Continuum"* document (1994). Approximate links are made to Early Stage 1, Stage 1, Stage 2 and Stage 3 as identified in NSW Board of Studies *English K-6 Syllabus*.

environmental print, such as wall print, big books based on real texts such as literary texts, information texts and so on; texts written by children; multiple copies of small books; and IT texts projected onto a large screen.

In modelled reading, teachers may demonstrate the following aspects of the code of texts written in English across print, IT and other media:

- how books are handled, including front and back covers, end papers, and so on
- how pictures, graphs and diagrams relate to words
- horizontal, left-to-right, top-to bottom directionality of English print in books;
- how sentences can be separated into words, signalled by spaces between words;
- how language can be separated into words
- how words can be separated into onset and rime
- how words can be separated into phonemes
- letter/sound relationships
- what individual letters look like
- what individual words look like, in terms of their length, shape, and letters
- knowledge and skills related to World Wide Web texts as identified in this chapter
- knowledge and skills related to email texts as identified in this chapter
- knowledge and skills related to Newsgroup texts as identified in this chapter.

These aspects of the written English code are most effectively modelled with real texts and real purposes.

As teachers read to children in modelled reading, they need to also model how they use prediction strategies to help crack the code. This means a teacher needs to talk aloud the processes going on in their heads, as they make predictions of what is next in the text; how they confirm or change their predictions; and how and why they monitor their reading and self-correct.

Guided reading

Here, teachers share code breaking responsibilities with children. This may be done in various situations, such as groups of children on a needs-basis; individual children in reading conferences; and whole class situations.

It is important here to choose texts which will neither frustrate children because it is too difficult, nor limit children because it is too easy or else can be read from memory. Texts need to strike a balance, so that they call on and further develop and consolidate children's code breaking skills. This means the teacher needs to know the capacities and potential of their children as code breakers well (see our later section on assessment in this chapter).

There are different ways in which guided reading may be conducted. In needs-based groups (ideally no more than six children)and individual situations, each child focuses on the same text, (either their own individual copies or one enlarged large copy which all participants can readily view). In small group or whole class situations, children may read together with their teacher. In individual situations, the child may read with the teacher or the teacher may use shadowed reading as previously described in our section on diverse readers.

Another strategy for guided reading involves children in completing oral clozes. A teacher masks words in the focus texts, with the use of such devices as post-its. Clozes may be constructed along a number of different lines as explained in our previous section on diversity. Below, we illustrate how on teacher has done this in a Year One classroom, where they are reading *Rosie's Walk* by Pat Hutchins (Hutchins, 1968):

T: [Reading and skimming with a pointer] 'Rosie the hen went for a – ? [stops at the next word which is masked].

C: 'Walk'

T: What else might it say?

C 'Run'

C: But Rosie doesn't look like she's running in the picture.

T: OK. Any other ideas on what this word might be?

C: Stroll.

T: Oooh, 'stroll' that's an interesting word. What does it mean?

C: Same as 'walk'. It means going for a walk.

T: OK. Well, let's look at the first letter of the word. [Lifts first part of the post-it to reveal the letter 'w'] What letter is this?

C: 'W'

T: What sound does 'w' make'

C: /w/

T: Have we predicted a word beginning with /w/?

C: Yes. 'Walk'

T: Well, let's see if that's the word. [Lifts the rest of the post-it to show the rest of the word] What does it say?

C: 'Walk'.

C: Yup, 'walk'.

T: Yes, but it could have been 'stroll', because it means the same thing as 'walk'. It would have made sense. Let's read on.

Independent reading

Building upon whole class interactions and shared experiences, teachers engage children in independent reading and related group tasks. Independent reading provides opportunity for children to read on their own and practise and apply their code breaking skills in meaningful and relevant contexts similar to those modelled in shared reading.

Effective language and literacy classrooms provide a rich and diverse range of reading materials from which children may make choices. These choices may be guided by themselves, peers or the teacher in terms of interest and readability.

Related tasks are accompanied by texts and include a variety of media through which children could express their thoughts and feelings. Children may be involved in writing text innovations and sequels, individual silent reading and reading to each other in pairs. More structured tasks may include labelling, cloze, sequencing, acrostics, crosswords and anagrams. Observing children as they engage in follow-up activities enables teachers to begin to understand the range of meanings in their classrooms, and to be in a position to negotiate these.

'Giant Pandas and Other Endangered Species': An Example of Contextualising Code Breaking Practices in a Year Four Classroom

Throughout this book, we continue to argue that reading practices need to be taught in classrooms in ways which are relevant and purposeful to children. Deciding what 'relevant' and 'purposeful' mean includes tuning into texts in children's home and community contexts, exploring texts necessary to success at school, and doing so in a way which integrates learning and is of interest to children.

This section provides a descriptive outline of how code breaking practices may be taught in a way which links these practices to the other three reading practices of text participant, user and analyst practices (detailed in the three chapters which follow). Our outline focuses on modelled, guided and independent reading and relates reading to print and IT texts. It does not indicate an exact time and sequence for implementing these strategies – these need to be finely tuned to children's needs. Rather, the outline provides a range of pointers to consider during modelled, guided and independent reading.

Thematic focus of unit
Giant Pandas and Other Endangered Species

Length of unit
Eight weeks

Integration of Key Learning Areas

Human Society and Its Environments
Countries around the world where endangered species dwell

Science and Technology
Environmental education: issues of conservation, protection and endangered species

English
Locating, reading and taking notes from information reports, reference books and WWW texts about endangered species
Writing information reports about endangered species

Creative and Practical Arts
Constructing collage images and murals

Objectives related to English
- to consolidate children's knowledge and skills related to library research
- to consolidate and extend children's knowledge and skills related to information reports
- to develop children's knowledge and skills related to conducting WWW searches
- to nurture children's sense of purpose in research and reporting of outcomes

Prior knowledge and background experiences

Children in this Year 4 classroom have had some experience with library research in both school and public libraries. They also have had quite heavily guided experiences with searches on the WWW, supported by their teacher's use of a 'selected bookmark strategy' (Ingvarson, 1997 – see Chapter 5 for a more complete description), whereby the teacher did the initial stages of a web search, culled results, and provided students with a starting point on a particular web site. Children also have read WWW pages, used links, and are familiar with the layout of web sites.

Modelled reading

Over a number of modelled reading sessions, a teacher can introduce the issue of endangered species as it relates to Giant Pandas in China. Begin by finding out what children know about this topic (as text participants) and collating this on chart paper for ongoing reference and additions throughout the unit. At the same time, find out what children know about where they might find information related to this topic. Their suggestions might include reference books and information reports that they have read or seen; they could also suggest other kinds of materials such as calendars published by the World Wildlife Fund which contains information about the WWF organisation and the issues they attempt to address. This could form another ongoing classroom display for ready reference and review.

Introduce relevant texts in modelled reading. Children can be made aware of their sources, be they library materials, privately owned materials, or materials downloaded from the internet. It is also important where possible to include texts which children bring to school, building on what is familiar to them and what are relevant texts in their own lives.

In relation to code breaking skills, review skills which these children have in relation to library research – such as reviewing use of library catalogues, shelf browsing, skimming and scanning, and text selection. These should be linked to text participant practices in terms of interpreting material and relating it to the task at hand; to text user practices in terms of using school and public libraries and reading for purposes of finding information and writing information reports; and to text analyst practices in terms of identifying position of texts in relation to endangered species and other conflicting interests and evaluating material accordingly.

Also in relation to code breaking, talk about ways of reading information reports, with examples at hand and in view for all to see. Review use of book summaries, tables of contents, headings, indexes and text sampling, with books borrowed from school library and from the community's public library. Here, links can be made to text participant practices in terms of interpreting information reports and relating them to the task at hand, developing topic knowledge, and developing knowledge about structures of information reports (see Chapter 5). Links can also be made to text user practices in terms of reading for purposes of writing an information report about Giant Pandas (see Chapter 6). Also link to text analyst practices in terms of identifying position of texts in relation to endangered species and other conflicting interests and using that to construct pros and cons in a discussion paper (see Chapter 7).

Modelled reading not only provides a time for revisiting and consolidating familiar skills and concepts. It also provides a time for introducing and demonstrating new learning. In relation to this unit's code breaking strategies for locating relevant information on the World Wide Web, and with a particular focus on Giant Pandas,

-   review children's access procedures for entering the World Wide Web
-   review search engines and where and how to find them
-   demonstrate searches in relation to Giant Pandas
-   demonstrate searches in relation to the World Wildlife Fund
-   demonstrate different types of searches and their impact on search results
-   demonstrate and discuss search results
-   demonstrate skimming, scanning, culling, and book marking of search results

When demonstrating any information technology texts, it is essential that all children can view the screen – ideally, a large projection screen is used. Alternatively, rotating small groups are used in these sessions.

In these demonstrations, links can be made to text participant practices in terms of interpreting material and relating it to the task at hand, developing topic knowledge, and developing knowledge about structures of web sites. Links to text user practices can be made in terms of conducting WWW searches and reading search results and selected web sites for purposes of writing an information report about Giant Pandas. A teacher can also link to text analyst practices in terms of identifying positions in WWW texts in relation to endangered species and other conflicting interests.

These modelled reading sessions have quite particular foci; ideally, they would be interspersed with opportunities for children to become familiar with the topic of Pandas and the whole concept of endangered species, through links to other curriculum areas such as HSIE and Science. Children ideally are allowed to pursue their interests in the topic through their own independent reading and research, as well as be actively involved in discussions and demonstrations of materials during modelled reading.

Guided reading

Guided reading provides opportunities for children to practise what has been previously modelled. For the purposes of this unit, shift the focus from Giant Pandas to another endangered species – preferably, negotiate this with the children.

Let's say that teacher and children decided upon whales. Involve children in talk and research about whales. Children may brainstorm and list what they know about whales and to identify key words and resources they may already associate with this topic.

Organise class visits to the public library for seeking out relevant materials. These visits should be planned in advance with the library to ensure, among other things, availability of suitable materials. Librarians can provide demonstrations of new skills (such as using non-loan reference materials like encyclopedias) and revisit old ones (such as locating information reports for loan). They can also work with you to model and guide children's use of the internet in small groups.

Have children gather their information and take notes (see Chapter 5 for various ways of doing these things) in the library and back in their classrooms. There should be plenty of mediating conversation about what they have found, what they've learned, and what continues to puzzle them – not only about the topic but about the code breaking practices used to locate information about the topic.

Information can be used as a basis for jointly drafting and composing an information report about whales as an endangered species. Ideally, children, by virtue of their research on the WWW and in the library, should have reasonable control over the content of the report; you should especially guide its structure and layout, which you would have previously modelled.

Independent reading

Independent reading allows children to spread their wings and to put into practices what they have learned from modelled and guided reading experiences.

For the purposes of this unit, have children work in small groups of say three, no more than four, children – keep in mind the need for them to work cooperatively at computer terminals.

The focus of their group work is to carry out research into an endangered species of each group's own choice, other than those used in modelled and guided reading. Arrange for the groups to use their school library, the local public library and the World Wide Web to research their topic. There should be plenty of opportunity for children to talk about their research to one another and between groups too in whole class discussions.

Children can continue to chart their project progress on classroom charts – noting as before what they knew at the outset, things they would like to find out about, what they are learning that is new, and any puzzlements that might still linger. As a classroom display for each group, this would be a dynamic document, changing with the course of the group's project.

As a culmination of their group work, have groups collate information into information reports, as previously modelled and guided. These can be shared with the rest of class. These reports can also be put on display in not only school but also public libraries. Negotiate the possibility of such a display with your local public librarian. This is especially appropriate because you incorporated the library in the planning and implementation of this unit. It is also desirable for it achieves greater links between your classroom and its surrounding community. Perhaps for greater visual impact, some children could re-work their reports as poster displays for this purpose.

Extension

As an extension of this group work and all that preceded it, and as a means of bringing all the projects together, children could be involved in thinking about the information they have collectively gathered as resource material for constructing a class discussion paper, or small group discussion papers, or individual discussion papers on endangered species.

Discussion is a particular text genre (see Chapter 6) whose purpose is to identify pros and cons to an issue, state a position and make recommendations. These discussions need to be both modelled and jointly composed before expecting children to independently write their own.

Assessing Readers as Text Code Breakers

In Chapter 3, we broadly described principles and procedures for assessing readers in classrooms. In this section, we include three examples of assessment tools which focus on assessing readers' code breaking knowledge and skills. Remember, these same tools can also be used to assess children's text participant, text user and text analyst practices, too.

These tools enable a teacher to put the spotlight on a particular set of practices. However, it is important to keep in mind that these tools need not and should not be used to separate the four sets of reading practices, as readers use these practices interactively.

Running record

As devised by Clay (1993), running records is a detailed and systematic form of observation which allows teachers to assess children's code breaking practices, specifically:

- children's use of semantic, syntactic and graphological/phonological information for identifying words and predicting meaning;
- children's monitoring of their reading strategies and self-correction of their miscues or errors;
- appropriateness of children's reading material.

Running records are rather time-consuming to administer, as they need to be done on an individual basis. Thus teachers need to be well organised to ensure other children are meaningfully engaged while teachers are with individual readers, and to involve support staff and volunteers in implementing this assessment procedure. Sometimes, teachers use this tool for particular children that they have concerns about (such as children who appear to be struggling or children who appear to be fixed on only one or two means of cracking the code, such as heavily depending on sounding out words). Other teachers may use this tool on a roster basis with all children over a period of several weeks, to monitor development of code breaking skills and their balanced use by children. How you use this tool will depend upon assessment needs and purposes in your own classroom. We have included an example of a running record in Figure 5.

Rating scales

A rating scale is an assessment tool which lists various traits or categories that allows the observer to indicate the importance of the observed behaviours. Rating scales can be developed for assessing children's code breaking skills. When used for this purpose, it allows teachers to assess patterns in children's skills – such as how frequently they use particular skills like predicting, sounding out, and self-correcting. It also allows teachers to determine if children are using a balanced approach, or whether some skills need bolstering to give children greater choice and flexibility. Figure 6 provides an example of a rating scale designed to assess children's use of code breaking skills.

Figure 5

An Example of a Running Record of a Reader's Code Breaking Strategies

<u>Name</u>   John Williamson   <u>Date</u>   18/9/2000

<u>Text</u>   "Henry and Amy(right-way-round and upside down)"
             by Stephen Michael King (1998) Sydney: Scholastic

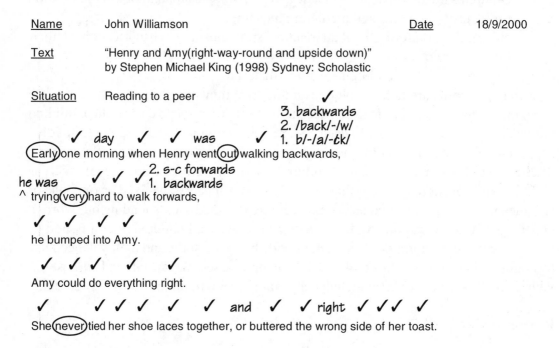

<u>Situation</u>   Reading to a peer   ✓
                                                           3. *backwards*
                                                           2. */back/-/w/*
         ✓ *day*   ✓   ✓ was   ✓ 1. *b/-/a/-ĉk/*
(Early)one morning when Henry went(out)walking backwards,

             ✓ ✓ ✓ 2. *s-c forwards*
he was   1. *backwards*
^ trying(very)hard to walk forwards,

✓   ✓   ✓   ✓

he bumped into Amy.

✓   ✓   ✓   ✓   ✓

Amy could do everything right.

✓   ✓ ✓ ✓ ✓ ✓ and ✓ ✓ right ✓ ✓ ✓ ✓
She(never)tied her shoe laces together, or buttered the wrong side of her toast.

<u>Interpretation</u>
John read this text for meaning. He made three omissions, none of which drastically changed the
meaning of the text. His substitutions still made sense and fitted the structure of the sentence in each
case. This could suggest he is using grammatical knowledge well. When he came across words he
did not know, he sounded them out. He self-corrected when he made a miscue which did not make
sense in the context of this text – this shows he is reading for meaning and monitoring his reading.

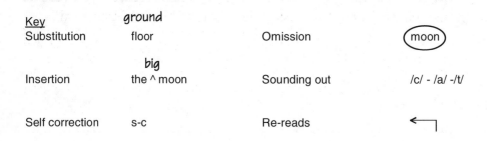

<u>Key</u>   *ground*
Substitution   floor   Omission   (moon)

                        big
Insertion   the ^ moon   Sounding out   /c/ - /a/ -/t/

Self correction   s-c   Re-reads   ⟵⌐

Figure 6

An Example of a Rating Scale for Assessing Readers' Skills as Text Code Breakers

<u>Name</u>   Melanie Stewart   <u>Date</u>   10/3/2001

<u>Situation</u>   Reading to peers; reading to teacher (six separate occasions)

Code Breaking Behaviours
(circle the appropriate response)

	Always	Often	Sometimes	Seldom	Never
Uses word attack skills: sounding out, blending, segmentation, syllabification	1	2	3	4	5
Uses word recognition skills	1	2	3	4	5
Samples text	1	2	3	4	5
Checking and monitoring predictions	1	2	3	4	5
Uses decoding skills to confirm or change predictions of words	1	2	3	4	5
Uses context, grammar and meaning to confirm or change outcomes of word attack skills	1	2	3	4	5

<u>Interpretation</u>

Melanie is very heavily focused on sounding out words she doesn't know. This occurs when she is reading to her peers and when she is reading to me. She especially focuses on initial sounds, but can blend some words quite well. Sounding out words takes time for Melanie at this stage and it seems to break the flow of her reading and the sense she is making. There are several words such as "were" and "was" that she doesn't readily recognise from one occasion to the next. She doesn't show much sign of monitoring her own reading, though, and when she makes graphophonic miscues that change the meaning of the text (such as "walk" for "work") or don't fit the sentence structure (such as substituting "with" with "went"), she doesn't appear to notice. I'll plan activities for her which ask her to think about the sense she is making from text, as well as activities to further enhance her word recognition and attack skills.

Checklists

A checklist is a list of behaviours that the observer identifies as present or absent. Often, these behaviours may be used in a developmental framework, such as our checklist example in Figure 7.

Figure 7

Checklist for Assessing Development of Readers as Text Code Breakers

	Emerging	Developing	Competent
Emergent Phase			
Displays book-handling skills	❑	❑	❑
Displays reading like-behaviours	❑	❑	❑
Recognises own name	❑	❑	❑
Recognises personally significant words in context	❑	❑	❑
Matches some written words in environmental print	❑	❑	❑
Early Phase			
Reads unfamiliar texts, with a focus on print	❑	❑	❑
Has a sight vocabulary of words which they recognise in different contexts	❑	❑	❑
Relies heavily on beginning letters and sounding out words	❑	❑	❑
Asks others for help with unknown words	❑	❑	❑
Skips words as they read	❑	❑	❑
Self-corrects	❑	❑	❑
Uses pictures and context to check understanding	❑	❑	❑
Integrates knowledge about text structures, language features, and subject-specific language	❑	❑	❑
Predicts, confirms, re-reads, reads on, and makes meaningful substitutions for words not recognised	❑	❑	❑
Fluent Phase			
Uses word identification strategies appropriately and automatically with unknown words	❑	❑	❑
Knows and uses word patterns, word derivations, prefixes, suffixes and syllables	❑	❑	❑
Integrates semantic, syntactic and graphophonic information	❑	❑	❑
Adjusts strategies for different text types (genres) and purposes	❑	❑	❑
Has metacognitive awareness of meaning and when meaning breaks down	❑	❑	❑
Slows down and sub-vocalises when meaning breaks down	❑	❑	❑
Self-corrects, re-reads and reads on	❑	❑	❑

When used within a developmental framework, checklists allow teachers to identify developmental trends in children's growth as readers, and so plan their instruction accordingly. The checklist shown in Figure 7 identifies code breaking indicators associated with emergent, early and fluent phases of reading (as previously seen in Figure 4). Where ticks in the box fall will provide a ready indication of where a reader's development is at and where, too, it is possibly heading. It will also allow teachers to diagnose strengths and weaknesses in children's code breaking repertoires.

Summary

Readers use code breaking practices to decipher written texts. In regard to English, readers need to be familiar with the code of written English texts. Code breakers draw on a range of strategies as they decode, predict, confirm, self-correct, and monitor the sense they are making from texts. Teachers need to provide explicit instruction about both the code of written English texts across different media such as print and computers, and strategies for cracking the code. Such instruction should be provided in meaningful, purposeful contexts with real texts.

Key Concepts

- text code breaker
- phonemic awareness
- print awareness
- graphophonic relationships
- sampling, predicting, monitoring, confirming and self-correcting strategies

- phonics
- phonemes
- word awareness
- graphological awareness
- phonological awareness

Tutorial Activities

A. In Chapter 3, we broadly described principles and procedures for assessing readers in classrooms. In this chapter on code breakers, we focused on running records, rating scales and checklists as tools for assessing code breakers. Choose one, two or three other tools from Chapter 3 and show how a teacher might use them to assess children's code breaking practices.

B. Choose a big book that you might use for modelled or guided reading. Examine its particular conventions and features. What features might you model in this book to develop code breaking knowledge and skills? Construct an oral cloze activity around this book, along the lines of what we have described in this chapter.

Further Readings

Adams, M.J., Foorman, B.R., Lundberg, I. & Beeler, T. 1998, *Phonemic Awareness in Young Children,* Paul H. Brookes, Baltimore.

Clay, M. 1979, *The Early Detection of Reading Difficulties,* Heinemann, Auckland.

Clay, M. 1991, *On Being Literate,* Bodley Head, London.

Derewianka, B. 1990, *Exploring How Texts Work,* Primary English Teaching Association, Sydney.

Derewianka, B. 1998, *A Grammar Companion for Primary Teachers,* Primary English Teaching Association, Sydney.

Gibbons, P. 1991, *Learning to Learn in a Second Language,* Primary English Teaching Association, Sydney.

Hancock, J. 1999, *Teaching Literacy Using Information Technology,* International Reading Association, Newark, Delaware.

Ingvarson, D., Ed., 1997, *A Teacher's Guide to the Internet – the Australian Experience,* Heinemann, Melbourne.

Chapter 5

READERS AS TEXT PARTICIPANTS

Opening Quote

*'Stories, from the perspective of narrative theory, are like
an adventure playground in which the nature of the game is
strongly influenced, but not wholly determined by the
structures available'*
(Williams, 1991, p.358)

Chapter Preview

This chapter focuses on readers as text participants. It explores what text
participants do and related knowledge and skills. We examine text genres
and topical knowledge which readers activate with particular texts and show
how this knowledge is culturally shaped. We explore diversity in relation
to text participant practices across different settings and implications for
what teachers do in classrooms. Developmental trends in growth as text
participants are identified and related classroom practices are described.
Procedures and criteria for assessing development of readers as text
participants are described

Focal Questions

- What are text participant practices? *– engage in trying to make sense of text*
- What does a text participant know and do?
- How may texts support the development of text participants?
- What are patterns in readers' growth as text participants?
- How may teachers support and assess the development of text
  participants?
- How may readers from diverse cultural and linguistic backgrounds
  best be supported as text participants?

Introduction

Working out what texts say is not an end unto itself – nor, we believe, should it be taught as such. Rather, breaking the code of a text gives the reader access to possible meanings in that text. This brings us to a second set of reading practices – that of text participant, as highlighted in Figure 1.

Figure 1

Model of Reading as Social Practices with Text Participant Practices Highlighted

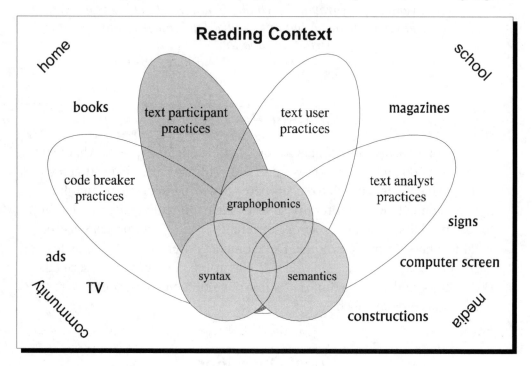

TASK

This task asks you to complete the following Directed Reading-Thinking Activity (a classroom activity genre introduced by Stauffer in 1969). You are asked to read the following text in sections; at the end of each section, you should stop reading and make predictions about what is going to happen next in the text. Remember to write down your predictions as you go.

'Practice makes perfect'

Stop reading. What do you think this text is about? What ideas come to mind? What do you already know about this topic? Jot down your thoughts, then read on.   ☞

2/ 'This activity requires careful observation, good timing and instruments which are in excellent condition. While at first it may seem daunting, remember, practice makes perfect.'   *discouraging*

> Stop reading. What do you think this text is about now? What do you associate this text with? Jot down your thoughts. Have they changed from your previous predictions? How and why? Now read on.

3/ 'Before you begin, collect your equipment. Protective wear is wise, for it is easy to be injured. Check your equipment to ensure it is clean and well honed.'

> Stop reading. What do you think this text is about now? What do you associate this text with? Jot down your thoughts. Have they changed from your previous predictions? How and why? Now read on.

4/ 'It is wise to begin by taking in the big picture. Look at the object overall – take in its shape and its immediate surroundings. Check for potential obstacles. Once you have done this, you can then decide on what parts you want to keep and what parts you want to eliminate.'

> Stop reading. What do you think this text is about now? What do you associate this text with? Jot down your thoughts. Have they changed from your previous predictions? How and why? Now read on.

5/ 'Direction of your action is crucial when eliminating parts. A good rule of thumb is to direct your action the same way as you wish the object to develop. Your action should be precise and crisp. Anything less may cause problems later.'

> Stop reading. What do you think this text is about now? What do you associate this text with? Jot down your thoughts. Have they changed from your previous predictions? How and why? Now read on.

6/ 'If you take the care and consideration described, then you will have pleasing results. But remember, this activity does need to be repeated to ensure that the desired result endures and thrives.'

> Stop reading. You have now read the final piece of the text. What do you think this text is about now? What do you associate this text with? Jot down your thoughts. Have they changed from your previous predictions? How and why?

(The topic of this text is revealed at the end of this chapter, under 'Summary')

What does this tell you about this aspect of reading and how it might be effectively taught in classrooms?

To read the above text you needed to crack its code, as described in our previous chapter. Code breaking practices involve the use of both visual information in texts, as well as non-visual information about written language and meanings. At the same time, however, you were also engaged in trying to make sense of the text -what does it mean? What is it about? As such, you were also engaged as a text participant which brings us to the focus of this chapter.

Being an effective text participant involves understanding meanings in a text. A text participant might implicitly or explicitly ask questions like, what is this text trying to say? what are its possible meanings? what do I already know about this topic?

As text participants, readers attend to how the text relates to the readers' prior knowledge and the way the text is constructed to make meaning. What meanings we make from a text are shaped by what we have read, seen, heard and experienced before. For example, what predictions you made about 'Practice makes perfect' would have been influenced by your own experiences.

Knowledge and Skills of a Text Participant

The kinds of knowledge and skills which text participants draw on are summarised in Figure 2.

As a text participant, a reader draws on two kinds of knowledge: knowledge of the topic at hand (content) and knowledge of how the text at hand is organised (structure). This set of reading practices then sees the reader engage with both meaning and structure of a text (after Freebody 1992, p.50). Knowledge of text structures and topics is in essence cultural knowledge. As Luke (2000, p.455) suggests, 'text participant practices are embedded in a reader's engagement with the cultures around them – residual and emergent, traditional and popular'.

Knowledge of how texts are organised

When readers encounter texts, they may ask, 'What kind of text is this?' Addressing such a question, whether asked explicitly or considered implicitly, allows a reader to narrow the options for what the text might possibly mean.

Each text excerpt in the following task has the potential of activating a particular genre schema (Wallace, 1992) in the reader. Schema refers to cognitive structures which enable us to organise information in our long term memory (after Widdowson, 1983). For example, if you read the words, 'Once upon a time', what kind of text do you think of? Probably fairy tales, which make up a text genre. Thus a fairy tale schema is activated and will let you anticipate what will follow broadly in the text. Of course, what genre schema are activated is partly cued by the text and partly cued by the readers' experiences

Figure 2

Overview of Text Participant

Definition

Text participants make meanings from texts

– making meaning:
what is this text saying?
what are its possible meanings?

Knowledge

Knowledge about the text's topic

Knowledge about the text genre – how it is organised

Intertextual knowledge

Knowledge about how Information Technology texts are organised

Skills

Retrieving literal meanings from text

Drawing inferences from text

Interpreting text

Constructing figurative meanings in text

Evaluating text

Innovating on text

Making links to prior knowledge and experiences

Reading pictures and other kinds of visual images across print, IT and other media

Based on Freebody (1992), Luke (2000), Luke & Freebody (1999) and NSW Department of Education and Training (1997) *Teaching Reading: A K-6 Framework*.

with particular texts and genres. If you are not at all familiar with fairy tales, then this could not be activated by 'once upon a time'.

TASK

If you came across the following texts for the first time and read their opening lines or titles, what kind of text would you anticipate and what might it be about broadly? Jot down your thoughts and reflect on why you have anticipated particular genres.

    'Once upon a time ...' — *fairy tale narrative*

    'Thrilling victory for nation's hero' *information*

    'Chicken pasta' — *Procedural*

    'A remake of a film first made in 1932, ...' *recount.*

    'An easy to grow perennial with an upright shape and compact foliage...' *explanation*.

What does this tell you about this aspect of reading and how it might be effectively taught in classrooms?

Text structures influence the pathways of meaning which readers carve out. For example, a narrative may begin with an orientation which puts the reader in the picture. This may be followed by events and complications which eventually come to some sort of resolution. The narrative may be rounded off by a coda. So, if reading a narrative, a reader will carve out a pathway of meaning which follows chronology of events and relationships among characters; settings and descriptions of characters will be attended to; complications will be anticipated and resolutions often will be guessed at even before they are at hand.

But what if instead a reader comes across an instructional text, such as a recipe, in order to make a cake? Then a different pathway of meaning will be constructed. Meanings in the text will be closely linked to the actions of the reader, as the text directs the reader to what utensils and ingredients to get out, how much of each ingredient to measure and add and what steps and in what sequence these actions need to be done. Readers may play with the text as many cooks do with recipes – but it is essentially a different kind of play with meaning than what readers may do when trying to second-guess motives and outcomes in a story.

Genre-related schema have a cognitive aspect to them, in terms of what mental structures are evoked in a reader's mind and how a reader's processing of text is subsequently influenced. However, knowledge of text genres is also essentially cultural

(Derewianka, 1990; Kress, 1985; Luke, 1993; Luke & Freebody, 2000; Wallace, 1992). It is sociocultural in the following ways.

- Knowledge of genres is gained through participation in and talk about particular genres in particular sociocultural settings. For example, in a study by Minns (1990), six year old Gurdeep was being raised by his Indian family in a working class community in England. In that family and community visits to the temple and exposure to traditional Indian tales as well as religious texts at bedtime were seen by Gurdeep's parents to teach him invaluable lessons about his cultural values, beliefs and way of life.

- What genres are and are not practised vary across sociocultural settings. For example, in Heath's study of three different sociocultural communities (Heath, 1983, 1986a), different genres emerged as part of everyday life. In middle class Afro-American Trackton oral story-telling was widely practised and highly valued; children were very much involved in such sessions. In Anglo-American working class Roadville reading the Bible as a didactic text was a frequent occurrence and the value of texts often was measured in terms of its truthfulness. In Anglo-American middle class Maintown narratives were a regular part of bedtime routines for children. The children in each of these communities were apprenticed into their respective community genres by way of immersion in them and talking about them. What happens, however, when children from different communities such as these come to school is a matter of concern – not in terms of inadequacies in the home, but rather in terms of school's failure to recognise and build upon children's home and community practices.

- What genres are valued and what genres are not valued vary across different sociocultural communities. For example, in mainstream school settings text genres such as narratives in the early school years is given much weight. As children progress through school, increasing emphasis is placed on factual information texts, arguments and discussions, with particular endorsed ways of reading and producing these genres.

Relevance of text structures to text participants extends to information technology texts. Take the *World Book* CD-Rom, for example (World Book, Inc. 1998, IBM Corp., 1998). Its initial organisation is along the following lines:

- Cover page (including IBM copyright)
- Home page:

Browse	*Search*
[icon] World Book	[icon] Topics
[icon] Media	[icon] Maps
[icon] Monthly Spotlight	[icon] Dictionary
	[icon] Time Frame
	[icon] What's online

Each icon represents a hyperlink and involves visual literacy to understand their meanings. For example, an eye next to World Book indicates the eye of a reader. An image of a CD next to Media represents various audio clips as well as photographs and other kinds of images which are found throughout the two volume *World Book* CD-Rom. 'Topics' is accompanied by an image of an open book with the heading 'Articles'; 'Dictionary' by an open dictionary; 'Maps' is represented by a globe; 'Time Frame' by an hour glass; and 'What's Online' by a satellite dish. Think about the cultural knowledge embedded in each of these images and necessary to recognising their meanings.

Back to organisation, each hyperlink takes a reader to sites, each of which have their own inherent organisation. For example, 'Media' page is organised as follows:

- a window to the left of the screen, giving options to click on Disc One or Two, which then shows a scrolling alphabetical list of images and audio clips for reader selection
- a menu bar across the top:

   InstructionsCaption   Go to Article   Browse   Overlay

A text participant needs to be able to interpret each of these menu items. What do 'instructions' mean in this context? How do they relate to the Media text at hand? In fact, they tell the reader how this page works. The 'caption' item, when clicked provides a caption from the *World Book* for the image or audio clip which the reader has chosen from the left hand window. Clicking on 'Go to article' takes the reader to the article in which the selected audio clip or image is to be found. 'Browse media' is the item the reader is currently using. A text participant needs to know that clicking on any of these items takes the reader to that site (as in 'Go to article') or brings that function to the present screen (as in 'Caption'); clicking them on again takes the function away once again.

Immediately above this bar is another set of menu items. Each is shown by an image; positioning the cursor on the image brings a word to the screen that explicitly identifies its function. For example, positioning the cursor on the image of a magnifying glass brings the word 'search' to the screen, denoting its search function.

A text participant also needs to know that some of these menu items are only able to be activated when the reader is in the articles of the *World Book*. For example, a reader can only choose a highlighter function (represented by an image of the tip of an highlighter pen) or a post-it note (represented by an image of a post-it) when an article is on the screen.

Those of us familiar with CD-Roms such as the *World Book* may take these systems of organisation for granted. However, over and beyond the actual print-like texts included (such as articles in the *World Book*), there are structures of organisation quite particular to Information Technology texts. Some of these organisational patterns are quite similar across various IT texts; others will vary. For CD-Roms, internet texts and the like to be used effectively in classrooms, teachers need to become familiar with the organisation of these materials, and model and guide children through their organisation in much the same way as they would with print-based texts.

Knowledge of text topics

When encountering texts readers not only consider the kind of text they have at hand, but what the text is about. This brings us to knowledge of text topics (also referred to as field knowledge). In this chapter's first task the title 'Practice makes perfect' conjured up various schema for many of you. Some of you might have activated sporting schema, others might have brought craft-related schema to bear. Whatever schema you initially activated, you would have kept this under review as you read this somewhat obscure text and tried to unravel its meaning.

Words in the text would have influenced your monitoring processes. Words like 'equipment', 'protective wear', and 'easy to be injured' may have evoked schema related to risky activity, such as high-risk sports. Actions described as 'precise' and 'crisp' may have helped confirm or disrupt your schema. Reference to 'shape', 'care and consideration' might have brought opposing schema into view.

Revisiting the text titles and beginnings in your previous task (set out below again for you), what words help cue you into what each will be about?

'Once upon a time ...' — n

'Thrilling victory for nation's hero' — inf.

'Chicken pasta' — ins.

'A remake of a film first made in 1932, ...' Me

'An easy to grow perennial with an upright shape and compact foliage ...' — ex

If you are familiar with fairy tales, then the first text extract, 'once upon a time' would have been readily recognisable as the beginning of a fairy tale. Having identified that then there are certain things you might anticipate about its topic, especially if you were to next read 'lived a beautiful princess'. You might expect the tale to be about a love story between a prince and a princess, complicated by the evil doing of a witch or a step-mother, but ultimately redeemed by the good of the protagonists who live happily ever after.

With reference to 'thrilling victory for nation's hero', the absence of 'a' before 'thrilling victory' and the sensational overtones of 'thrilling' and 'hero', suggests a newspaper headline to those familiar with newspapers' style of reporting. 'Chicken pasta', if recognised as a name of a dish, suggests a recipe.

Reference to 'remake of a film' implies a film review text and words 'perennial' and 'foliage' elicit to those familiar with garden books and television programs a text about gardening.

In all cases, a reader's recognition of text genre and topic will be shaped by what they have encountered as part of their own reading histories – what we might refer to as intertextual histories, which we explore a little more in the next section.

Multiple and Possible Meanings in Texts

Texts can be thought of as not only those physically present but also those texts and fragments of ideas and experiences which are remembered and constructed in a reader's mind (Pearson & Tierney, 1984, cited in Hartman, 1995). What genres and meanings any one text evokes, once it has left the hands of its author and is taken up by a reader will be shaped by many intertextual influences.

For example, if you were to come across the word 'duckville' what meaning would you give it? Your response might be blank, or you might have one or even more possible associations. What you associate with this word will be shaped by other texts you have read, viewed and listened to.

'Duckville' was a word uttered by six-year old Lenny in a classroom study by this book's first author (Harris & Trezise, 1999, p.371). Its occurrence was puzzling for Lenny did not explain beyond this one word what he meant, and there seemed to be nothing in the book he was reading to explain where 'duckville' possibly could have come from. Let us visit this episode here:

Lenny, a first grader, was reading a book of stories about families in silent reading time in his classroom. He came to an illustration which showed an extended family of animals in a tree. Each animal was labeled in terms of its family role, such as 'mother', 'father'. Lenny turned to me and asked:

Len: Do I have to read this?
Pau: Do you want to read it?
Len: [nods] [reading] 'mother' ... 'father' ... 'brother' ... 'sister' ...
         I don't know this one [pointing to 'nephew']
Pau: 'Nephew'.
Len: Duckville ....
Pau: No, it says 'nephew'.

I had not understood Lenny's intention, nor was I familiar with 'Duckville'. Fortunately, Lenny persevered with me and, in doing so, revealed understandings I otherwise would have overlooked:

Len: Yeah, I know, but that's like 'Louie' and 'Dewey'. I've got a book about it.
Pau: What's its name?
Len: 'The Giant Pearl'

In elaborating on his 'Duckville' utterance, Lenny drew intertextual connections across space and time to a remembered text and to situational contexts at home and school:

Len: I'll bring it in for News tomorrow ... oh, except you won't be here.
Pau: Perhaps you can bring it in next Monday, I'll be here then.
Len: Yeah, but News will be over by then.
Pau: Oh.
Len: When do you go?
Pau: I leave when you go out for Recess, for little lunch.
Len: When you go, I can ... when I get my little lunch, I can show you before you go.
Pau: OK.   (Harris & Trezise, 1999, p.372)

In many ways this interaction illustrates the intertextual nature of reading – and for the purposes of this chapter, text participant practices specifically. Intertextuality was originally conceived by Kristeva (1984) as a way of showing how every text is shaped by other texts. If texts are intertextual, so too is the act of making sense of them. Making sense can occur in a blink of an eye – as was the case with Lenny. He said "duckville" very quickly and spontaneously before the association was even fully formed in his mind. This, in fact, typifies how meaning making works for many readers (Harris & Trezise, 1999; Kristeva, 1984). Harris and Trezise (1999, p.372) went on to elaborate:

'Once unpacked, condensed utterances like 'Duckville' reveal substantial understanding and insight. Lenny was …

- *identifying a link between a classroom reader-type text encountered at school and the cartoon texts encountered in print and on television at home;*
- *drawing an analogy between the family tree in the classroom text and the family situation of Donald Duck and his nephews in Donald Duck texts; and*
- *shifting from the general labels on the family tree, e.g., 'uncle'; 'nephew') to particular examples, that is, Donald Duck as Uncle and Huey, Dewey and Louie as nephews (after Hasan,1996).*

These reveal levels of higher-order thinking about texts, as suggested by Ruddell's model in Ruddell and Harris (1989).

These higher-order levels of thinking are closely related to Bloom's taxonomy (Bloom, 1956) which identifies five levels of thinking. These may be applied to levels of making meaning from texts, which we show below:

1. Knowledge – this is the simplest level in Bloom's taxonomy and is defined as recall of facts and ideas. In relation to text participants, this may be used to refer to direct and literal retrieval of what is in a written text, such as main ideas, facts, dates and definitions of terms in factual texts; sequence of events, settings and characters' actions in narratives; materials and actions in instructional texts like recipes; and so on.
2. Comprehension – this refers to understanding and includes knowledge at the previous level. In relation to text participants, includes interpreting written texts, as well as engaging in inferring implicit meanings, making predictions, and explaining relationships such as cause-and-effect.
3. Application – this refers to the ability to use ideas and principles in new situations and includes comprehension and knowledge of the previous two levels. In relation to text participants, this may include applying new insights gained from reading a novel to new situations, applying new concepts read in a factual text to undertaking a new activity and so on.
4. Analysis – this is defined as identifying parts of a whole, and includes knowledge, comprehension and application of the previous three levels. In relation to text participants, this involves process such as analysing, comparing, contrasting and classifying.

5. Synthesis – the highest level in Bloom's taxonomy, refers to putting parts together to make a whole and includes knowledge, comprehension, application and analysis of the four previous levels. It involves processes such as creating, constructing and predicting.

There are, of course, other taxonomies which have been developed since Bloom (such as the one by Ruddell in Ruddell & Harris, 1989, which we previously read). Regardless of the taxonomy *per se,* we need to keep in mind these levels of thinking, as they plan interactions around texts, in order to ensure their questioning and discussion about texts achieves this balance and genuinely fosters higher order thinking in their students. We return to this point later, as we examine modelled and guided reading.

How Picture Book Narratives Work and their Influence on Text Participants

When selecting texts to nurture children's text participants practices, it is important to select texts which cater to a child's ability and inexperience (Williams, 1991, p.361). Texts which do this most effectively are those whose stories may be simple, but they are not simply told. Texts define roles for readers in different ways, especially in terms of what a reader has to do to construct a story (Williams, 1991, p.361)

A key to this is the ways in which pictures can relate to words. Picture book narratives can present various relationships between words and pictures, as has been quite extensively explored by Margaret Meek (1988) and Judith Graham (1990). We briefly explore these below.

Pictures confirming words

To begin with, pictures may have a quite direct and straightforward relationship with the words. As such, they *confirm* what the words say and together with the words, they create what seems to be a unified narrative. For example, pictures may quite directly *echo* the words. While it is always inevitable that pictures provide an interpretation of what the words say, pictures may do so without substantially adding new information or changing what the words say. For example, in *Maisy Goes to Playschool* by Lucy Cousins (1992), the words say 'Maisy dances like a ballerina'. The illustration directly shows Maisy dressed as a ballerina and in ballerina pose. The reader can even contribute to this direct meaning by moving a tab to make Maisy indeed dance like a ballerina!

Pictures may expand upon what the words say, by showing background and situation, how characters are feeling, what they look like and so on. A good example of this is found in *Where the Wild Things Are* by Maurice Sendak (1963). While the words describe Max's adventure to 'the place where the wild things are', the illustrations show both this as well as Max's feelings as he progresses on his journey. The reader is vividly shown Max's feelings of mischief as he chases his dog down the stairs, his feelings of indignation when sent to bed without his supper, his feelings of glee and anticipation as a forest takes over his room, his feelings of empowerment as he takes charge over the monstrous 'wild things', his feelings of loneliness when longing for home and his feelings of calm and composure when returning home once more.

In expanding upon the words, pictures may also unlock themes that may be too difficult to express in words – themes such as friendship, jealousy, even death, as in *John Brown, Rose and the Midnight Cat* (see Graham, 1990, for a detailed analysis of this book.

In all these examples, where pictures confirm what the words say through echoing, focusing and expanding their meanings, the reader as a text participant is positioned by the text to directly retrieve meanings from the words and look to the pictures for additional information as cues to meaning and as bases for interpretation and anticipation.

To be a text participant means reading pictures as well as words. The ability of the reader to think and to anticipate are valued by such texts as *Where the Wild Things Are* and *John Brown, Rose and the Midnight Cat* by Jenny Wagner and Ron Brooks (1977). These texts offer rich layers of meaning, which may be peeled back with each visit to the book. Re-reading such texts, then, serves a purpose beyond repetition for the sake of developing code breaking skills alone. Rather, reading serves a real purpose of extracting more meaning and exploring possible and even contradictory meanings, yet at the same time affording the opportunity to practise and refine code breaking skills.

Pictures disrupting words

Instead of confirming what the words say, pictures may actually disrupt what the words directly say or suggest. Pictures may introduce elements which create disturbance or ambiguity not suggested by the words. Possibilities are created which somehow are at odds with the words.

For example, in *Rosie's Walk* by Pat Hutchins (1968), the words describe an uneventful stroll which Rosie the hen takes around a farmyard. The pictures show Rosie in unchanged pose as she appears to take her casual stroll, head slightly upturned in the air. However, the pictures do more: they introduce threat, a complication in the form of a predatory fox in cunning pursuit of Rosie. Time and again he tries to catch her, only to fail each time. Thus the pictures disrupt the semblance of an uneventful stroll. The tension between words and pictures provide gaps for the reader as text participant, inviting them to ask questions like 'what is really going on here?'. There is more to the story than first meets the eye – the reader might wonder, perhaps, if Rosie knows what is going on. Or does the fact that the words do not mention the fox suggest to the reader that Rosie does not know what is going on behind her back? Williams (1991) refers to books like *Rosie's Walk* as providing 'space to play' for readers. If the reader chooses to play, then further layers of meaning may be constructed.

Pictures contradicting words

Going beyond disrupting what the words say, pictures may in fact contradict what the words say – producing in the most extreme cases a 'divided narrative'. For example, in John Burningham's picture book,*Come Away from the Water, Shirley*, the words report on what two vigilant parents are saying to their daughter as she plays in the water at the beach. The illustrations on the left side of each page are consistent with these words – showing Shirley's parents in their deck chairs, looking over Shirley. However, on the right side of each page a different story altogether unfolds in pictures. Brightly coloured, the pictures tell a story of Shirley's adventure at sea, complete with pirates, treasure chest and walking the plank. Thus the picture book constructs a story of contrast between an adult-controlled world and a fancy-free world of childhood imagination. This construction is, of course, culturally laden – many refugee children, after all, would find Shirley's daydreams about pirates a nightmare instead.

TASK

Explore one, two or three picture books in terms of how words and pictures relate to each other. How might you describe their relationships, in terms of the relationships briefly described in this chapter? What potential effect does each relationship have on the functioning of the reader as a text participant? How might you use the text in modelled and guided reading sessions?

Information Technology and Text Participant Practices

In many ways, text participant practices related to Information Technology texts are not so very different from those related to print. Knowledge about topics and text structures are relevant in IT contexts. If anything, hypertexts make more explicit what readers do with most texts they read – making links as they go and carving out pathways of meaning through the links they select and pursue.

Doing searches on the World Wide Web

Knowing how to use search engines effectively on the World Wide Web is not so very different from knowing how to do searches in libraries or in information books and reference materials. They all require some degree of background topic knowledge – what a reader already knows about the topic will determine how specific they can be in terms of breakdown and scope of the topic at hand. A reader may know little of the topic and so do a broad search which the reader needs to cull as they make judgements about relevance to the topic at hand.

Alternatively, a reader may know enough about the topic to break it down into sub-topics, key words and phrases which will facilitate the success of the search. They may be able to adjust the scope of their search with addition or deletion of key words and authors they know work in the field of their inquiry.

Another aspect of WWW searches that is similar to library searches is understanding the search results, initially from title and URL, and from the brief blurbs that are provided. Similarly, in libraries, online catalogues may provide some preliminary information that may allow a reader to cull or continue to pursue items.

Searching the WWW can be overwhelming, however – much more than libraries and reference material, because of the sheer vastness of the Web (and the many distractions which can occur along the way when pursuing links). Ingvarson (1997, p.29) has developed a 'Selected Bookmark Strategy' which we previously mentioned in Chapter 4. Designed for classroom use, this strategy involves a teacher conducting an initial search which yields a number of possible references. With reference to ages of the children in the class, the topic at hand, the number and type of reference books listed, a teacher may then:

- quickly visit sites and bookmark those considered suitable – children can then use these sites as starting points; or
- print out the search results list and allocate various references to various children or groups for follow up; or
- select references containing further external links – allocate one primary reference from list to each group or individual and require them to follow up secondary or tertiary links from the original, collecting material from each site visited.

A question of meaningful access to the World Wide Web

The issue of access to relevant, safe, and good quality resources is a contentious issue for classroom teachers. We argue that there is a fine line between teachers taking proactive steps to ensure meaningful access and disenfranchising students from the process of discerning quality and relevance for themselves. We continue to explore this issue in our Chapter on Text Analysts.

Massie (1997) advocates the use of local area networks (LAN) to create an 'intranet'. This involves teachers selecting material they deem relevant and of good quality from the WWW, and placed on the LAN in a WWW-like format. The objective of this approach is

> *'to allow students access to a wide and rich range of curriculum specific material, but in an environment that teaches comfortable familiarity with current WWW facilities such as browsers, hotlinks and searching techniques. If the long-term aim is for students to surf the wide open seas of the Internet, we choose to teach them the basics of survival and navigation in a paddle pool.' (Massie, 1997, p.53)*

Massie (1997, p.54) also explains that the choice of material extracted from the WWW and placed on the LAN is 'entirely the prerogative of those who guide the curriculum at the school'.

We support concerns with safety in terms of child protection on the internet and measures to address these concerns such as ensuring appropriate levels of supervision within the classroom; withholding identifying information over the WWW; and encouraging children to advise their teacher if they receive inappropriate messages (N.A.E.Y.C, 1999). Teachers might also consider the use of Internet filtering software for added security.

Also, the idea of reducing the quantity of information available in a WWW format may have its merits in terms of what children can manage.

However, when it comes to matters of relevance and quality of information, we ask you to critically consider the following question:

> Should children have a role in the process of selecting information from the World Wide Web or should this rest with teachers alone? Why/why not?

From our point of view, judging relevance is an important part of being a text participant, for these judgements are based on topic knowledge and influence how that knowledge develops. We would certainly caution against electronic spoonfeeding and instead advocate the development of learners' active roles in this decision-making process. What is 'meaningful' to one reader may not be meaningful to another reader.

These judgements also relate to text user practices in terms of reading purposes – relevance of a particular text will depend on the reader's purpose at hand and how they themselves perceive relevance (as we explore in our next Chapter).

In relation to quality of information, judgements about quality tie in with analyst practices, as we see in Chapter 7 – for example, who defines 'quality'? Whose purposes and agendas are being promoted when some materials are selected and others are kept at a distance?

We also believe that it is important to remember that children may access the WWW outside the classroom, and perhaps the classroom should be the very place where the skills to make such judgements are nurtured in appropriate ways.

Developing Readers from Diverse Cultural and Linguistic Backgrounds as Text Participants

For all children from all cultural and linguistic backgrounds, it is essential that teachers tune in and build upon readers' schema and intertextual histories which they bring to texts. Sometimes this is a challenge for teachers, as children do not always make their meanings clear at the outset (as we saw with 'Duckville'), and because when teachers ask questions, they already have preconceived answers that they are looking for. This is evident in the following extract from the first author's research (Harris & Trezise, 1997). In a Kindergarten classroom children and their teacher are focusing on the picture book narrative, *Meg's Eggs*, by Nicoll & Pienkowski (1975). The story is about the comical misadventures of a witch called Meg. In the extract below the teacher reads a spell within the story and asks the children to identify its genre:

'T: *Listen to this. "Lizards and newts, three loud hoots, green frogs' legs, three big eggs." What does that sound like?*

Cathy: *Like a rock-a-bye.*

T: *It doesn't sound like something that would put me to sleep.*

Edward: *It's a spell.*

T: *Good boy. What's a spell?'* (Harris & Trezise, 1997 , p.197)

Like yourselves when reading the various text extracts in this chapter, children in this class had different associations with the same text. Cathy's response made sense, especially in light of her home experiences where nursery rhymes featured as a very substantial and enjoyable part of her bedtime routines.

When choosing texts in classrooms, it is also important to assess their cultural relevance and to be aware of how texts may be interpreted differently according to different cultural frames of reference. Gibbons (1991, p.76) has made this point quite vividly:

'Content which is quite alien to children, or has a different connotation for them, will be much more difficult to understand. Refugee children who have encountered real pirates will not bring to a pirate story the same associations of adventure, excitement and fun that the topic may evoke in the minds of Anglo Celtic children.'

Ways of making meaning which are valued and foregrounded vary across different sociocultural contexts. For example, in Heath's study which we have already mentioned, (1983, 1986a) parents in white middle-class homes encouraged children to talk about and relate books to their own experiences. In contrast, parents in working class homes focused more on code breaking practices rather than talking about possible meanings in a text. Indeed, the Bible featured as a predominant text in many homes and in such instances the single truthfulness of text was prioritised. In yet another contrast, families in Afro-American middle class homes focused more on participating in oral story telling events, which were judged in terms of embellishment and dramatic effect even if based on real-life events.

From Heath's study, and other such studies (Minns,1990; Reid, 1998), four key implications for teachers emerge:

- teachers need to recognise the many and diverse ways of making meaning from texts which children bring to school;
- teachers need to build on these diverse practices to provide continuity of experience and to validate children's histories;

- teachers need to include a range of home and community text participant practices in their classroom repertoires; and
- teachers, at the same time, need to explicitly orient children to text participant practices which are critical to success at school.

When working with NESB children Gibbons (1990) highlights the need to explicitly talk about the language of questioning about meaning. This requires teachers to identify the language demands of their questions and to model forms of questions and answers to children. Some examples follow:

- describing, e.g., 'What is [a character] like?'
- evaluating, e.g., 'Do you think [a character] was treated fairly?'
- inferring, e.g., 'Why do you think [an event] happened?'
- generalising, e.g., 'Do all spiders have these features?'
- predicting, e.g., 'What do you think will happen next?'
- making links, e.g., 'What does this text remind you of?'
- sequencing, e.g., 'What happened next?'
- comparing, e.g., 'How is that the same as ...?'
- contrasting, e.g., 'How is that different from...?'
- giving/following instructions, e.g., 'First, do...'
- classifying, e.g., 'How are all these the same?'
- recounting, e.g., 'Describe what happened.'
- summarising, e.g., 'What was this text about, in your own words?'
- giving an opinion, e.g., 'What do you think about...?'
- personal response, e.g., 'How did that make you feel?'
- arguing, e.g., 'Do you agree or disagree? Why?'
- discussing, e.g., 'That's one point of view. What's another?'

The types of questions asked by teachers and children about texts will of course, be influenced by the type of text at hand. For example, if a class is talking about a narrative, then there may be quite a few questions which focus on personal response, description of events and characters, and evaluating actions in the story. A recount, on the other hand, may focus talk more on sequence and description of events. Factual texts such as information texts will likely evoke questions which involve generalising, classifying, and recalling information, and so on.

While many children from diverse social and linguistic backgrounds are able to develop competency as text participants through explicit and systematic demonstrations in modelled and guided reading sessions, teaching practices need to also incorporate reflective practices. Guided and modelled reading sessions may enhance disadvantaged children's understandings about text topics and structures. However, follow-up questions are just as important for they not only continue to model this set of reading practices, they also stimulate and facilitate children's insights into texts and hone their emerging interpretations.

It is also important that teachers allow children to volunteer their own thoughts and ideas, as they come to hand. Research by Harris and Trezise (1999) and Oyler and Barry (1996) show the greater levels of meaning which children can reach when freed from the constraints of always having to answer questions which someone else asks. In being able to spontaneously make their own comments and ask their own questions, children are able to establish and pursue their own pathways of meaning. Teachers should be prepared to guide the children on their journeys of meaning-making, taking the child's lead at times and providing sign posts to help children navigate their way.

At the same time, it is important to realise that not all children will come to class ready to interact in this way. Many children, for example, may come from backgrounds which directly discourage children interrupting the teacher and asking their own questions; they may be much more accustomed to being the respondents to teachers' questions instead. Teachers need to be aware of this and explicitly model through their own interactions and those of other children in the class, ways of contributing to discussions around texts.

Classroom Practices for Supporting Text Participants

Developmental trends in becoming a proficient text participant are shown in Figure 3, along with related classroom practices.

Below we elaborate further on some of these practices. We begin with some suggestions on conducting modelled and guided reading sessions in ways that most effectively engage readers. This is followed by a description of other classroom activities.

Modelled and guided reading *prior knowl*

When conducting modelled and guided reading (as explained in our previous chapter), there are a number of considerations which teachers may keep in mind. Each of these are detailed below.

Make links to children's prior knowledge and experiences (semantic)

As Pearson and Tierney (1984, cited in Hartman, 1995) indicate, texts can be thought of as not only those physically present but also those texts and fragments of ideas and experiences which are remembered and constructed in the mind. Teachers who effectively develop text participants are those who make links to children's experiences and understandings as they make meaning from books. This activation of prior knowledge and experiences has been shown to be a critical element of reading (Ruddell & Unrau, 1993) and provides a pathway to a higher order thinking about texts.

Focusing children's attention is an important first step in doing this. For example, from a study by Harris (1998), a Year One teacher drew on local knowledge and asked questions about children's personal experiences with the question, 'Do you think this

Figure 3

Developmental Trends of Text Participants and Related Pedagogic Practices

Indicators	Pedagogic Practices
Emergent Phase *(includes Role-Play &Experimental Reading; approximately links to Early Stage 1)**	
• Realises that print carries a message, but each time they read the same print,message may change	• Encourage children to talk about their meanings and to go beyond literal recall
• Focuses on the meaning of media and electronic as well as print texts such as a television program or story	• Praise children's divergent thinking, and avoid seeking consensus of ideas about what a text means
• Makes links between such texts and their own personal experiences	• Allow children to see there are many ways of interpreting a text, and invite different interpretations among children
• Focuses on meaning rather than accuracy	
• Comes to use prior knowledge of context and personal experience to make meaning	• Re-read favourite texts, to allow children to explore new layers of meaning
• Children's responses to various texts reflect understanding and interpretation	• Model how you interpret words and illustrations
	• Guide children's interpretations through open-ended questioning and prompting
	• Make links between texts and children's own experiences and texts they have read
	• Use various forms of print purposefully and on a daily basis
	• Encourage children to express their responses to what they read, view and hear through drama and visual arts.
Early Phase *(includes Early and Transitional Reading; approximately links to Stage 1 and into Stage 2)**	
• Can re-tell major content from visual and printed texts	• Ask about ideas and information children have found in books
• Uses pictures and knowledge of context to check their understanding of meanings	• Provide opportunities for children to individually conference with you about what they are reading, and what meanings and responses they are making
• Comes to re-tell and discuss interpretations of narrative texts, in relation to plot, characters, main idea and supporting details	• Provide opportunities for children to demonstrate their understandings of and responses to texts, through activities such as story maps, semantic webs, readers theatre, reader response, directed thinking reading/listening activities, read and re-tell, drama, and visual arts
	• Encourage use of personal experience to make meaning
	• Develop a shared language to talk about how different kinds of texts are organised

Pat Hutchinson
Rosie Walk.

Fluent Phase (*includes Independent and Advanced Independent Reading; approximately links to Stage 3*)*

- Reads and comprehend text that is abstract and removed from personal experience
- Makes inferences based on implicit information and justify these
- Makes connections between old and new knowledge
- Returns purposefully to different sections of a text to make connections among them
- Reading becomes purposeful and automatic
- Proficient in making connections between new and old knowledge

- Discuss prior knowledge of text types (genres), text structure and language appropriate to text type
- Help children to anticipate and select appropriate reading strategies
- Engage children in a range of activities to explore and express their meanings and responses (see those listed under early readers for text participants)

[in addition to those strategies identified for emergent and early readers]

* Emergent, early and fluent labels are derived from Mooney (1990). Role Play, Experimental, Early, Independent and Advanced labels are derived from the Western Australian department of Education's *First Steps – A Reading Developmental Continuum* document (1994). Approximate links are made to Early Stage 1, Stage 1, Stage 2 and Stage 3 as identified in NSW Board of Studies *English K-6 Syllabus*.

is Benjamin Park?' (adjacent to their school). As children responded they were asked 'Why do you think so?' As they explored similarities and differences among their responses and between the park in the book and their local park, children's thinking was raised to inferential levels.

These shifts in thinking beyond literal meanings were facilitated further by teachers' links to shared experiences.

Provide and utilise shared experiences

There are times when teachers try to unsuccessfully interpret children's responses in light of what they believe to be their personal experiences.

Harris (1998) found that teachers make more appropriate interpretations when they base these on shared texts and experiences. For example, when talking about the picture book 'Crocodile Beat' (Jorgensen & Mullins, 1988), in modelled reading, one teacher made links to the following experiences which the class had shared:

- a text about crocodiles on the classroom's listening post;
- a previous classroom visitor who brought a baby crocodile; and
- a future activity when the children would be making collage pictures similar to those in the book.

At the same time children volunteered their own links to shared experiences. These included: links to rhyming stories; links to another classroom text, links to a class song, 'The prehistoric animal brigade', links between rhyming words and things children themselves had said, links to word lists on display, links to a class television program; and links to a previous class excursion.

In making links across children's personal and instructional experiences, teachers provide very explicit signals of what the children can anticipate and on what the children can build new learning. This supports children in making connections, thereby moving beyond recall to interpret and transfer meanings within and across texts.

Provide opportunity for peer input and feedback

Children also serve as agents in fostering one another's thinking as they take up one another's meanings. We can see this illustrated in the following excerpt where children and teacher are discussing if Rosie knew about the fox in *Rosie's Walk* by Pat Hutchins (1968):

Jim:	I think Rosie doesn't know about the fox.
Geo:	Same here.
Fel:	Yeah, but how do you know?
Geo:	'Cause, um, 'cause she's just walking along, like, um, like walking around the pond and looking up at the sky.
Jim:	Yeah, like there [going to book and turning to page showing Rosie walking around the pond]
T:	How do you think she feels there?
Geo:	Um, good, pretty good.

Fel: Yeah, I think she feels good, too, but, um, you know, um, she's not dumb!

Jim: Sure she is. All chooks are dumb.

Geo: Yeah! My uncle has chooks, and he's always going mad at them, they're always getting out and getting caught.

T: Felicia, why do you say Rosie's not dumb? What makes you think that?

And so they continued. Children extended, corroborated and even challenged one another's interpretations. The teacher used the children's ideas as the basis for her own questioning which seeks to clarify and raise children's thinking to higher interpretative level.

Children's participation in this way is enabled by the freedom the teacher gives them to make spontaneous contributions (this has been shown to be particularly important in a classroom study by Oyler & Barry, 1996).

In this way, a sense of a meaning-making community – as also seen in Cairney (1990; 1992) – is fostered. In this community children share with their teacher authority in verifying or indeed challenging one another's meanings. There is no one right answer – no answer that is in the teacher's head that children try to guess. When the teacher takes up a child's contribution and when children do the same for one another, children's meanings are implicitly validated. Such activity, according to Ruddell and Unrau (1993), enables readers to perceive and engage in text participant practices as processes of exploring and possible meanings.

Allowing children to spontaneously contribute their ideas in such a way that shapes the interactions around the text, validates and accepts children's ideas and enhances their engagement – provided it is balanced across all children. However, ground rules must be established to manage this effectively and to ensure all children have an opportunity to contribute, if and when they so desire. It also means the teacher needs to expect the unexpected – and to be prepared to explore children's ideas, even if initially they don't make much sense to the teacher – such as in our earlier 'Duckville' example.

Adjust questioning and prompting to meet where the child is at

Asking open-ended questions where there are no necessarily right or wrong answers is important to nurturing text participants. Open ended questions allow readers to draw on their experiences and knowledge as broadly as possible and to share one another's thinking about such experiences. As teachers continue to talk about texts with children, they may find that as they tune into what children are saying they need to tailor their questions more specifically.

Guided reading

There are a number of ways that teachers scaffold children's meaning making in guided reading. One is through asking questions which prompt children to make predictions, relate texts to their own experiences, focus on particular aspects of a text, apply what is in the text to other situations, and so on.

There are also interactional formats which may serve to structure this scaffolding in particular ways. We explore briefly three such formats below: Directed Reading-Thinking Activity, ReQuest and Tell Me Reader Response.

Directed Reading-Thinking Activity (DR-TA) (Stauffer, 1969; Rapp Ruddell, 1993) is a means for guiding readers through the process of activating and reflecting upon the knowledge about text structures and topics which they bring to any one text. It is appropriate to both fiction and non-fiction texts. The text, 'Practice makes perfect', at the beginning of this chapter, is an example of this activity.

DR-TA may also be adapted to become a Directed Listening-Thinking Activity (DL-TA), where a text is read in sections to children who make predictions orally after each section in the same way as DR-TA.

Rapp Ruddell (1993) describes a particular procedure she calls 'Content DR-TA' to use with non-fiction texts (Rapp Ruddell, 1993, p.140). Before the title is read the teacher may give children the general topic and ask them to list everything they know about that topic – such as 'cricket'.

Next, the title is read/heard, and/or the specific topic is announced- such as 'how to bowl in cricket'. Children are asked to stop and think about what kind of text it might be (text structure and genre) and what it might be about (text topic). Children are asked to review the list they made in the previous step and tick what they think will appear in the text and add any new predictions.

Children then read/listen to the text. If they do so in segments, then children stop after each segment and review their predictions. If they read the text all at once, then at the end they note how well they predicted. They may tick again what things they predicted that actually appeared in the text and add new things they learned or had not anticipated.

This then forms the basis for a discussion of children's various experiences with the same text. It is always important that children are given the opportunity to discuss their processes and predictions with one another. Such discussion can provide invaluable lessons about text participant practices in terms of the many and possible meanings which texts may evoke: how possibilities may be confirmed, narrowed or opened up as a reader reads on, and how the meanings we make impact on how we proceed to crack the code of the text.

ReQuest is another interactional format for guiding the process of making meanings from texts. It is a particularly appropriate approach for teachers to guide children's reading of factual texts such as information reports. Originally developed by Manzo (1969) and described in some detail by Rapp Ruddell (1993), it is a form of reciprocal questioning in which teachers use questioning to engage children in purposeful reading. It may be done in a one-to-one situation between a child and teacher/expert peer or in small groups. Like DR-TAs, a text is read in segments. Its steps are summarised below (from Rapp Ruddell, 1993, pp.79-84):

1. Teacher and children silently read the first segment of the text. Then the teacher invites children to ask as many questions as they wish about the text. The teacher answers these questions as best they can.

2. Once the children have finished asking their questions, the teacher takes a turn to ask questions about the same segment in the text. The children answer these questions as best as they can. Rapp Ruddell (1993, p.81) recommends the following balance of questions over the course of a ReQuest (alternatively, you could also strike a balance of questions across Bloom's levels, previously described):

   – questions for which there is an immediate answer in the text, e.g., 'How many planets make up the Solar System?'

   – questions which draw on 'common knowledge' (keeping in mind, of course, that any knowledge is culturally influenced and we must therefore be careful in assuming anything about 'common' knowledge) and for which answers can be reasonably expected from what the teacher knows about the children, e.g., 'Without seeing illustrations of 'Orion the hunter', 'Orion's belt' and "Orion's sword", what might these star shapes look like?'

   – questions for which the teacher is not expecting a correct response but for which the teacher can provide related information, e.g., 'Have you ever heard the word 'constellation'? Do you know how it relates to the word 'stellar'? Well, let me tell you ...'

   – questions with no right answer but which are worth pondering, e.g., 'I wonder if the day will come when we can all travel to the moon like we can travel now to other countries?'

   – questions of a personalised type which only individual children can answer because they relate to their own personal experiences and responses, e.g., 'What do you already know about this topic?' and 'What do you find the hardest thing to understand about ...?'

   – questions which need further reference to another source, e.g., 'I wonder how frequently Hailey's Comet comes around?'

   – questions which need translation, e.g., 'In your own words, how would you explain ...?'

3. Children and teacher read the next segment of text silently, at the end of which children and teacher ask questions of one another, as above.

4. This continues, segment by segment, until children can reasonably predict what the text is about, what follows next and so on. At this point, the teacher changes tact, and begins asking the children to predict, with questions like, 'What do you think the rest of this text will be about?' and 'What question can we ask that you think might be answered by the end of this text?'

Tell Me Reader Response is an activity developed by Chambers (1993), for the purpose of scaffolding children's discussion of fiction in teacher guided situations as well as independent situations. We refer you to Chambers' text (see reference at the end of this chapter) for more detailed information.

Briefly, the 'Tell Me' format consists of four groups of questions which are intended to make discussions about books open-ended:

1. 'Basic questions' which focus on children's personal reactions to what they have read. Questions include 'Was there anything you liked about the book?' (Note that this does not assume a child likes what they have read, and is a significant departure from the less open question, 'What did you like about the book?'), 'Was there anything that puzzled you?' and 'Were there any patterns or connections that you noticed?' (Chambers, 1993, p.88).

2. 'General questions' which further explore children's related experiences and personal responses in terms of the book at hand. Questions can include 'Have you read other books like this one?', 'Has anything that happens in this book happened to you?', and 'What will you tell your friends about this book?' (Chambers, 1993, pp.88-89).

3. 'Special questions' which explore in depth the story at hand. Examples of questions include, 'How long did it take the story to happen?', 'What character interested you the most?' and 'Who was telling or narrating the story? Do we know? How do we know?'(Chambers, 1993, p.90-92).

Independent reading

When teachers guide children's reading as text participants through their own line of questioning or through formats such as the three we have described above, they are providing templates for children to continue making meaning when reading in independent situations and when discussing what they've read with their peers in independent small group situations.

Across all ages and settings, independent reading and related discussions and activities provide opportunities for children to interact with a wide variety of texts. Key features include children's choice of what they read and provision of a comfortable space to read.

Independent reading includes silent reading, which is important for allowing children to quietly engross themselves with texts of their own choosing – including texts such as books and displays which they or their peers have written and illustrated.

In addition to silent reading other forms of independent reading allow children to discuss their books and to assist one another. It is important for teachers to allow children to share with their peers what they have read as well as their reactions to what they have read.

One means of doing this is 'literature circles', such as those used and described by classroom teacher Ahang (1999) with her Years 6 and 7 children. Generally, 'literature circles' are small groups of children getting together in their classroom to discuss books they have read – possibly along the lines of what we described under 'Guided Reading' above. Usually these groups run independently, although teachers may observe, monitor and mediate as required.

In Ahang's classroom of 11-13 year old children, Ahang developed a particular procedure for using and monitoring explicit processes and strategies for making and sharing meanings from books among peers. Key points which emerged from her classroom are:

- At the outset children chose the books they wanted to discuss in small 'literature circle' groups. These books may be chosen from what a teacher makes available, but we would argue that the range should include books which are relevant to children, which they themselves perhaps bring in and which are used in their home and community lives. In her classroom Ahang aided children's identification of books by orienting them to the books in question, by reading summaries on back covers and so on. Children then listed their first, second and third preferences on a recording sheet. These preferences became the basis for forming the literature circle groups: children were placed with peers who had the same first or second preference as their own.

- To get the literature circle groups going and to be explicit about what was expected of the groups, the teacher distributed a reading checklist of activities. These activities were to be completed over a set time, say, five weeks. Time, of course, depends on length and complexity of the focal book, as well as children's interest levels and so on. Such checklists may include agreed upon target pages to be reached each week, work to be completed in reader response workbooks, which each student in Ahang's class was given, participation in discussions, and final presentations which bring the experiences over the weeks together and allow children to share their group experiences and outcomes with the rest of their class.

- Children had input on how frequently their groups met. In Ahang's classroom they wanted to meet daily and so they did. During this time each day, they read silently in their groups, talked about what they had read and their responses to it, as well as write about these things in their reader response work books. What happened in each group varied for they were self-directing in this sense.

- While children had a degree of choice and self-direction in Ahang's classroom, they were held accountable for the work they completed. As they completed particular activities, these were checked off on their checklist. These activities were scheduled on a weekly timetable to aid pacing.

- Children's experiences in these literature circles were brought together in a final presentation project. In Ahang's classroom children were given a choice, which the teacher modelled to the children. Such activities may include dioramas, story maps, dramatisations, readers theatre, painting murals, and so on. Some of these activities are described a little later in this chapter.

Individual and Group Activities

Teachers should provide a range of experiences which allow children to explore their understandings and responses as text participants. Ideally, these experiences encompass a range of media – such as puppetry, drama, readers' theatre, visual arts (e.g., painting a mural), and music (e.g., creating a 'soundtrack' of *Where the Wild Things Are* with percussion instruments).

There is an abundance of activities which teachers may provide in classrooms to further develop children's text participant practices. Some of these are briefly described below, with further readings suggested at the end of this chapter.

Two points about these activities which we wish to make are: one, across lessons and activities teachers need to ensure they take account of various levels of meaning-making in texts, and two, it is important to provide opportunities for children to express their understandings and responses through a variety of media such as art, craft, drama, and mime.

Again taking account of diverse backgrounds, it is essential that teachers explicitly model (without necessarily prescribing) how these activities are carried out – for they each form a particular classroom activity genre).

Working with non-fiction texts

There are several activities and strategies for engaging and supporting children as they work with factual texts such as information reports. Creenaune and Rowles (1996), in the book *What's Your Purpose?*, have provided a framework for the role such activities can play in different phases of working with factual texts. We summarise their framework and related activities below:

- Activities which orient children to the text at hand:
  - semantic maps or concept maps which are a visual means of representing key ideas and the relationships among them. Figure 4 shows an example based on reading an information report about floods. Figure 5 shows an example of a visual map based on reading articles and following hyperlinks in a *World Book* CD-Rom (1998).

Figure 4

A Semantic Map Based on Reading an Information Report about Floods

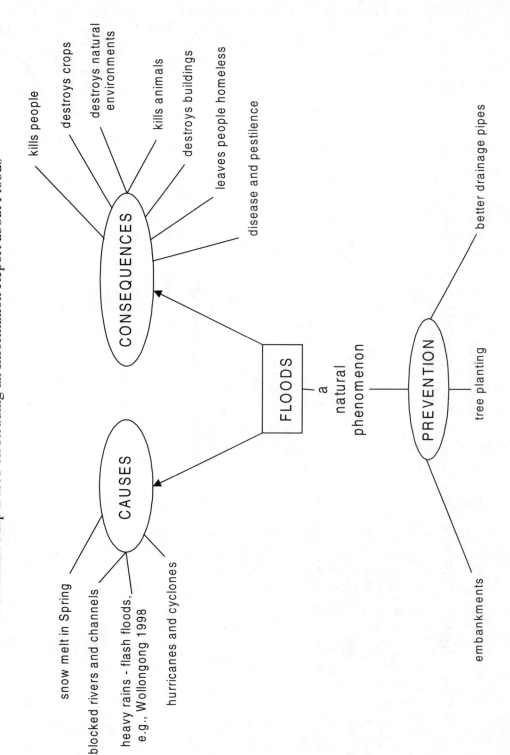

Figure 5

A Visual Map Based on Reading Articles and Following Hyperlinks in the *World Book* CD-Rom (1998) about the History of Libraries

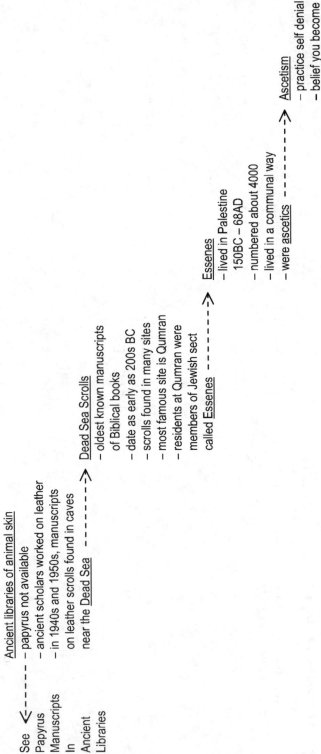

Note: Underlined words represent hyperlinks; broken lines represent point at which hyperlink was followed. Points under each link represent key ideas from the particular article.

- prior knowledge charts which involve children in listing what they know about the topic at hand. This may be done by groups of children brainstorming their ideas or by individual children listing what they know and then sharing these with one another. Rapp Ruddell (1993) describes an extension of this in terms of a 'K-W-L Plus' mapping technique from Carr and Ogle, 1987, cited in Rapp Ruddell, 1993, p.156). This technique involves children working with non-fiction texts, including Information Technology texts on CD-Roms and the World Wide Web. It begins with children brainstorming (individually, in small or large groups) what they know about the topic. This is followed by a list of what they want to find out. Next, they read the text and re-visit their K-W-L Chart to review and record what they learned that was new. We have included an example of a K-W-L Plus activity in Figure 6, based on an information report about crocodiles.

- Activities which focus on extracting information and ideas:
  - skimming, scanning and identifying key words
  - taking notes, identifying the main idea, and summarising
  - turning sub-headings and statements into questions, to guide reading
- Activities which represent information graphically:
  - diagrams which show comparisons and contrasts
  - diagrams which show cause-and-effect relationships
  - diagrams which show problem and solution relationships
- Activities which involve children in organising information:
  - flow charts
  - time lines
  - life cycles
  - concept maps
  - outlines (as illustrated in Figure 7).

Figure 6

An Example of a Know/Want to Know/Learned Chart Completed Prior to and after Reading an Information Reports about Crocodiles

Know	Want to Know	Learned
Crocodiles are reptiles	Why do crocodiles attack people?	Crocodiles are related to dinosaurs
Some live in saltwater	How do they swim?	They are different from alligators
Some live in freshwater	What do they eat?	They have ribs like dinosaurs
They attack people		They eat snakes, birds, frogs and smaller reptiles
		Saltwater crocodiles are called estuarine because they live in estuaries where the river meets the sea.
		Crocodiles swim by using their tails.

Figure 7

An example of an outline for organising information read in an information report about koalas

KOALAS

1. General classification

    a) mammal – marsupial
    b) marsupials breathe with lungs, are warm blooded, have pouches and give birth to live young

2. Appearance

    a) small
    b) similar to possums, but they are not bears
    c) short tail
    d) have pouch for baby koalas
    e) sharp claws for climbing trees

3. Feeding

    a) herbivores – eat plants
    b) drink from eucalyptus leaves

4. Habitat

    a) bush areas in eastern Australia
    b) in Eucalyptus trees

Working with narratives

Below we have identified a few activities which foster meaning making with narrative texts. This is by no means exhaustive. We have listed further readings at the end of this chapter for more information about these activities.

*   **Story maps** are designed to explore and reconstruct setting in narratives, as well as chronology of events and relationships such as cause-and-effect relationships. Story Maps may be done on an individual or group basis and may range from small sketches to large murals. We have included an example of a story map in Figure 8, based on a child reading the picture book narrative, *Where the Wild Things Are* by Maurice Sendak (1967).

    As children talk about story maps they need to be able to negotiate their own interpretations of the particular story, again providing important experiences in text participant practices. However, it should not be taken for granted that children know how to complete story maps or how to negotiate their interpretations. Teachers need to explicitly model both to children.

- **Readers Theatre** is a means of dramatising narrative text by either reading the original text or reworking the original text as a script. Unlike a complete dramatisation where lines need to be remembered and there is a full staging of the text, readers' theatre relies on readers reading hand-held scripts which they themselves have developed from the original text and the use of minimal but symbolic props and actions to represent characters, events, settings and relationships. Readers Theatre develops text participant practices by requiring children to step into the text and even reworking its structures to suit. As children are required to think about props, actions, positions and vocal expression, they become involved in exploring nuances of meaning and dimensions of characters and their relationships to one another, to capture what they find to be the essence of the story. For further reading, we recommend Hill (1990) and Dixon *et al* (1996).

- **Read and Re-tell** is a means for children reconstructing the sense they have made of a text they have read without the constraints of predetermined questions which have "right" answers. Brown and Cambourne's book, *Read and Re-tell* (1987), provides a very detailed coverage of this classroom activity. It starts similarly to DR-TA, in that children are initially asked to read the text's title and predict its genre and content (alternatively, genre may be supplied by the teacher). Children then share their predictions with one another and make comparisons. Having done this, children read the whole text. They then compare the actual text with their earlier predictions. Next, children are invited to re-read the text a number of times to be sure they have understood it. Then they are asked to tell or write the text in their own words, providing as much information as they can so that someone else can enjoy and understand what they write. Emphasis is put on children's own words and interpretations and it needs to be made explicit there is no one right re-tell.

Assessing Readers as Text Participants

When assessing children's text participant practices, we are focusing on their growth as text participants (for which developmental trends in Figure 3 provides one guide), the repertoire of actual practices that they use and the texts they read. Following, we describe three means of assessment by way of illustration.

Portfolios of children's work samples

Portfolios provide a means of organising, dating and monitoring ongoing development of children. Farr (1999, p.49) has described portfolios in the following way:

Figure 8

An Example of a Story Map Based on a Child's Reading of *Where the Wild Things Are* by Maurice Sendak (1967)

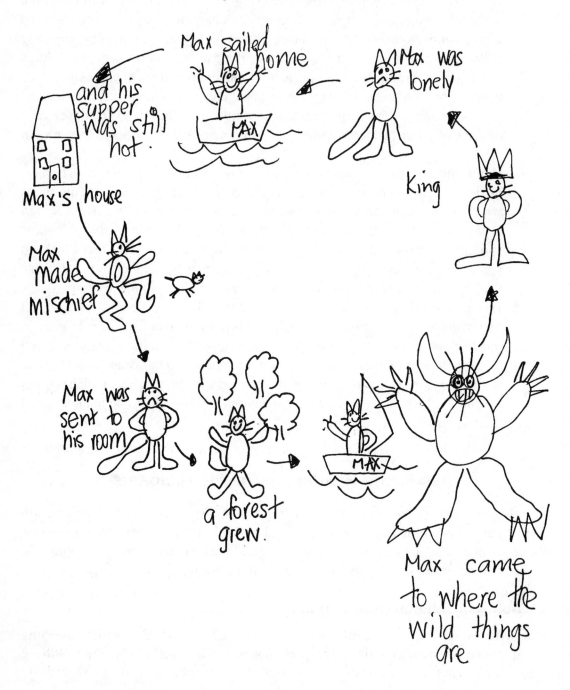

'For [portfolio] collections, students and teachers select numerous samples from drafts and final versions of various kinds of a student's writing [our addition: as well as visual texts such as story maps, charts and such as we've described elsewhere in this chapter]. The idea is to demonstrate the student's progress and development in the combined process of reading, thinking and writing. Thus many of the samples in the portfolio are responses to reading. The portfolio is reviewed and discussed regularly by the teacher and student, who may arrange it for others to examine.'

For portfolios to work well, they need ongoing and consistent attention. This means samples of a child's work need to be added and as it grows, older samples may systematically need to be removed. All samples should be dated to clarify the picture of the child's development.

They also require discussion or conferencing with children. Portfolio conferences may be done on a one-to-one basis between teacher and child. Small groups can also discuss their portfolios with one another. Both forms are recommended, for the former allows the teacher to see what is going on, while the latter allows children to share their progress and ideas with one another.

Key elements that make portfolios a desirable form of assessment include the following:

- they contain material which is completed in the normal business of the classroom and so do not require extra assessment work to be done for this particular purpose;
- children have a choice about what they put into the portfolio which provides them with a sense of ownership;
- more than a means of display, portfolios are a working document for each child, as it not only contains work samples they complete over the course of a term or year, but also traces growth in their knowledge and skills;
- the teacher plays a key role in helping to guide children in what goes in the portfolios and in reflecting on the learning that these samples indicate.

Valencia (1999, p.113) has made a useful analogy with an artist's portfolio:

'developing artists rely on portfolios to demonstrate their skills and achievements. Within the portfolio, they include samples of their work that exemplify the depth and breadth of their expertise. They may include many different indicators: work in a variety of media to demonstrate their versatility; several works on one particular subject to demonstrate their refined skill and sophistication; and work collected over time to exemplify their growth as artists.'

To relate this analogy to assessing children's reading, then:

1. samples of children's work as outcomes of the kinds of activities we have described in this chapter are appropriate and will reflect children's development as text participants (among other reading practices)
2. as we have previously recommended, these samples should be done across a number of media to allow children the opportunity to express their meanings in a variety of ways, some of which may lend themselves more strongly than others to what children intend

3. a number of samples which focus on one particular text, to allow the child to show the depth of their response

4. samples collected over the duration of a school term or school year, a substantial period to allow signs of growth to emerge.

A further consideration for implementing portfolio assessment is the need to explicitly model its forms and purposes to children. Vizyak (1999) did this with children as young as Year One; her approach is applicable to classrooms K-6. She began by introducing and explaining the term 'portfolio' to children. She contextualised this with an example of her own portfolio, which she modelled to the children (which took the form of a manila folder which she decorated to reflect things which were personally significant to her, e.g., a drawing of her family and a drawing of her favourite story book). She also shared the contents of her portfolio and explained why each one was there and what it showed about herself as a learner.

Next, she gave children a manila folder each which they decorated and shared with the class. Then their entries began. As they completed particular work they chose to put outcomes into their folders.

To continue supporting the process, she provided what she called 'mini lessons' (Vizyak, 1999, p.138) on portfolios. These included focusing on the contents of portfolios and why they were there, thus modelling language of self-reflection, choosing work which were best samples, and choosing work which highlighted other reasons, such as,

something you have learned (growth), something that took a long time (effort), something that was challenging (risk-talking), and something that showed interests outside of school (holistic learning)' (Vizyak, 1999, p.138).

Portfolios provide a whole picture of children's functioning as readers in relation to all four sets of reading practices. While children's work from activities such as we have described in this chapter can be used to assess their functioning as text participants, they will also reflect aspects of code breaking, text user and text analyst practices. Thus portfolios allow the teacher to assess how the child is developing across the four sets of practices.

Assessing classroom texts

Although this section is called 'Assessing Readers as Text Participants', teachers cannot carryout such assessment without also assessing the reading materials provided for children in classrooms. Questions related to text participant practices include:

*   is the text appropriate to readers' background knowledge?
*   what experiences does a teacher need to provide to develop relevant topical and textual knowledge?
*   is the genre one with which children are familiar or do I need to explicitly develop knowledge about this?

- is the topic of relevance and interest and how might I need to develop appropriate field knowledge?
- are the texts in my classroom inclusive of genres and topics relevant to and valued by children's home and community contexts?

Summary

Text participant practices focus on making meaning from texts, both fiction and non-fiction, across different media. These practices are based on knowledge of text genres and structures as well as text topics. Such knowledge is culturally shaped and needs to be explicitly developed in classrooms. Texts place different demands on text participants, depending on their genre, topic, the ambiguities they create and space they provide for the reader to engage in higher levels of meaning making. There are a number of formats for scaffolding children as text participants which help children predict meanings, relate texts to their own knowledge and experiences and share one another's interpretations. Portfolio assessment provides an important way of assessing text participant practices and doing so in a way which integrates all four sets of reading practices. Assessing classroom texts is an equally important aspect of assessment.

(**Note**. The text in this chapter's first task was about pruning rose bushes.)

Key Concepts

- text participant
- reader response
- levels of thinking

Tutorial Activities

A. In 3-5 groups, students are given a book and a different classroom activity designed to develop children as text participants.

Group 1 – group story maps

Group 2 – readers theatre

Group 3 – reader response (Chambers)

Group 4 – DL-TA

Group 5 – text innovation

At end of the workshop each group is to:

–   display their outcomes to the rest of class

–   report on how the activity works to the rest of class

–   describe specific benefits of activity in developing text participants

B. In small groups of no more than six students, carry out a Directed Reading (or Listening) – Thinking Activity, and/or a ReQuest activity, with non-fiction texts such as information reports. On completion of these activities reflect on and discuss how you functioned as a text participant. Describe how you might use these activities in the classroom, with what kinds of texts and for what purposes.

Further Readings

Barrentine, S.J. (Ed.), 1999, *Reading Assessment – Principles and Practices for Elementary Teachers,* International Reading Association, Newark.

Brown, H. & Cambourne, B. 1987, *Read and Re-tell,* Nelson, Melbourne.

Chambers, A. 1993, *Tell Me – Children, Reading and Talk,* Primary English Teaching Association, in association with Thimble Press, Sydney.

Creenaune, T. & Rowles, L. 1995, *What's Your Purpose? Reading Strategies for Non-fiction Texts.* Primary English Teaching Association, Sydney.

Dixon, N., Davies, A. & Politano, C. 1996, *Learning with Readers Theatre – Building Connections,* Peguis Publishers, Winnipeg.

Gibbons, P. 1991, *Learning to Learn in a Second Language,* Primary English Teaching Association, Sydney.

Graham, J. 1990, *Pictures on the Page,* Australian Reading Association, Carlton, Vic.

Hancock, J. (Ed.), *The Explicit Teaching of Reading,* International Reading Association, Newark, DE.

Hill, S. 1986, *Books Alive – Using Literature in the Classroom,* Nelson, Melbourne.

Hill, S. 1990, *Readers Theatre – Performing the Text,* Eleanor Curtain, South Yarra.

Meek, M. 1988, *How Texts Teach What Readers Learn,* Thimble Press, Stroud.

Chapter 6

READERS AS TEXT USERS

Opening Quote

*'Not only do people learn about the technology of script
and about how to work out the meaning or possible
meanings of written texts, but they also learn through social
experiences what our culture counts to be adequate reading
for school, work, leisure or civil purposes.'*
(Freebody, 1992, p.53)

Chapter Preview

This chapter focuses on readers as text users. It explores what text users do and related knowledge and skills of a text user. We look at the social purposes which different kinds of texts serve. We also consider how these purposes are fulfilled by ways in which texts are organised and the language features that they contain. Developmental trends in growth as text users are identified and related classroom practices are described. We emphasise the importance of including home and community texts in classrooms and to provide explicit and inclusive experiences. How teachers might effectively and inclusively scaffold children's development as text users are described, along with learning activities and assessment.

Focal Questions

- What are text user practices?
- What does a text user know and do?
- What are the different purposes served by text genres?
- How do text genres serve their purposes?
- What are patterns in readers' growth as text users?
- How might teachers support and promote the development of text users?
- How might teachers support and assess the development of text users?

- How might readers from diverse cultural and linguistic backgrounds be best supported as text users?

Introduction

So far in this book we have examined how readers decipher texts as text code breakers, and make meaning as text participants. This chapter focuses on another inter-related set of reading practices – that of text user practices, as highlighted in Figure 1 below. It explores how readers as text users use texts in social situations to achieve social purposes.

Figure 1

Model of Reading as Social Practices with Text User Practices Highlighted

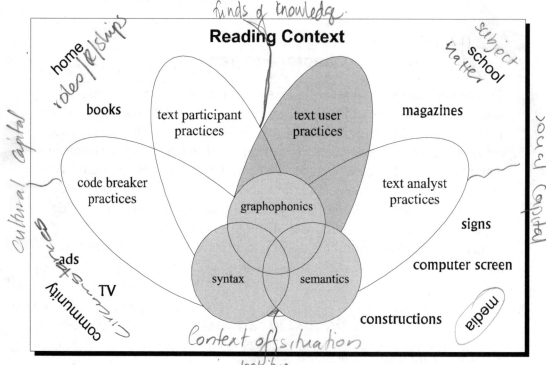

text user involves readers concerning themselves with the way the text ... action – What do I do with this text here and now? What are my ...s? For what purpose(s) am I reading this text? What kind of text ... et my need? (after Freebody, 1992; Luke, 2000; Luke & Freebody, ...ctices also include participating in literacy events and, at school, ...ers in the classroom around the text.

TASK

Read the following word:

CONCENTRATE

As a text code breaker, were you able to decipher the text? What does the word say?

As a text participant, what meaning did you make from the text?

Now, as a text user, consider what is the purpose of this text? Where might you find this text? How does its possible context influence the purpose and meaning you infer?

Suppose you found this word on an overhead in a lecture theatre? What purpose might it be serving?

What if you instead found this on a bottle of orange fluid in a pantry? What might its purpose then be?

What lessons about text purposes can you infer from the above task?

What relationships among reading as a text code breaker, text participant and text user can you infer from the above task?

What does this tell you about this aspect of reading and how it might be effectively taught in classrooms?

From the above task we hope you can see that being a text user involves inferring or being already aware of purposes which texts serve. Being a text user interrelates with being a text code breaker and a text participant. For example, deciphering and attaching meaning to text is helped by knowing what a text's purpose is. Knowing what a text's purpose is further aided by understanding the context in which it was produced and is found.

Knowledge and Skills of a Text User

To engage with any text is to take part in a social activity. Therefore, the kinds of knowledge and skills which text users apply to their reading are social and cultural in nature; they are overviewed in Figure 2.

Figure 2

Overview of Text User

Definition

– using text for social purposes:
what do I do with this text?
for what purpose has this text
been written?

Knowledge

Knowledge about different types
(genres)of texts
Knowledge about social purposes
which different text types serve

Skills

Using texts in social and personal
situations to achieve purposes
Interacting with others about texts
Participating in reading events
Selecting texts to suit reader purpose
Adjusting reading strategies to suit text
type and reader purpose

Based on Freebody (1992), Luke (2000), Luke & Freebody (1999) and NSW Department of Education and Training, 1997,
Teaching Reading: A K-6 Framework.

Proficient text users know that different kinds, or genres, of texts exist – for example, narratives, information reports, instructional texts and recounts. As argued by Luke (2000), different genres are valued in different sociocultural contexts, as we have seen in our previous chapter on text participants.

TASK

Cast your mind over the reading which you have done over, say, the past month. Make a list of specific titles which you have read. Don't forget to include texts which may seem incidental, such as timetables, TV programs, directions, labels and signs, as well as magazines, novels and University reading.

When you have finished your list, categorise your titles according to kind or genre of text, such as narrative, factual information, procedural and so on.

What patterns emerge? Do some text genres occur more frequently than others? Do some genres appear to play a more significant part in your life than others? Why might that be so?

What does this tell you about this aspect of reading and how it might be effectively taught in classrooms?

Along with awareness of different text genres, text users also know that different genres serve different purposes. All texts are socially constructed, each a product of a writer with a particular purpose in mind. For example, narratives serve to entertain, instructional texts to explain how to do or make something, recounts to describe past events and so on (as we also saw in Chapter 4).

Knowing the purposes of text genres comes into play when:

- a reader needs to choose the kind of text needed to suit their own needs;
- a reader draws broad external inferences about why a particular text has been written – what broad social purpose does it serve; and
- a reader adjusts their code breaking strategies according to text purpose and reader purpose.

TASK

As a reader, think about and jot down a description of the kinds of reading strategies you use when reading a novel for leisure's sake. Next, think about and jot down a description of how you read a magazine, again for leisure's sake. Do similarities and differences emerge between reading a novel and a magazine. Now, think about how you go about reading texts in preparation for a University essay. What are your reading strategies? What similarities and differences emerge between this and reading a novel and magazine?

What does this tell you about this aspect of reading and how it might be effectively taught in classrooms?

Outcomes of this last task should illustrate for you how readers use knowledge of text genres to recognise the kind of text at hand and to adjust reading strategies accordingly. Herein we can see an important interaction between two sets of reading practices: text code breaking practices (selecting reading strategies) and text user practices (recognising genre so as to choose appropriate strategies).

As we saw in our chapter on text participants, knowledge of how texts are organised is part of engaging with meaning and structure of a text (after Freebody 1992, p.50). Text organisation goes hand in hand with text purpose – purpose influences how a text is organised, and how it is organised furthers its purpose. Thus another key relationship emerges between two sets of reading practices – text participant practices (knowing about text organisation) and text user practices (knowing about text purposes).

Texts contain particular structures and language features which fulfil their generic purposes. For example, the purpose of information reports is 'to document, organise and store factual information on a topic. Information reports classify and describe the phenomena of our world. We use them when we want to talk about a whole class of things.' (Derewianka, 1990, p.51). An information report on gardening, then, will classify and describe flowers, herbs, vegetables, trees, shrubs and so on.

The purpose of an information report is realised by the way it is structured. It typically begins with a general statement or classification, such as,

'Roses have always been a favourite flower in the garden. They were cultivated by the ancient Babylonians, Greeks and Romans, and no other flower has received more attention from gardeners through the ages.' (Yates Garden Guide, 1995, p.298).

Information reports then typically proceed to identify and elaborate upon facts about various aspects of the topic. In the case of roses, the *Yates Garden Guide* includes general facts about situation and soil, planting roses, general maintenance and types of roses. Sub-headings are usually used to indicate how the topic is being broken down and paragraphs further aid the organisation of information. Often diagrams and/or illustrations are included, along with captions and labels. In the Yates text about roses, photographs and illustrations of different kinds of roses are included.

The Yates Garden Guide example being used here raises another important point about text genres and purposes: more than one genre may be found in the one text or book. For example, brief instructional texts are embedded in the information report about roses. One is how to plant roses, the other how to prune roses. Each instructional text includes detailed diagrams and step-by-step description of procedures. The presence of these texts is consistent with the multi-purpose nature of this text: not only to provide information about garden phenomena, but to explain how to garden.

Texts further achieve their purposes through their language features. We have already explored language features of text genres in Chapter Four, when focusing on code breakers. There we saw how readers might reasonably expect to find certain language features in a text, given its membership to a particular genre. We continue to explore this here, too, for language features serve to fulfil text purposes and cue the reader into what the text is for – what social purpose it serves. Thus we find another instance of how reading practices interact with one another – in this case, code breaking and text user practices.

We illustrate here the interaction between text purpose and language features with reference to information reports. Because information reports serve to provide facts on phenomena in our world, then they include generalised participants. The roses text, for example, is not about the particular roses growing in my garden or your garden, rather, it is about roses generally. Thus, it contains generalised participants (nouns) such as 'roses', 'bush roses', 'rambling roses', 'climbing roses', 'miniature roses', 'fertilisers', 'pests and diseases' and so on. Action verbs may also be included if a type of behaviour is described. In the roses text such verbs are used in relation to roses (e.g., 'grow', 'climb') as well as their maintenance (e.g., 'prune', 'water', 'mulch', 'fertilise'). Linking verbs are also typical in reports, such as 'Most shrub roses <u>are</u> hybrids' (*Yates Garden Guide*, 1995, p.303) and 'Good drainage <u>is</u> necessary' (*Yates Garden Guide*, 1995, p.299). Timeless present tense is used in reports, as is descriptive language of a factual nature – for example, 'Miniature roses look like tiny floribundas, but have miniature leaves and flowers in perfect proportion' (*Yates Garden Guide*, 1995, p.303). Technical terms are also a feature, such as 'floribundas', 'hybrid', 'weedicides', 'bud union', 'briar shoots' and so on.

We have taken some space to explore how texts achieve their purposes through their overall structure and specific language features, for teachers need to make these explicit to develop text users in their classrooms, as we explore in the next two sections on diversity and classroom practices.

The Internet and Text User Practices

If we take as part of text user practices, the ability to understand social purposes and ways of using various kinds of texts, then this has clear relevance to how readers use the internet. Below, we have identified a number of features of text user practices in regard to email, World Wide Web, and Newsgroups. It is not our intention to provide a detailed coverage, but rather to flag key points and contextualise these in terms of text user practices as they relate to information technology. There are many classroom-oriented resources available for further reading on this subject, such as Ingvarson (1997) and Hancock (1999).

As we explore uses of the internet, we need to keep in mind differences in experience and perceptions in relation to what happens at school and home. Snyder (1999, p.25) has noted a 'discernible gulf' between computer user practices in schools and in home and community contexts. This gulf, Snyder maintains, arises from a number of sources. These include: some parents assume that their children's skills in using information technology is being covered at school; many parents may use IT at work and feel confident in their own use and that of their children; other parents may not share this experience or confidence; parents may be informed about IT through television programs and private reading, while others may not; and many parents provide computers and related software programs and games for their children.

Email

Email provides users with the opportunity to send and receive messages, chat in real time, and to join mailing lists. Email can also be used to start and join groups such as educational groups (see Ingvarson, 1997). Learning to be an effective text user of email involves learning about its appropriate use in ways that IT users expect and ordain.

What constitutes appropriate use includes a number of understandings and practices. One such understanding is that the broad purpose of email is to send and receive messages. At the same time, users also need to understand the specific purposes of sending any one message through this means. Ingvarson (1997) found that children may initially send messages for their own sake, before moving to a greater appreciation of specific purposes, which then sustains their ongoing use of email.

Another set of understandings concerns the purposes for which email can validly be used in different settings. For example, in most institutions it is not appropriate to send out 'all point bulletin' emails for personal reasons such as trying to sell something, for which special address lists are created. There is a connection between specific purpose of message (e.g., to communicate to an individual person; to advertise an item for sale; to argue a point of view to a community of email users about an issue which impacts on that community) and to whom the email might be addressed (e.g., an individual person's email address; 'Classifieds' email group; 'Forums and Debates' email group).

Email users also need to understand issues of confidentiality of texts which are transmitted by email. They need to discern when this is an appropriate form of communication and when other forms (such as hard copy letters or face-to-face conversations) might be preferred.

A perhaps controversial understanding is that what one puts in an email is actually in writing. It is a potentially permanent record, especially if saved or printed out by the recipient. Its quick turnaround (in contrast with written letters) and its semblance of being interactive (in contrast with a telephone conversation) make it seem more like spoken language. In their review of research related to this issue, Hawisher and Selfe (1999) noted that researchers agree that online communication (sometimes called 'networked discourse') uses language which falls somewhere in the middle of a continuum between spoken and written language.

However, the spoken language-like qualities of email are illusory and can mislead users into writing inappropriately, running the risk of defamation and inflaming readers on the receiving end of emails written in haste. Hawisher and Self (1999) note that when writing to a screen, a writer can lose sense of audience. There is also considerable variety on how writers compose email messages. While some may write quite tersely and even use abbreviated forms, truncated sentences, and be quite telegraphic, other writers may write quite profusely. While these aspects of email communication relate to writing, they obviously impact on readers when receiving various email messages.

Two other aspects of effective email use is awareness of potential for spread of viruses through email attachments and ways of minimising this risk; and awareness of spamming problems, such as intruding on email lists in order to promote one's own interests instead of the interests of the elist.

World Wide Web

The purposes of the World Wide Web are many and varied. To be effective WWW users, children need to learn about the range of purposes met by the Web and how to use the Web effectively to meet their purposes. These purposes include:

- seeking information, often an overwhelming activity given the vastness of information available on the Web. Often, too, users can become addicted to browsing itself, which can distract a user from the specific purpose of the search at hand.
- shopping online
- publishing material on the Web
- joining special interest groups on the Web
- pursuing special interests over the Web
- participating in chats over the Web.

The World Wide Web overall provides access to a far wider range of information and resources than would be usually available in classrooms. Users of the WWW need to be able to discern when to use the Web and when to use other sources such as print-based or CD-Rom reference books. For example, if researching spiders, reference books may be a more useful source (Moore, 1999). If using the WWW and doing a search with a search engine, users also need to decide what to do with search results in light of their purpose.

Other issues related to appropriate use of the Web include:

* how to acknowledge sources of information to avoid plagiarism
* censorship, safe interaction guidelines and control of access
* understanding the structure and purpose for conducting a search on the Web
* knowing when to use book marks effectively.

Newsgroups

Newsgroups provide a means for people to come together in cyber space around a common focus. Their purpose is to allow users to write to one another on a specific subject, and to read one another's texts on same. Users can slot into a pre-existing Newsgroup or else create their own. Frequently asked questions (FAQs) are usually included, their purpose being to allow individuals to keep informed on issues that arise time and again, while still allowing the interests of the group to move forward.

Supporting Readers from Diverse Cultural and Linguistic Backgrounds as Text Users

The kinds of classroom practices we have described are based on the recognition of diverse community text user practices and so are equally applicable to all children from all kinds of cultural and linguistic backgrounds. Teachers need to ensure inclusive selection of genres, relevant to children's personal, home and community as well as school lives.

Shepherd (1999) was teaching a Year 2/3 class in a school 'where 75% of the families receive government support because of low income. Twenty-five percent of the students are from non-English speaking backgrounds, 15% are Aboriginal, and 50% have been identified as having several learning difficulties.' (Shepherd, 1999, p.39). Shepherd sought to build bridges between home and school texts by focusing on popular texts such as magazines. She began with a very important step that all teachers should carry out – she found out what her children read at home. Making a comparison of children's reading at home and school, she found that while books were predominant at school, they were not so at home; in her words, 'I realised that the most popular forms of reading at home were those least valued at school' (Shepherd, 1999, p.41). To address this concern, and to make reading more accessible and enjoyable for children, she focused on popular texts. Magazines became a focus as they were the most commonly read by children in their homes.

She generated much talk and activity about magazines. This included: comparing books with magazines, talking about the different kinds of texts found within magazines, why children preferred books, magazines or both, who helps children read magazines at home and what do children look at first when reading a magazine. In doing these things, the teacher put herself in a position where she had something to learn from her children and they had something to 'teach' her that no-one else could – that is, their own text user practices. By doing this, the students' practices were validated and they were empowered in their classroom because their 'cultural capital' was valued. (By 'cultural capital', we mean the resources and predispositions children bring to classrooms, after Bourdieu & Passeron, 1977).

As we have previously said, teachers also need to provide explicit instruction about text genres, in terms of their social purposes, the kinds of situations in which they are usually found and how their text structures and language features achieve their purposes. Indeed, such an approach, often referred to as a 'curriculum cycle' (Painter, 1991) arose in a region of schools where children were perceived to be at a disadvantage when schools did not make explicit information about texts with which the children had no or limited prior experience.

Working in Australian Aboriginal contexts, Walton (1993) has documented well the difficulties with classroom practices which fail to make text practices explicit. She has written:

> '...Bourdieu and Passeron (1977) suggested implicit models of teaching were among the practices used to keep outsiders excluded from valued knowledge. They hypothesised that the greater the cultural and linguistic distance between the home and the school, the less successful will be the learning/teaching of the school.' (Walton, 1993, p.41)

Implicit models of instruction do not work in the face of sociocultural diversity. Texts used at school and taken to be central to school learning come to be seen as familiar, even natural, and accessible to all (Fairclough,1989). However, this is not the case in reality. If teachers act on this false assumption, however, they continue to marginalise children who do not have experience in those school genres and do not understand their purposes, structures and features. Walton (1993, p.42) cites her own earlier study (1986) which showed that the use of implicit models of teaching with disadvantaged Aboriginal children served only to perpetuate that disadvantage, for they did not have to assume knowledge and experiences to be able to tune into classroom activity.

Teachers, therefore, need to be explicit about what texts have been selected and why. They need to explicitly model and talk about how texts achieve their purposes and what those purposes are. Children need to actively engage in talk and activity which links texts to contexts – for example, in what kind of social context and for what

Figure 3

Developmental Trends of Text Users and Related Pedagogic Practices

Indicators	**Pedagogic Practices**
Emergent Phase *(includes Role-Play &Experimental Reading; approximately links to Early Stage 1)**	• Use different kinds of print for different purposes
• Reads for enjoyment	• Re-read familiar texts for enjoyment, for information, and for other purposes
• Engages in shared reading which nurtures bonds with significant others	• Read texts which relate to children's interests and purposes
• Shows interest in print	• Link texts to children's purposes
• Incorporates print into their play	• Develop a shared language for talking about different kinds of texts and their purposes
• Understands print has a general purpose of communicating something, but meanings change from reading to reading.	
Early Phase *(includes Early and Transitional Reading; approximately links to Stage 1 and into Stage 2)**	• Ask children about how their purposes have been served by particular books
• Can identify and talk about different kinds (genres) of texts	• Provide a broad range of text types (genres)
• Comes to select reading materials which suits particular reading and social purposes	• Talk about purposes of different text genres
• Comes to adjust reading strategies to suit different types of texts and purposes	• Develop a shared language to talk about text genres and purposes
Fluent Phase *(includes Independent and Advanced Independent Reading; approximately links to Stage 3)**	• Model to and guide children to select appropriate text types, compile reference lists, summarise and take notes, compile bibliographies, and generate their own questions
• Can recognise and discuss elements and purposes of different types of texts, such as reports, narratives, procedural texts, and so on	[in addition to those strategies identified for emergent and early readers]

* Emergent, early and fluent labels are derived from Mooney (1990). Role Play, Experimental, Early, Independent and Advanced labels are derived from the Western Australian department of Education's *First Steps – A Reading Developmental Continuum* document (1994). Approximate links are made to Early Stage 1, Stage 1, Stage 2 and Stage 3 as identified in NSW Board of Studies *English K-6 Syllabus.*

purpose might one find an information report? How might a reader most effectively read such a text? What purposes do texts serve? How might a reader identify a text's purpose and read the text effectively in context?

Classroom Practices for Supporting Text Users

We have overviewed developmental patterns in text users and related classroom practices in Figure 3.

Employing text user practices in school settings involve the student becoming familiar with and accomplished in a range of genres that are considered to be authentic and valid in that setting. These school-based genres are composed of both factual and literary texts which are commonly used in classrooms and seen as central to school learning. They include narratives, information reports, procedural or instructional texts, recounts, argument and discussions.

However, by focusing children's attention predominantly, even exclusively, on these genres, teachers run the risk of conveying that these are the only authentic, valuable genres and that other genres occurring in communities have little or no value. To promote that viewpoint, even inadvertently, would be naive in the extreme. We also read for real purposes in a variety of other arenas, related to personal, work, home and community lives. Many of the types of texts at work in these arenas are powerful, such as advertising brochures, magazines, posters, signs and symbols like traffic signs, television, video games, comics, newspapers and computers.

Inclusion of home and community texts

Luke and Freebody (1999a, 1999b, 2000) advocate the use of a range of text user practices within classrooms that also embrace a range of more community-based genres, so that children may come to understand:

'the social relations around texts; knowing about and acting on the different cultural and social functions that various texts perform both inside and outside the school and knowing that these functions shape the way texts are structured, their tone, their degree of formality and their sequence of components.' (Luke & Freebody, 1999a, p.7)

If we subscribe to the notion that literacy itself is a social practice, then we need also concede that:

'it is subject to the play and power relations of local face to face contexts – of classrooms, communities, workplaces, places of worship, homes and so forth.' (Luke & Freebody, 1999b, p.3)

Classroom teachers are to a great degree responsible for the power relations in their classrooms. Each classroom contains a collection of individuals which reflects the diverse nature of the communities it serves. These children need to be introduced to a wide range of text genres that not only include school-based genres but also genres which are prevalent and powerful within home and community contexts.

Exploring mass market booklets

How teachers might do this is illustrated by classroom teacher Jennifer O'Brien (1998), in her use of a mass market booklet, 'A Lady in Smurfland' in her Reception-Year Two composite class. This book chronicles the adventures of a male Smurf and a female Smurf and is widely available at supermarket checkout counters. A child brought the book to school and O'Brien used it as a springboard to discussion and activities which focused on characters, events, roles and relationships in the book. These learning experiences were significant for a number of reasons which are listed below:

- The experiences were initiated by a child bringing in a book from their home/ community context to which children had broad access.
- The experiences placed the children in the role of 'expert' and the teacher in a 'novice' role, as the children knew a great deal more about this book than their teacher. The children contributed to class discussions by drawing on other aspects of their experiences with Smurfs, such as television programs, other Smurf books, and related merchandise.
- The experiences used a powerful community-based text which had links to a wide range of cultural products such as a television program, figurines, crockery, manchester and so on.
- The experiences provided a basis for bringing children's cultural knowledge from playground and community contexts into the classroom which then framed their critical discussions of the text. Children were able to move into a critical discussion of the book because it formed a part of their own social worlds. In so doing, important links between text user practices and text analyst practices (further discussed in Chapter 7) were made.

As O'Brien discusses, she could also have focused on the social and economic contexts in which these types of texts are read. This could focus discussion on aspects of where the books are sold, who reads them, who doesn't read them and other products to which they are linked and why.

Exploring cereal boxes

Another example of community texts in the classroom comes from the work of Comber and Simpson (1995), who describe their use of cereal boxes. They contend that children,

'learn to read, not only from the book and lessons of early schooling, but from McDonalds signs and Coke bottles, confection wrappers and toy boxes. In doing this, they learn to read the world as well as words, as versions of lifestyle and identity are constructed through what is presented and how.' (Comber and Simpson, 1995, p.2)

They used four different types of cereal boxes in a Year 4/5 classroom. They examined these texts to discover how the print and visual features of these texts are manipulated to sell cereal. Such texts could be used in a range of activities across the curriculum and both these activities and related assessment could focus on such things as:

- the language features of texts, including words, logos, charts and pictures
- the purpose and audience of the types of messages the texts carry
- designing a cereal box
- using nutritional charts and information in Maths and Science lessons to construct tables of various cereals, and comparing fibre, sugar, vitamin and mineral content
- construct a questionnaire to survey the school, with questions like, 'What is your favourite cereal, and why?' and 'How much does the packaging effect your choice?'

As children discuss and work with these multiple cereal box texts, teachers may monitor and assess children's text user practices by observing their participation in discussions, noting their ability to do things like list nutritional information and interpret messages, signs and symbols on the packaging of cereal boxes. How children uncover inferences in these texts, especially given their commercial appeal to young and older audiences, could also be a point of assessment, as well as children's discussion of reasons for choice of visual images on these packages.

Explicit demonstration of text purposes

Classroom teachers are also responsible for determining whether the range of practices emphasised in a reading program 'was indeed covering and integrating the broad repertoire of textual practices required in today's economies and cultures' (Luke & Freebody, 1999b, p.3).

Teachers need to explicitly demonstrate and explain the purposes of various text genres, and how these purposes are achieved through text structures and language features (such as we saw with the information report about roses). This is not to present this information as formulaic, but rather to explore and even challenge conventional writing structures and to deconstruct how texts achieve their purposes. Such instruction also assists readers to make meaning from and produce such genres. Perhaps more importantly, children need to understand that it is the writer's initial purpose for constructing the text that leads to the choice of a particular textual genre. Teachers also need to be aware that the majority of texts we encounter daily are not purely one genre but are often a combination of genres – such as we saw in the roses text earlier.

TASK

Find texts which combine two or more genres. Examples include cereal boxes, television guides and magazines. Focusing on one such example, such as a cereal box, identify and describe the various genres which are included and the purposes they serve. Describe how might you use your sample text in modelled and guided reading to explore and develop text user practices.

Community based texts are a rich source of variety that can be introduced into the classroom to provide children with a diverse range of reading experiences. Many teachers are introducing community texts for they provide a bridge between the academic types of texts which are seen as legitimate and valuable at school and community texts which have powerful influences on children's daily lives.

Modelled, guided and independent reading and mediating activities

School and community texts alike can and should be explored in modelled, guided and independent reading. Modelled and guided reading are times for teachers to provide explicit demonstrations of text purposes and how they are achieved. In the following example, a Year Two teacher focused on how narratives are structured to achieve their purpose of entertainment. They started out talking about stories generally, as they had been spending quite a lot of time looking at stories. Then, they focused on a book initiated by one of the children; it was called *Alexander and The Terrible, Horrible, No Good, Very Bad Day* by Judith Viorst (1972):

T:	We've been spending quite some time now looking at stories. What is another name for stories?
Ji:	Narrative.
T:	OK. Who can tell me what they know about narratives?
Ka:	Well, they are stories, and they can be stories like, um, fairy tales, and books like some of those books we have in the reading corner.
T:	What kind of books in particular?
Ka:	Um [turning around to look], like 'Wilfred Gordon McDonald Partridge'.
Cr:	Yeah, and 'Where the wild things are' and 'Alexander and the terrible, horrible, no good, very bad day'.
Hu:	Ha-ha, that's a good story.
T:	Why is 'Alexander' a good story, Hayley?
Ha:	It makes me laugh.
Jo:	Yeah, all those things go wrong for Alexander.
Ha:	Yeah!

T:	Mm, we were only reading that book this morning, weren't we? Can you remember how the story started?
Ji:	It started like, with, it started with Alexander saying he's having a bad day.
Jo:	Yeah, when he was going to bed and he had gum in his hair!
T:	OK, that's the beginning of the story. And what's the beginning part called?
Cr:	Orientation.
T:	Orientation. OK. Then all these things started to happen, didn't they. Lots of things went wrong for Alexander.
Eu:	Well, the next day, he had his cereal and he didn't get any toys in his cereal box, like everyone else did!
Ji:	And when they went to school he got squashed in the car and no-one cared. And then he got into trouble at school and he had a fight with his friend—
Ka:	Yeah, and he wanted to move to Timbuktu because of that.
T:	OK, when all these things go wrong, what's that part of the story called? Patrick.
Pa:	The complication.
T:	And as Hayley said, those complications made her laugh.

In this sequence the teacher is careful to allow children to take some initiative throughout the discussion, and for children to expand on one another's contributions. As the teacher does so, she also is using their previous experiences with narratives to carefully develop a language with which to talk about texts (which is called a metalanguage). That is, she moved from common-sense terms like 'beginning of the story' and 'lots of things went wrong' to more precise and technical terms like 'orientation' and 'complications'. Because these terms and the concepts behind them had grown out of shared experiences with many narratives in the classroom (including those brought in by children) and were first talked about in common sense terms, then they took on meaning for the children. The bridges that this teacher was thus building are important to children's later school success.

Given the pragmatic nature of text user practices, activities which mediate and link these reading sessions further support learning. These activities should allow children to explore various facets of texts which contribute to their purposes and use these texts in ways which reflect their use in social settings.

There are a variety of ways that teachers may do this in their classrooms. For example, if the focus is on instructional texts (e.g., recipes), then it helps to involve children in the kinds of action which go with such texts, like cooking, doing something or making something.

We will explore this a little now with reference to comics and cartoons in classrooms. In a Year 1/2 classroom, Simms (1997) used a range of cartoons and comics to explore how their particular features and structures achieve their often powerful effect. Such a focus is relevant to middle and upper primary classrooms; as we explore their use in a lower Primary classroom, we encourage you to think about how you might use similar texts with older children.

In Simms' classroom the unit on comics and cartoons was resourced by the children bringing in comics, as well as videotaping cartoons in children's television viewing time. It is important to note that Simms took the time and care to explain her unit to the children's parents, so as to foster both their co-operation and the teacher's understanding of how cartoons and comics are used in children's home settings.

The children initially looked at comics and brainstormed what they knew about these texts. This knowledge was compiled into a classroom list. In pairs, the children then examined a range of comics to discuss how they tell a story. Later, a whole class list was created to show aspects of characters and settings. Again in pairs, children used a range of comics to discover and record the ways characters speak to each other in this text type. Children were able to distinguish between the type of balloon used when a character is speaking (a round shape with a point end) from the type used for thought (little bubbles joining a larger bubble or cloud). They also described the various shapes which sound bubbles like POW and KBOOM have.

Issues of the types of words used to convey sound were also investigated and how words at times described both sound and movement (e.g., 'whoosh', 'zap'). Children then revisited class lists which had documented their background knowledge of comics. This is important to build for it continues to show children the links between old and new knowledge and helps them identify and build continuous pathways of learning.

Following this, the children then used many of the features of comics which they had discussed to create their own comic strips, first planning their work with a partner.

In the next section of the unit children were shown snippets of cartoons on videotape. As a whole class, the children brainstormed what they knew about cartoons. The children were shown excerpts of a range of cartoons, pausing to discuss characters, music, colour, setting, sound effects and storyline. They generated a set of observations and conclusions regarding each of these aspects of cartoons.

Focus was then given to link music to different stages of the cartoon such as opening titles and opening sequences. Children drew their favourite cartoons and a class list of cartoon elements was made, as with comics previously. The unit thus culminated in a comparison of comics and cartoons.

The teacher assessed children's learning in this unit by observing children as they worked in pairs and held small group discussions with focus on such things as speech, thought and sound bubbles. Work samples were collected to assess children's use of speech and sound conventions, characters, story development and segments within the comic.

Partnerships between Public Libraries and Schools

Being effective library users is a substantial part of text user practices in a broad sense (such as knowing how to use a library and for what purposes); and libraries themselves involve a range of text user practices (such as using catalogues and reading various kinds of materials).

Public libraries are much more than places where books are housed. They constitute a dynamic community resource which provides public access to diverse reading materials across different genres and media. These materials include those for loan as well as reference material which otherwise may not be readily available for families – such as encyclopedias, comprehensive atlases, dictionaries in various languages, and so on. These materials are regularly reviewed and updated. Access to current material has been greatly enhanced in recent years by the installation of computers and internet access in many public libraries.

Libraries also provide outreach programs to the communities they serve and educational programs for children. These programs include partnerships between public libraries and schools.

When describing text user practices in relation to home, school and community texts, then, it is important that we include public libraries in our description – and in our classroom reading programs. As Meek (1991, p.175) has written, 'in the information-laden contexts of new curricula the library plays a central role'.

Libraries carry extensive collections across key curriculum areas. They also provide access to document delivery services such as inter library loans – a service which needs time and for which libraries may charge a small fee. These materials provide invaluable resources for classroom use and project work.

Use of public libraries has been shown to benefit children's reading from an early age. In her landmark study of children who started school already able to read, Clark (1976) found that in most cases, these children were frequent library users. Her findings revealed the important role which local libraries play in providing for children's interests and stimulating their reading. Children were actively involved in their own borrowing choices and processes. Through their local library, children were able to access a broad range of materials. For example, one child read a wide range of daily newspapers available in her local library.

Even though these children's homes provided literacy rich environments, the range made available in libraries often surpassed what could be made available in homes. For example, while many parents purchased encyclopedias, these become outdated over time, especially in regard to some of the children's interests; as well, expense was a substantial consideration. Perhaps in the 2000s today, we might argue that families can access encyclopedias on the internet in their own homes – but this assumes private computer ownership and brings us back to a question of access once again.

Clark (1976) also documented the benefits of children's access to material that is often deemed too difficult – such as material found in the adults' part of the library. Through this access, children's reading for enjoyment and information was extended and their personal interests nurtured in positive ways.

In her conclusions, Clark conveyed a strong message to teachers, librarians and parents alike:

'The findings with regard to accessibility of different types of reading material, layout, advice and flexibility of regulations all have implications for libraries concerning ways of ensuring that children with potential but without the continuing support of a kind available to most of these children have access to reading material to suit their developing interests.' (Clark, 1976, p.103)

She went on to advocate

'...greater links between school and local library in order to provide wide enough resources is certainly an aspect worthy of further consideration.' (Clark, 1976, p.103)

Meek (1991, p.175) has written that 'librarians are a special breed of literates'. In terms of this book's framework, we could say that librarians have a range of specialist text user sills. This is **not** to say that they live in ivory towers where they jealously guard their expertise. Rather, by virtue of their professional development and experience, they have expertise in an increasing range of resources such as online catalogue programs, library research facilities on CD-Roms, information about copyright regulations and procedures, and so on.

Teachers can work productively with librarians to develop children's expertise in these areas, so that they might become not only effective and discerning library users but also enjoy broad access to information.

Activities and Strategies for Library User Practices

School projects

Libraries provide a wide range of resources suitable for school projects. Teachers, however, need to communicate with libraries about pending projects ahead of time so that libraries can ensure access to relevant materials. Without this communication, libraries can find themselves under considerable pressure when they face unexpectedly heavy demands on one part of their collection. With this communication, ways that libraries can ensure access include putting relevant materials in a Reserve collection or Special Projects collection for use only in the library, and/or reducing their usual lending periods for project-related materials to be taken home.

Communication about school projects also allows library staff to make useful suggestions for teachers and students to consider.

Library skills workshops

School projects and such both require and develop children's library user skills. Children need to find out how to find out and learn to be systematic in this research (Meek, 1991).

Being an effective library user involves skills such as:

- using catalogues to locate materials by author, title, topic, key words or other search strategies
- recording call numbers form catalogues and matching these to those on shelved material
- using classification systems and call numbers to locate key areas within a library's collection – for example, 'junior non fiction'
- browsing shelves to read book spines, back cover blurbs and so on
- skimming and scanning various materials such as books, leaflets, video cases, audio-cassette notes, and reference books, to check suitability and interest
- reading for different purposes and selecting texts to suit these purposes, such as daily newspapers, weekly magazines, information brochures, fiction, non-fiction, reference materials, and so on;
- making judgments about material located from a library search – for example, what do I do with it? does it suit my purposes? where does it fit? is it reliable? (this last question brings a reader into the realm of text analyst practices)
- requesting material to be placed on hold;
- requesting inter library loans;
- framing reference inquiries appropriately so that library staff can understand and meet requests for information;
- borrowing material;
- keeping track of library loans; and
- returning material.

Teachers can talk with staff in their local libraries to invite them to talk to children at school about library research, and to arrange visits to the local library for demonstrations and guided use of these skills.

Library programs

Public libraries provide various programs for readers. These include Story Time for young children which typically involves reading aloud and listening to picture book narratives in print or other media, and participating in follow up activities which are taken home or displayed in the library. Other programs provide for older readers, allowing them to get together to share, talk and reflect on what they're reading.

In addition to these regular programs, libraries also provide special programs and holiday programs to their communities. It is wise for teachers to keep abreast of these programs. From time to time libraries arrange visits from children's authors, story tellers, puppeteers, cartoonists and so on. Programs built around these visitors include performances (e.g., a story teller narrating a tale to a group of children), conversations (e.g., a children's author talking about their own reading and writing experiences with children), and hands-on workshops (e.g., a cartoonist conducting a series of workshops with children, involving children in learning about various features of cartoons and in composing their own cartoons). Book Week and other special events are also included in libraries' special activities.

Generally, libraries publicise information about their upcoming programs in fliers to schools, posters in the library, and feature articles and ads in local newspapers and other media. Teachers can arrange class visits to such programs with public library staff.

Nestle 'Write Around Australia'

Geared for Years 3-6 children, this program involves children submitting pieces of narrative writing to a panel of judges. Typically, book authors are involved in visiting libraries to talk to budding writers about their work, as well as share their own writing experiences. In this nationwide program, links are made between reading and writing and provides opportunity for children to talk with professional authors.

Mobile library services

These services provide information in smaller communities which may be located some distance from a branch library. Mobile services also provide holiday programs which teachers can find out about and encourage their children to become involved in.

'Olympics/Paralympics Cyber Reporters' Project – a library/school partnership in action

An innovative internet education project was developed between Wollondilly Shire Library and a local primary school, St Anthony's at Picton. The focus of the project was the Sydney 2000 Olympics and Paralympics Games. The class involved was a Year 3 and the teacher Rasheeda Flight.

We describe this project here for two purposes: first, to illustrate how teachers, librarians and children may work together in literacy and technology partnerships; and second, to reflect on the potential benefits of such a partnership to children's reading.

Prior to the start of the project, Wollondilly Shire Library Service had established a 'Sister Library' relationship with Tifton-Tift Library County Public Library in Georgia, U.S.A.[1] The purpose of this relationship is to provide opportunities for the communities of both libraries to exchange print-based and interactive forms of communication about events and people of local, national and international interest.

---

1. The Sister Library Project was launched as an initiative from the White House in Washington, D.C. and is administered by the National Council of Library and Information Services in U.S.A. Wollondilly Shire Library Service became involved through the Public Libraries Branch of the State Library of New South Wales.

The Co-ordinator of Library Services at Wollondilly Shire Council, John Daley, seized upon the Sydney 2000 Olympic and Paralympic Games as an ideal focus for such exchange. Through the local schools in the Shire, he invited teachers and children to write about their experiences of the Games and have them displayed on a special web site maintained by the library, as well as sent overseas for print-based displays in Tifton-Tift Library. Given its interactive involvement with the internet, the program was dubbed the 'Olympics/Paralympics Cyber Reporters Project.

In the first instance, St Anthony's Primary School at Picton responded. Children at this school had already been involved in an 'Adopt a Paralympian' program. In this program, children and teachers alike were emailing a Paralympian athlete from Canada, Courtney Knight, in the lead up to the Games. They exchanged email and snail mail regularly. With weeks to go, this correspondence turned into a daily event. Courtney Knight shared her feelings of nervousness and excitement about the Games. The children attended the Welcome Reception for the Canadian Paralympic Team where they first met her. Later, she was to visit the children at their school.

Thus the children brought enthusiasm, involvement and sense of purpose to the 'Olympics/Paralympics Cyber Reporters Project. At the outset, this project was guided by four objectives:

- to encourage children to reflect on the Sydney 2000 Games in terms of a meeting of cultures from around the world and in terms of elite athletes with disabilities
- to use the Sydney 2000 Olympic and Paralympic Games for providing a window into how one small NSW town viewed and reacted to these events, through the words of children communicating their reflections and experiences in reports on the internet
- to encourage children's literacy development by involving them in writing reports about the Sydney 2000 Games and reading one another's reports over the internet
- to develop children's skills with information technology.

The children drafted and revised reports of their time at the Games. These reports included children's reflections of the visit made to their school by Courtney Knight, as well as their other experiences of the Games. Along with photographs of Courtney Knight's visit, these reports were emailed to the Library. From there they were emailed to Tifton-Tift Library for further responses and discussion over the internet. They were also sent in hard copy for a print-based display in the overseas library.

J. Sara Paulk of Tifton-Tift Library reported that their school-aged library users had read the print-based displays of reports written by the children of St Anthony's. These displays were enjoyed as well as used to get a sense of another community's experiences of and insights into an international event. Tifton-Tift's enjoyment of these displays was further bolstered by inclusion of children's art work depicting the Paralympic Torch Relay passing through the local community, submitted by another school in the Wollondilly Shire. As time went on, reports were written by individual students and classes from other schools in the Shire about the Sydney 2000 Games.

Children's cyber reports were also posted on a web site through an e-list and so journeyed through cyber space to reach destinations all around the world. (For purposes of the Web, children's identities were suppressed in the interests of safety.)

We include two samples of children's reports and a teacher-led report in Figure 4.

Figure 4

Samples of Year 3 Children's Cyber Reports

Clare and Emily write ...

When we met Courtney Knight at the Welcoming Reception it was the best day of our lives. She took us round to meet all the other Canadian Paralympians and they gave us their autographs. We got to bed at 1.00am so Mrs Flight said we didn't have to do any homework.

Brad wrote ... 'Our Olympic Experience'

The Olympic Torch Relay came right past St Anthony's. The whole school lined the street to watch. All of us cheered and cheered. I couldn't believe that I held the torch. The Sydney Olympics are the best in the whole world.

Photos attached [not included here]

1. this is a photo of me and the lady who ran with the torch

2. Photo of some of us lining the street

3. The best is Sydney 2000.

'Our Paralympic Experience' by St Anthony's Cyber reporters from 3R

Earlier on in the year the Education Officer from Ryde City Council in Sydney invited Year 3 to adopt an elite Paralympian from Canada. We were thrilled.

Her name is Courtney Knight and we have 'walked with her' as she has prepared for the most important and exciting venture in her life. We emailed and snail mailed her regularly and she replied immediately. We got to know her very well.

A few weeks before she arrive in Australia we took turns to email her daily. She would tell us how nervous and excited she was because she had never had anyone 'adopt' her and she really wanted to meets us. She said that knowing we would be watching her made her train harder and more determined to do her best.

When she arrived in Australia we met her at the Welcome reception for the Canadian Paralympic Team. The school children from Ryde sang and danced and there were lots of speeches and yummy food.

The photos attached are of the Welcome reception for the Canadian Paralympic team.

Other schools and individual students (both Primary and Secondary) in Wollondilly Shire were to later become involved in the project and so it continued to evolve. Further joint library/school projects being pursued includes involving local school children in correspondence with community figures of their 'Sister' community, in relation to matters such as indigenous affairs by emailing local indigenous figures to interview and set correspondence in motion around a particular purpose; or focusing on sports and emailing a local sporting figure to learn of individual experiences. It was foreseen that the two Libraries in the 'Sister Library' relationship could facilitate putting children in touch with appropriate individuals for this kind of dialogue through cyber space.

What is the potential for such a partnership to develop children's reading?

This project provides an excellent example of how library/school partnerships has great potential to benefit children's reading practices in an integrated, meaningful fashion. Children benefited from the program in many ways. Rather than reiterate specific benefits here, we stand back and describe potential and possible directions for developing reading practices within the framework of this book. From this, we hope you can draw a more general picture of the value of library/school partnerships in the community.

Potential to develop code breaking practices

Children's code breaking practices, for instance, may be further nurtured by being oriented to: world wide web texts and their conventions for links to pages within the site and to other sites; the mechanics for operating a browser such as pointing and clicking the mouse until it turns into a hand in order to use a hyperlink; forms of world wide web addresses; layout of computer keyboards and functions of keys; and forms of written language when drafting, editing and publishing Games reports. In this, the connection between reading and writing further supports children's learning in this kind of scenario.

Code breaking practices are also a focus when talking about visual symbols and what they represent – such as the three Paralympic shapes which represent mind, body and spirit. This is able to be supported with children's library research.

Flags and their symbolism in terms of colour, design and images make another focus for code breaking and their link to other reading practices and library research. For example, with the identification of flags by their colour, design and imagery, their meanings can be discussed as text participants (such as the religious connotations of the green, white and orange bands on the Republic of Ireland flag; or what the black and red bands and yellow circle represent on the Australian Aboriginal flag).

Potential to develop text participant practices

Focusing now on children's text participant practices, these were enthusiastically fostered by using children's direct experiences of the Games to compose texts and to read one another's reports. At the same time, such a project provides opportunities to draw on other sources of information about the Games, such as television coverage, newspaper reports, magazine articles, and historical texts about the Games, all of which are available in public libraries.

Potential to develop text user practices

Children's text user practices benefit from projects like this by becoming familiar with newspaper report genres – their purposes and features. As well, children may further hone their skills of writing for an audience and therefore write like a reader; using the World Wide Web for reporting on the Games to people far and wide; and learning about people's experiences in other times and places, such as from their email with their 'adopted' Paralympian.

The Olympic and Paralympic Games were able to stimulate interest in countries that otherwise might be obscure in children's minds. For example, the sole race swam by Eric Mossambani from Equatorial Guinea, reported on by some children, can lead to further research in atlases and encyclopedias to locate this country and learn something of its history, economics and culture.

Purposes of flags can be discussed as text users – such as signalling national identities of teams as they parade in the Opening Ceremonies of in the Sydney 2000 Games, and consolidating national pride when flags are raised in medal ceremonies.

Flags can be further explored through library research. Looking up atlases to locate countries involves skills specific to this kind of text, as does looking up other kinds of reference material to explore histories of countries. For example, the historical significance of the unified march of athletes from North Korea and South Korea in the Opening Ceremony of the Olympics can be better appreciated when familiar with the history of conflict between these two countries.

Potential to develop text analyst practices

In relation to text analyst practices, children were involved in constructing a position as writers by virtue of writing a newspaper-style report – for example, a position which supports the wonders and enjoyment of the Sydney 2000 Games. Constructing position in texts as writers enhances understanding of how we are positioned as readers.

Meanings of flags can be further deconstructed as text analysts. Possible issues arising for text analysts could include: the importance of the mind, body and spirit alliance to the Paralympian movement; historical reasons behind the inclusion of the Union Jack on the Australian flag and how this relates to the Republic debate in Australia; and the significance of Cathy Freeman carrying both the Australian and Australian Aboriginal flags when doing her lap of honour.

TASK

Identify a hypothetical class project. Describe ways you would implement this project in co-operative partnership with the public library located in the school's community.

Assessing Readers as Text Users

Marshall (1999) in reporting on a reading program for at-risk students in a secondary school, described procedures and criteria for assessing children's projects on travel brochures. The assessment criteria were made explicit to the students at the outset and indeed students had input on these criteria. This is an important principle of assessment that is equally applicable in primary classrooms.

Anecdotal records

Anecdotal records describe a specific event or product and report on it as a basis for later interpretation and assessment. Often they are recorded after the event, although it is wise for the sake of accuracy not to let too much time lapse. An example of an anecdotal record is shown in Figure 5.

Anecdotal records allow teachers to capture incidents that they may not have anticipated and in situations where they were not set up to take observations on the spot. They also let teachers be spontaneous in their assessment, as well as more planned as they systematically rove their classrooms, focusing on particular children or groups of children and looking for incidents of interest which add insight into children's practices and learning. What is noted down in an anecdotal record is descriptive, somewhat brief and can be related to other things known about the child/children.

Rhodes & Nathenson-Mejia (1999) have formulated a general observation guide for the purpose of making anecdotal records. Below we have adapted this guide in order to develop a similar guide which focuses specifically on text user practices – this, however, is not exhaustive. (From this, we encourage you to develop similar guides for making anecdotal records about children's code breaking, text-participant and text analyst practices, too).

- functions served in children's reading in the classroom
- functions served in children's reading in home and community contexts (as spoken about by children)
- the kinds of texts children read in the classroom
- the kinds of texts children read in home and community contexts (including those they bring to school)

Figure 5

An Example of an Anecdotal Record for Describing Text User Practices

<u>Name</u>:   Cathy   <u>Date</u>: 3/3/2000

<u>Situation</u>:   Modelled reading session with class, and then talking to Cathy after modelled
reading session

Description – I was modelling spell texts today, with spells in 'Meg's Eggs'. When I asked
the children what the spells were like, Cathy answered, 'Like a rock-a-bye'. I didn't think
that the spell sounded like a rock-a-bye, and said this. But when I thought about it later, I
thought I should find out what Cathy meant.

Later, I asked her to explain her answer, and she talked about nursery rhymes she had at
home. It turns out Cathy is read nursery rhymes every night before she goes to sleep. She
expressed much enjoyment of these rhymes, usually read by her mother.

Interpretation – It seems that while I was modelling spells as an example of an instructional
text, for Cathy, their rhyming nature conjured up nursery rhymes instead. Obviously she is
much more familiar with rhymes than spells. I'll provide nursery rhymes in the classroom
for Cathy, so as to make stronger links to her home experiences. I'll also ask Cathy, as well
as other children, to bring in any texts that they or family members might use to make or do
things, so as to ensure relevance and to build children's understandings about instructional
texts on the basis of their home experiences.

- how talking about text genres, text purposes and links to text structures and
  language features affects what children say and do as text users
- how children use texts in their classroom
- how children talk about texts in the classroom, and with whom
- what kinds of situations do children use texts in
- how children use texts before, during and after reading
- comparisons between what children say and what they do
- what children say about texts and their relevance to their lives

Questionnaires and interviews

Simple questionnaires and interviews provide a way for teachers to find out about
children's text user practices. Parents/caregivers and children alike can be involved in
providing this information and they may do so in the context of completing a simple
and short written questionnaire, and/or talking with parents on information exchange
sessions, and/or talking directly with children themselves individually or in small groups.
An example of a written questionnaire, which may also be used as a basis for an
individual or small group conversation with children, is shown in Figure 6.

Figure 6

An Example of a Written Questionnaire to Assess Children's Text User Practices in Home and Community Contexts

<u>Name</u>:   Eric Brown   <u>Date</u>:   March 2001

1.   What kinds of texts do you read do at home and in the community?

❏ billboards	❏ junk mail
❏ books	❏ letters
❏ catalogues	❏ magazines
❏ cereal boxes	❏ music
❏ charts	❏ newspapers
❏ comics	❏ notes and notices
❏ computer	❏ posters
❏ computer games	❏ puzzles
❏ dictionaries	❏ recipes
❏ food labels	❏ rhymes
❏ games	❏ shopping lists
❏ greeting cards	❏ television guides
❏ jokes	❏ television programs
	❏ traffic signs
❏ other (name)	❏ video cases

_____

_____

_____

2.   From your answers to Question 1, what three things do you most prefer to read, and why?

3.   When and where do you usually read? (For example, at night in front of the television; in the supermarket; …)

4.   Do you choose what you read?

5.   Does anyone else help choose what you read? If so, who?

6.   Why do you read?

7.   Do you belong to a library? If so, how often do you go and what kinds of things do you like to borrow or do there?

8.   Do you use a computer at home or somewhere else like a friend's home or the library? If so, what kinds of things do you do on the computer?

Note: These questions instead may be used for conversation with small groups of children.

Getting to know what kinds of texts children read in their home, community and school contexts will be aided by questions which focus on:

- what kinds of texts children read?
- when do children read these texts?
- in what kinds of situations do children read particular kinds of texts?
- who chooses the texts children read?
- do children choose their own texts?
- what do children read for?
- do children belong to a library? If so, how often do they go there and what kinds of texts and for what purposes do they borrow?
- do children use a computer, and why?
- what kinds of reading do children do on the computer (e.g., computer reading texts, surfing the net)?

Assessing the repertoire of text user practices embraced in the classroom

As we have said time and again, assessment should not just focus on what the children are doing and how they are developing; teachers' own teaching practices and the reading environment they provide should also be assessed. A checklist or simple survey can be developed for this purpose, based on questions like:

- what do I know about the kinds of texts children read at school?
- what do I know about the kinds of texts children read in their homes and communities?
- am I building on the kinds of texts children read outside the classroom?
- am I explicitly introducing children to genres they need to succeed at school?
- what kinds of texts does my classroom provide?
- do I encourage children to bring texts to school, and do I value and use these in my reading program?
- how do I use children's home and community texts in my program?
- do I allow children to talk about their home and community texts, and to 'teach' me and one another about these text?

Summary

Text users recognise social purposes which texts serve and choose texts to meet their particular needs. Text user practices are founded on the knowledge of purposes served by different kinds of texts and how these purposes are achieved by a text's structure and language features. In the classroom it is important that the range of texts reflect the range and diversity in children's homes and communities. At the same time it is necessary to include those texts which are important to children's success at school and adult life.

Key Concepts

- text user
- text genre
- text purpose
- text and context relationships

Tutorial Activities

A. Students work in small groups. Each group is provided with 2-3 texts belonging to the same genre. Each group works with a different genre of texts and is to:

- explore each text

- compare similarities and differences

- identify common purposes

- examine how they are organised

- identify their language features.

B. Bring to your tutorial a range of community texts. These might include magazines, travel brochures, real estate guides, manuals, cereal boxes, television guides, hypertext printouts, catalogues, advertisements and so forth. In groups, share your texts and talk about the purposes they each serve, how their structures relate to their purposes, to what kind of audience are they each geared and their visual features such as font, colour, imagery and composition. From this discussion, what implications for classroom practices which relate to text users can you identify?

Further Readings

Comber, B. & Simpson, A. 1995, Reading cereal boxes – analysing everyday texts, in *Texts – the Heart of the English Curriculum, Series 1,* Curriculum Division, Department for Education and Children's Services, South Australia.

Derewianka, B., 1990, *Exploring How Texts Work,* Primary English Teaching Association, Sydney.

Hancock, J. (Ed.) 1999, *Teaching Literacy Using Information Technology,* International Reading Association, Newark, Delaware, U.S.A.

Ingvarson, D. (Ed.) 1997, *A Teacher's Guide to the Internet – the Australian Experience,* Heinemann, Melbourne.

Luke, A. & Gilbert, P. (Eds.) 1993, *Literacy in Contexts,* Allen & Unwin, Sydney.

Luke, A. 2000, 'Critical literacy in Australia: a matter of context and standpoint', *Journal of Adolescent and Adult Literacy, vol. 43,* no. 5, pp.448-461.

O'Brien, J. 1998, 'Experts in Smurfland', in M. Knobel & A. Healy. (Eds.), *Critical Literacies in the Primary Classroom,* Primary English Teaching Association, Sydney.

Shepherd, L. 1999, 'Building on cultural capital: linking home and school literacies with popular texts', in J. Hancock (ed.), *The Explicit Teaching of Reading,* International Reading Association, Newark.

Simms, J. 1997, 'More than words – exploring comics and cartoons: speech, sound and movement', in *Texts – the Heart of the English Curriculum, Series 1,* Curriculum Division, Department for Education and Children's Services, South Australia.

Chapter 7

READERS AS TEXT ANALYSTS

Opening Quote

'Books, as enduring, concrete and wide-reaching cultural artifacts, carry a weight of authority beyond that which might be attributed to a particular teacher.'
(Gilbert, 1989, p.21)

Chapter Preview

This chapter focuses on readers as text analysts. It explores what text analysts do and the related knowledge and skills of text analysts. It looks at ways in which texts written for children construct worlds of childhood and shapes sense of identity and systems of values and beliefs. It examines various definitions of this set of reading practices and discusses a set of philosophic parameters by which teachers can begin to think about planning and programming. Developmental trends in growth as text analysts are identified and related classroom practices are described. How teachers might effectively and inclusively scaffold children's development as text analysts are described, along with learning activities and assessment.

Focal Questions

- What are text analyst practices?
- What does a text analyst know and do?
- How do texts construct ideological meanings?
- What are patterns in readers' growth as text analysts?
- How might teachers support and promote the development of text analysts?
- How might teachers support and assess the development of text analysts?
- How might readers from diverse cultural and linguistic backgrounds be best supported as text analysts?

Introduction

So far in this book we have explored what readers do as text code breakers, text participants and text users. This chapter brings us to a fourth and final reader set of reading practices – text analyst practices, which we have highlighted in Figure 1.

Figure 1

Model of Reading as Social Practices with Text Analyst Practices Highlighted

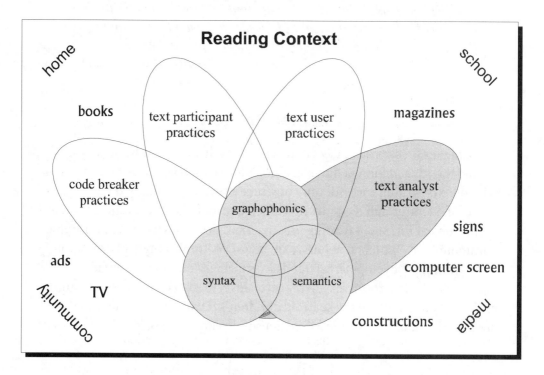

As text analysts readers move beyond the meanings they make from texts to consider what it is a text wants the reader to do, think or believe.

Text analysts may reflect on questions such as: What is this text trying to do with me? What does it want me to believe? Whose interests are being served? Whose voices are heard? Whose voices are silent? (after Freebody, 1992; Luke and Freebody, 1999; NSW DET, 1997)

TASK

Let us step in to the shoes of a text analyst by applying these kinds of questions to the extract which begins the bestselling autobiography, *Angela's Ashes*, by Frank McCourt (1996, pp.11-12). Read the extract, then take time to reflect on the questions which follow.

'People everywhere brag and whimper about the woes of their early years, but nothing can compare with the Irish version: the poverty; the shiftless loquacious alcoholic father; the pious defeated mother moaning by the fire; pompous priests; bullying schoolmasters; the English and the terrible things they did to us for eight hundred long years.

Above all – we were wet.

Out in the Atlantic Ocean great sheets of rain gathered to drift slowly up the River Shannon and settle forever in Limerick. The rain dampened the city from the Feast of the Circumcision to New Year's Eve. It created a cacophony of hacking coughs, bronchial rattles, asthmatic wheezes, consumptive croaks. It turned noses into fountains, lungs into bacterial sponges. ...

The rain drove us into the church – our refuge, our strength, our only dry place. At Mass, Benediction, novenas, we huddled in great damp clumps, dozing through priest drone, while steam rose again from our clothes to mingle with the sweetness of incense, flowers and candles.

Limerick gained a reputation for piety, but we knew it was only the rain.'

What is this text trying to do with you as a reader? What does it want you to believe? Whose voices are heard? Whose voices are silent?

What does this tell you about this aspect of reading and how it might be effectively taught in classrooms?

Texts invite the reader to share and take on particular views and experiences of the world. The above extract draws the reader into the author's past lived experiences. In so doing, it positions the reader to feel and so be convinced of the abject poverty and suffering which prevailed at that time and place. Its vivid descriptions of images such as the sodden clothing, the people's maladies and the uncaring religious figures, dispel any possible myths about a rosy Irish childhood and devout Irish Catholic piety. The text shows, not just tells, how these myths are not necessarily true.

As texts portray world views and experiences, they give voice to some social groups of people while other voices remain silent (Luke, 1993). In the above extract, the voice of Frank McCourt, on behalf of himself and the people who shared his experiences (such as his family) is heard. Other voices are silent – for example, voices of other residents in Limerick and of the Catholic Church.

This comment about voices does not falsify this text. Rather, it points out that this text, like texts generally, is one person's version of events – it is one construction of reality, not reality itself. This concept is fundamental to being a text analyst for it provides the basis for a reader to question texts and to think about what is read from alternative points of view.

Knowledge and Skills of a Text Analyst

Our brief visit of the above extract draws out ways in which texts position readers to feel particular emotions, to take up particular perspectives and/or to hold particular values. One of the tasks of successful reading is to learn to detect this reading position and deciding whether to accept or reject it. Thus, text analysts detect a text's position and choose to accept and endorse that position, or to question it, or to challenge it, or to reject it and adopt an alternative position. For example, do you accept or reject the text's position in the above extract? Why?

Knowledge and skills of a text analyst are summarised in Figure 2. A text analyst understands that texts are constructions of reality (and not reality itself). The meanings of a text are shaped by the context in which the text has been produced and in which a reader reads. For example, the extract above is one person's construction of growing up in Limerick. That construction is shaped by the personal experiences of the author, his place in the social order, the happenings and interpersonal relationships in his family and community, his Catholic context and so on. Had a Catholic priest from the same time in Limerick written this text, no doubt it would be a very different version of events.

A text analyst also understands how texts are crafted to construct overt and hidden meanings. Linguistic choices contribute to this crafting of text – such as choice of descriptive words and choice of verbs (for example, who engages in action, who is more passive, who does what to whom).

The extract from *Angela's Ashes* vividly describes poverty and suffering, with phrases like 'miserable Irish Catholic childhood', 'poverty', 'shiftless loquacious alcoholic father' and 'pious defeated mother'. Likewise, the effects of the rain on people's health is graphically portrayed. This suffering is juxtaposed to the Church which remained dry and provided refuge for anyone within its walls. But this refuge is also viewed by the text somewhat cynically – the church flowers and candles which are described set up a rather shameful contrast to the living conditions of the parishioners once they leave the sanctuary again. This is further underlined by the text's description of 'pompous priests', 'bullying schoolmasters' and 'the English'.

Figure 2

Overview of Text Analyst Role

Definition	Knowledge	Skills
Text analysts seek and identify ideological meanings in texts:	Texts are culturally crafted objects	Reflecting on a text's ideological meanings
	Texts construct ideological meanings	Interrogating texts
what does this text want me to believe, feel, do?	Texts position readers to take up particular actions, beliefs or ideas	Detecting a text's position
what do I think about that?	Texts carry opinion, bias and point of view	Taking a position - accepting, rejecting, or challenging a text's position
what are alternative positions?	Different texts may treat same topics or themes differently	Recognising and talking about opinion, bias and point of view in texts
	Readers may agree or disagree with a text's position	Constructing alternative positions to those in texts
	Different readers might interpret a text differently, and reasons why	Recognising and describing ways in which a text is crafted through such means as choice of words, grammatical structures, overall organisation and layout, and visual images

Based on Freebody (1992), Luke (2000), Luke & Freebody (1999) and NSW Department of Education and Training, 1997, *Teaching Reading: A K-6 Framework*.

How Children's Texts Construct Ideological Meanings

Be they in the guise of fiction or non-fiction, texts written for children construct particular beliefs and values, which are inherent to the particular sociocultural contexts in which texts are produced. That is, they construct ideological meanings.

For example, the picture book narrative, *Titch* by Pat Hutchins (1971) tells the story of a family awaiting the arrival of a fourth child. The words tell of Titch growing out of his clothes and being given hand-me downs from his older brother and sister. The words make no mention of the expected baby. The illustrations show the mother sitting by a window, knitting baby clothes. As the mother holds up her knitting needles, with father standing by her side, the reader's gaze is directed by the needles to a scene outside the window, where birds are building a nest and seedlings are planted in the garden bed. As time moves on in the story, the mother's belly grows larger, the nest becomes more established and the seedlings grow. When the baby is brought home, baby birds are seen in the nest, the new plants are in flower and Titch is given a new set of clothes. The underlying theme is one of growth and expansion in a nuclear family, a theme aligned with the natural order as it is seen outside the window and therefore seen as good. Thus the reader is positioned to accept this view of family as truthful and unproblematic.

In this, we see an example of the argument that texts may normalise and naturalize representations of social identity, relations and actions (Luke, 1993, p.39). The themes of growth and change in *Titch* could be portrayed in other family contexts – such as single-parent families, extended families, families where both parents work and so on. The choice of a two-parent nuclear family impacts upon the ideological meanings which are constructed – meanings not just related to change and growth, but also to social identities, roles and relationships.

TASK

Locate a children's narrative which portrays everyday situations such as family life. Examine the book in terms of questions like: What is this text trying to do with me? What does it want me to believe? What do I think about that? How is its position constructed through its words and its pictures?

What does this tell you about this aspect of reading and how it might be effectively taught in classrooms?

Texts which challenge traditional ideological meanings

A reader's previous experiences, both lived and with other texts, influence the positions they detect and take up or reject in texts (Davies, 1989).

TASK

Suppose you were about to sit down and read a traditional fairy tale. What kinds of characters might you expect to find? Jot them down. Perhaps even draw them. What do they look like? How do they dress? What do they wear? What are their characteristics? Now, think about the kinds of relationships among these characters? What kinds of relationships might you expect to find in this fairy tale?

What does this tell you about this aspect of reading and how it might be effectively taught in classrooms?

The previous experiences you have had with fairy tales will influence your expectations. Likewise, your previous experiences will to some extent have influenced your view of the world. As argued by Davies (1989, p.43) wrote, 'the moral order is deeply embedded in that fanciful world' of fairy tales. Acts of courage and virtue are rewarded, usually by a prince and princess finding each other through such acts and living happily ever after. These values are reinforced by their recurrence across a number of different texts.

However, children's narratives such as *The Paper Bag Princess* by Robert Munsch (1980) turn the traditional fairy tale upside down. In *The Paper Bag Princess*, Princess Elizabeth's castle was burned down by a dragon, who carried Prince Ronald away. The only thing left for Princess Elizabeth to wear was a brown paper bag. Donning the bag, she went off to rescue her prince in distress. By cleverly outwitting the dragon she rescued Prince Ronald, who immediately expressed not his thanks but rather his disgust at Elizabeth's untidy state. Telling her to go away and only come back when she is dressed like a proper princess, Elizabeth promptly dumped her Prince and skipped off into the sunset – alone.

This text positions the reader to accept the importance of being your own person and not being misguided by expectations based on limiting, stereotyped views of gender. Davies (1989) explored children's responses to this upturning of the traditional fairy tale. She found that five-year-olds' uptake of the text's position was shaped by their choice of taking on Elizabeth's or Ronald's or the dragon's perspective, by their understandings about gender roles, and by their own experiences of working mothers. Thus, some children (all girls) took up Elizabeth's perspective, although one thought she should have done what Ronald asked in the end. The boys took up with either the Prince's or the dragon's perspective. The boys went beyond the words to infer from the pictures meanings about Ronald as a champion tennis player and in possession of admirable prowess – thus downplaying the fact that he was the dragon's victim and dependent on Elizabeth to save him.

Children's fiction which focuses on social issues was closely investigated by Lewison, Leland and Harste (2000). Fifty children's books were examined. Social issues children's books were portrayed as having some of the following characteristics (Lewison *et al*, p.10):

- they invite discussion about unfair treatment of people and why some people are marginalised in society
- they do not have 'happy ever after' endings
- they explore how differences in culture, language and so on make a difference in terms of what happens to people in society and how they are treated and perceived
- they give voice to people and groups of people who traditionally have been marginalised or silenced – for example, indigenous peoples and people with disabilities
- they make visible the social systems which attempt to maintain the status quo of inequities because such systems serve the interests of power groups in society
- they explore dominant systems of meaning which belong to and are promoted by power groups in society and their effect on how people are positioned – where they are deemed to 'fit' – in society

A small sub-category of these books fell into a group called 'multi-view books' (Lewison *et al*, 2000, p.9). These books have characters who have very different perspectives and world views and tensions arise in these stories when different characters interpret the same event in different ways. An example of a multi-view book dealing with social issues for older readers is *Making up Megaboy* (Walter, 1998); an example of a picture book narrative for younger readers is *Voices in the Park* (Browne, 1998).

In *Voices in the Park*, Browne presents four very different versions of the one encounter at a park. A wealthy woman and her young son and dog go to the park, as well as an out-of-work man and his young daughter and dog. They each share their view of what happened that day. Each view is clearly shaped by their own sociocultural background, including prejudices and views of the way things are and should be.

Consequently, four very different stories emerge, showing how different individuals perceive the same set of events and one another very differently and so construct very different 'realities' out of the same situation.

In exploring multi-view, social issues books and teachers' and students' responses to them, Lewison *et al* (2000, p.11) found that

'Books for children that invite multiple perspectives and interpretations go against the grain of social convention and the search for single, right answers.'

Children's texts may also advocate a stance on environmental issues and animal rights. For example, *Where the Forest Meets the Sea* (Baker, 1987) advocates an environmental position in relation to saving the rain forest. Its exquisite crafting of collage images, for which Baker is renowned, draws the reader in to marvel at these images and to so marvel at the real-life environment that they represent which is under threat. The words provide a simple commentary on the images, told through the personal experience of a child who travels with his father to the rain forest and learns of its long natural history, now threatened by urban development. The final image of a holiday resort superimposed on the natural landscape positions the reader to see the imminent threat and so take up a 'save the rain forest' position.

Texts like this invite questions like, 'Whose story is this?', 'Who stands to benefit from this story?' and 'Whose interests are being challenged and why?'

TASK

Choose a children's text which advocates a position on a particular social issue. As you read the text, consider what the text's position is, what you think about the position and how the text puts forward that position through words and images.

What does this tell you about this aspect of reading and how it might be effectively taught in classrooms?

Non-fiction texts

While we have so far portrayed fiction as someone's version of events which construct deeper values and serve larger group interests, the same also applies to non-fiction. All non-fiction texts represent some voices, while others remain unheard. Non-fiction texts serve some group's cultural and/or economic interests, while others are not served or indeed ill-served.

Think about non-fiction texts which report on Australian history – such as the 'discovery' of Australia by Captain Cook. Even seemingly innocent words like, 'Captain Cook discovers Australia' are not innocent at all, nor are they necessarily factual. The word 'discovers' in such historical texts tends to imply discover 'for the first time', as if no-one had gone before. Statements like this marginalise Australia's indigenous peoples who came to Australia some 40,000 years before Cook. Such texts can tend to gloss over what happened to these indigenous peoples after Cook's arrival. In the current debate over Reconciliation in Australia, historical reconstructions of events and the groups they represent take on tremendous significance.

Rather than elaborating further here on such texts, we hand this task over to you. We ask you to explore how texts that are labelled 'non-fiction' and are deemed to be 'factual' position readers.

TASK

Locate a non-fiction text about a topic with which you are quite familiar. Alternatively, locate two or three texts on the same topic and compare their coverage of that topic. As you read the text, think about and note down the information it includes and, as importantly, the information it doesn't include. Why do you think some information is left out? What is its potential effect on whose voices and interests are served by the text?

What does this tell you about this aspect of reading and how it might be effectively taught in classrooms?

The Internet and Text Analysts

Being able to 'read between the lines' and know whose interests are being served, what information is reliable and how a reader is being positioned are critical skills in readers' use of the internet. Based on the writings of cultural critics Hawisher and Selfe (1999, p.40) state that

'computers fundamentally shape and are shaped by, cultural values. Hence these machines continually magnify and reproduce the complex social conditions connected with those values... Computers, then, far from encouraging change, can also serve to support stasis within the existing educational and cultural systems'

Over the email and other forms of internet correspondence, readers may find themselves subjected to inappropriate canvassing of views and products – inappropriate because of ill-chosen email group listings (such as using a listing of individuals brought together by a common community or sporting activity such as the local cricket to advertise goods for sale) or because of intruding upon Newsgroups and elistings to promote one's own personal campaign that has no relevance or place in that group. With these thoughts in mind, we now explore some text analyst issues as they relate to readers using the internet.

Access to the internet

Access to the internet is another issue which needs consideration by readers as text analysts. By access, we do not just mean physical access, such as having a computer on your desk at home or access to computer labs at University. Nor do we just mean access to internet service providers. These certainly are access issues. Over and beyond these, however, is the fact that once on the internet, gatekeepers are implicitly present, with decisions made about what information can be accessed.

These gatekeepers are not disinterested parties and it is possible for them to limit internet users' access. As noted by Moore (1999, p.56), 'every inch of [the internet's] millions of miles of network is owned by someone and, with rare exceptions, users must pay access to it.' Internet users may find their access limited, or indeed may have it limited without realising it:

'Just who makes those decisions and on what basis, is often very difficult to discover, an issue in itself for readers and users of Internet texts.' (Moore, 1999, p.56)

Shopping online

Shopping on the internet is fraught with issues such as:

- fair trading issues – what you see is what you get and so on
- consumer credit card fraud
- division between 'haves' and 'have nots' on basis of credit card ownership
- consumer protection laws do not apply across international or even State borders and while a consumer may reside in a particular State and Country, they may not be protected as they assume when dealing with traders on the Web without borders.

The National Association for the Education of Young Children (NAEYC, 1999) explicitly advocate that children be taught the pitfalls of this and other uses of the internet from an early age:

'Teach children that everything they read on-line may not be true – offers that sound "too good to be true" probably are.'

Choice magazine has provided a set of guidelines specifically related to online book shops (*Choice*, November, 2000). Relevant to this discussion about text analysts, online book shops were analysed and evaluated according to the following criteria:

- variety and range of book stock are present;
- information about and reviews of books for sale are included;
- ease with which users can navigate the site;
- ease with which users can locate a book;
- ease with which users can order a book; and
- ease with which users can monitor their order.

A little later in this chapter, we briefly describe how teachers might use this kind of information for bringing online shopping into the classroom for close scrutiny.

Making judgments about information on the internet

The World Wide Web is made up of sites maintained by companies, universities, government bodies, non-profit organisations and individuals. Each group has its own particular focus, concerns and agendas to promote. These include their explicit missions which are apparent on their home pages in some form or another; they also include more implicit or hidden agendas.

As text analysts, readers need to make judgments about information they locate on the internet. The State Reference Library of New South Wales (Cao, 2000) has provided criteria for selecting electronic reference resources. While geared to librarians, many of these criteria are relevant to text analysts:

- the information is accurate and relevant
- information is regularly updated
- source of the material is well documented, including authorship
- the site is maintained by a reputable organisation or publisher.

When going to a new web site via a link, a user does not need to know its address or source – a simple clicking of the mouse will get the user there. A user can easily be mislead about the authenticity of sites if not consciously stopping to check this. Clicking on links is quite different from a more conscious process of conducting a search via a search engine and critically sifting through results on the basis of some preliminary evaluation that takes account of source. Both ways are valid and readers need to be encouraged in both cases to critically reflect on the quality of information they find.

Catering for Children from Diverse Social and Linguistic Backgrounds

Catering to the needs of readers from diverse cultural and linguistic backgrounds, it is important to include:

- texts which are composed and dictated by children, for text analyst discussions, such as what children want the reader to think or do
- texts written in children's first languages
- texts written in children's own cultural contexts, to examine the positions they construct for readers
- texts which portray social identities, role and relationships across different cultural contexts
- texts which report factual information about similar topics from different sociocultural standpoints
- multi-media texts as well as print texts (e.g., television, video) for the purposes of developing text analysts.

Scaffolding should be based on understandings and inclusive practices in relation to children's sociocultural backgrounds. For example, texts which challenge traditional family roles such as *Piggybook* (Browne, 1986) might resonate with children in different ways, depending on their own family structures and their views of those structures, shaped as they are by values inherent to their cultural contexts. Or, in response to *Voices in the Park* (Browne, 1998), different children might take up and validate different versions, shaped as their decision is by their own backgrounds.

By virtue of developing readers as text analysts and all that such instruction entails, a teacher is working towards implementing inclusive practices which take account of social and cultural variation and interests. Analysing texts in order to uncover their positioning of readers and the social groups whose interests they promote or silence, empowers readers and serves the interests of inclusivity.

More specifically, whether working with children from different or similar backgrounds, it is important that such variations are accounted for in the texts chosen for instruction and the knowledge and skills which are developed.

In regard to readers from diverse backgrounds and their development as text analysts, it is important to provide opportunity to understand and for children to articulate their own sociocultural backgrounds and the way this shapes their views and reactions to what they read, Indeed, the same is true for all readers.

As teachers focus on these aspects of functioning as text analysts, they need to develop a language with which to talk and think about texts in this way – for **all** children. This language needs to be mutually understood and carefully negotiated over time. It is not appropriate to leap immediately into using technical terms without first expressing them in common sense terms. We saw this in the previous chapter's examples which showed teachers taking time to develop language about how different kinds of texts are labeled and structured.

Teachers may develop this metalanguage through their own talk-aloud commentary as they share texts with children – for example, making self-directed comments like 'I think this author wants me to think about ways to save the rain forest' and posing self-directed questions like 'I wonder why saving the rain forests is important to this author?' This common sense language over time can give way to introducing more technical terms – for example, 'This author's position is about saving the rain forest' and 'I wonder whose interests are being served by this position?' Metalanguage such as this is further developed through its continued use and glossing as teachers and children together talk about texts – for example, 'What is this text's position – that is, what does it want you to think?' Over time, once children have all grasped the meaning of technical terms used to analyse texts, such glossing becomes redundant. Teachers can monitor children's understanding of technical terms through the way children use those terms in the comments they make as text analysts.

Classroom Practices for Supporting Readers as Text Analysts

Choosing texts

When choosing texts for our classroom reading programs, in order to develop children as text analysts, we need to think about individual texts as well as their collective impact. We are not talking about censoring classroom collections because of concerns with political incorrectness, for example. Indeed, according to Gilbert (1989, p.21),

> *'Texts which are considered less than ideal in terms of content may serve the function of helping children to learn to read critically. Perhaps in this way, teachers can take advantage of the way in which inequities are made tangible and therefore accessible, when translated into print.'*

It is important for teachers to be aware of the meanings each text constructs and how it construct those meanings, so that teachers may model and guide children through processes of identifying and discussing that position.

Equally important is careful consideration of the range of texts teachers make available to children. As argued by Luke (1993, p.28), many print texts create patterns of mutually reinforcing references. For example, in a collection of texts designed to be used to teach children to read in the early school years, Baker & Freebody (1989) found that similar social roles and relationships across these books were repeatedly constructed on the grounds of age and gender. Similarly, Gilbert and Rowe (1989), in their study of books deliberately designed for beginning reading instruction at school, found that stereotypes on the basis of gender prevailed across these books. In both studies, recurring portrayals of individuals on the bases of age and gender both propagated and confirmed social stereotypes.

In this way, texts intertextually reinforce the truthfulness of their meanings. Some implications for teachers arise. Teachers need to model ways of identifying these stereotypes when reading to children. Teachers also need to model how texts construct these stereotypes through words and pictures. In addition, teachers need to invite children to critically talk about these stereotypes and relate them to their own experiences.

While we saw above that texts may intertextually reinforce the truthfulness of their ideological meanings, some texts go out of their way to bring this alleged truthfulness into question. For example, *Archie the Big Good Wolf* (Baillie & Bentley, 1999) presents an alternative version which constructs the wolf as an innocent victim of misguided gossip and misunderstanding. Such texts show the reader that texts are not definitive in the realities they present.

When choosing texts for your classroom reading program, to support the development of text analysts, consider:

- texts which make visible their textual practices for constructing values, beliefs and for positioning the reader – such as those we previously discussed.

- texts which innovate on or manipulate elements in another text or text genre that is known. Children can be asked to reflect on what has changed and what is the effect on how we now view those characters and events.
- texts which are different versions of the same tale or theme or topic, such as texts about family-related themes. Children can be encouraged to think about similarities and differences, drawing up charts to show recurring themes and points of departure, as well as connections to their own views and experiences.
- texts which embrace diversity and inclusivity and include traditional and alternative points of view.

The inclusion of such texts provide opportunities for children to be initiated in interrogating texts, taking on an active and interpretive role by enabling and inviting them to do so and understanding the constructedness of texts.

TASK

Make a selection of five children's texts which you believe together (not necessarily individually) meet the above criteria. Explain how your collection meets these criteria. Describe how you might use these texts in classrooms.

Inclusion of community texts in classrooms

We made the point in our previous chapter that teachers are responsible for including texts which are functional and powerful in the lives of children in their classrooms, in order to develop their text user practices. The same applies to the development of text analyst practices.

Here, we provide a brief summary of how a Year 5/6 teacher, Jane Pitt (1997), used women's magazines to encourage children to explore the types of messages they convey.

The children studied the ways that women are perceived through examination of literacy devices such as photographs, advertising and the articles chosen for the magazine. Although there are various components of magazines that could be explored, Pitt focused her unit on the use of widely accepted stereotypes about what women should look like and do; and on the use of gimmicks to sell products.

Three well known national women's magazines were chosen and copies provided for classroom use. Children were expected to achieve the following outcomes:

- make predictions about the purposes, content and audiences of the magazines
- check their predictions against the actual content of the magazines under focus
- analyse the photographs in the magazines
- consider the techniques used by advertisers in magazines.

The children initially generated lists of predictions in pairs about the main purpose of the magazines and the types of readers; why and where these magazines are read; and the types of articles they contain. They then shared their lists with the class and created one class list which included:

- who reads the magazines?
- what is the main purpose for reading the magazines?
- what sections would you expect to find in the magazines?

These predictions were then tested as individuals used copies of the magazines to check and confirm (or change) their predictions. The findings were then discussed by the whole class.

The photographs used in the magazines were analysed too, so as to encourage children to think about how photos convey messages about what makes women successful. Discussion was also generated about the types of images of women projected in the magazines; how realistic these images were; and their possible effect on readers. Questions also were asked about the groups of women who were <u>not</u> present in these photos and why and if there were any similarities or differences between those groups represented and those not.

The children also focused on the advertising techniques used in the magazines. The emphasis was on assisting children to read through the ads and uncover the hidden messages in both the written and visual texts which perpetuate stereotypes and target women as consumers. Again the children used a predict-check-confirm/change format, recorded the information in their reading journals and then met as a whole class to discuss the implications of their findings.

A teacher might assess such units by keeping anecdotal and observational records on children's ability to discuss stereotypical images, advertising techniques and categories of articles in magazines. Rating scales, checklists and/or work samples could determine children's ability to recognise how magazines could be produced differently and whose interests are served by the different ways in which magazines are and could be produced. These assessment procedures could also focus on children's understanding about formats and content in magazines and links between this and projected readership.

Text analyst practices

Beyond immersing children in texts which support and stimulate their practices as text analysts, it is equally important to actively involve them in being text analysts. Involving children as text analysts means focusing on such aspects as those identified in *Teaching Reading: A K-6 Framework* (NSW Board of Studies, 1997):

- purposes of texts, in terms of what texts seek the reader to think, do or believe
- opinion, bias and point of view in texts
- different texts' treatment of same topics or themes
- agreement and disagreement with texts

- identifying position in texts
- endorsing or challenging positions in texts
- constructing alternative positions to those in texts
- understanding why different readers might interpret a text differently
- understanding how the way in which a text is crafted through such means as choice of words, grammatical structures, overall organization and layout and visual images, contributes to the text's ideological meanings.

Teachers' scaffolding needs to be based on understandings about trends in the development of text analysts. Indicators of growth in readers as text analysts are summarised in Figure 3, along with related teaching practices.

These trends are only intended as a guide; they do not prescribe how each and every child does or should develop as a text analyst.

Modelled reading

Modelled reading provides a venue for teachers to explicitly demonstrate how texts function to position readers and how readers function as text analysts. After the NSW Board of Studies' guidelines (1997) a teacher's role in this situation includes reading a text and showing, explaining and instructing its ideological meanings and how those meanings are made. Children in this situation listen to and view the text, following it as it is being read, as well as asking questions of the text and participating in talking about its position.

In preparation for modelled reading, teachers need to carefully select their texts, based on criteria we've earlier described. It is also important to build students' knowledge which is relevant to the text. This way, children can make informed decisions about a text's position and their response to that position. For example, if the text is focusing on environmental issues, it may be appropriate to provide information on the environment, as well as providing a forum for those issues to be identified and discussed.

As a teacher begins a modelled reading session, they may orient the children to the text's topic and make links to what children know about that topic. This orientation can also include an exploration of why the author may have written the particular text. Children themselves may make some judgments on this based on what they know about the topic an related issues. Links may also be made to previous texts they have encountered, on similar topics and issues. Having done so, they may be invited to compare how different texts present different or similar positions on the topic at hand.

Working with the text as text analysts during modelled reading also involves the teacher providing an explicit commentary on how the text constructs its ideological meanings. This commentary may include self-directed questions. Questions and comments may focus on the point of view found in the text (e.g., saving the rain forest); what groups of individuals might agree or disagree with that point of view (e.g., environmentalist groups, politicians, loggers, developers); reflecting aloud on why other

Figure 3

Developmental Trends of Text Analysts and Related Pedagogic Practices

Indicators	Pedagogic Practices
Emergent Phase *(includes Role-Play & Experimental Reading; approximately links to Early Stage 1)**	• Select print, TV and videotexts which embrace social and cultural diversity
• Can form opinions about texts, including TV/video as well as print	• Share with children times when you challenge or disagree with texts
• Can relate texts to own experiences	• Encourage children to respond critically to what they read, view and hear
• Can agree and disagree with texts	• Discuss instances of stereotyping in texts, relating these stereotypes to children's own experiences
• Can see patterns across different texts	• Share different versions of the same text, to see how different characters, events, and ideas are constructed
	• Involve children in visual arts and drama to explore points of view
	• Use projection questions like "What do you think?"
	• Encourage children to share and listen to one another's points of view
	• Immerse children in texts which reveal their constructedness
	• Use common-sense language to talk about texts
Early Phase *(includes Early and Transitional Reading; approximately links to Stage 1 and into Stage 2)**	• Encourage a range of opinions and reactions to texts
• Demonstrates understanding that all texts, both fiction and factual, are written by authors who are expressing their own ideas and point of view	• Discuss stereotypes and generalisations in texts
• Comes to recognise that characters can be stereotyped in a text	• Encourage children's interrogation of texts
• Comes to discuss how stereotypes may be changed	• Create an environment which fosters critical thinking
• Comes, with teacher support, to comment on and criticise texts	• Help children be aware of the view of the world being present in a text and how that view affects them
• Can recognise bias in texts	

- With expert support, can detect position and construct alternative positions

Fluent Phase *(includes Independent and Advanced Independent Reading; approximately links to Stage 3)**

- Makes critical comparisons between texts
- Discusses alternative readings of a text
- Offers possible reasons why a text may be interpreted differently by different readers and viewers
- Identifies and elaborates on author's purpose across factual and fictional texts, including more abstract texts
- Discusses at length opinion, bias and point of view
- Explains and discusses how choice of words, grammatical structures and text structures ad formats construct ideological meanings

- Develop a more technical metalanguage for discussing texts
- Involve children in debates on topics with which they are familiar
- Involve children in manipulating elements of a text to achieve a different view
- Involve children in re-telling/illustrating/enacting a text from another perspective
[in addition to those strategies identified for emergent readers]

- Encourage critical thinking about texts
- Model and guide the identification of different points of view within and beyond texts
- Examine, analyse, deconstruct and discuss texts
[in addition to those strategies identified for emergent and early readers]

* Emergent, early and fluent labels are derived from Mooney (1990). Role Play, Experimental, Early, Independent and Advanced labels are derived from the Western Australian department of Education's First Steps – A Reading Developmental Continuum document (1994). Approximate links are made to Early Stage 1, Stage 1, Stage 2 and Stage 3 as identified in NSW Board of Studies English K-6 Syllabus.

people might interpret the text differently (e.g., to protect their economic interests, political agendas or altruistic concerns); and comparing the text with other texts which convey alternative positions (e.g., re-working an environmental text from a logger's point of view).

Modelled reading does not end with just one visit with the text at hand. Several readings on different occasions allows teachers and children to peel back its layers of meaning, so as to get a firmer grasp of the text's underlying ideological messages. These readings may be interspersed with appropriate activities which are described below:

- Visualise an unseen picture book narrative without pictures. Compare and contrast with the original. How did your values shape what you visualised? How were they different from the text? What does this say about what the text values and assumes?
- Debate social issues, to articulate, clarify and justify one's own position and to be aware of and consider alternative points of view.
- Explore and talk about how texts are crafted and their effect on the reader. Explore different ways in which the text might have been crafted, such as different words chosen, alternative ways of presenting images. Implement some of these alternatives through creative arts experiences.
- Manipulate elements of a text, such as changing gender or material conditions of characters, or reverse roles.
- Re-tell or enact a text from another point of view, supported by role-play and simulation.
- Compile charts which analyse narratives in terms of social identities, roles and relationships.
- Compile charts which analyse factual texts in terms of whose perspective is used to report the information; whose perspectives are not included; what information is included; what information is excluded; what is fact and what is opinion or emotion.
- Share different versions of the same text and identify recurring patterns and the effect these have on the reader.
- Rewrite a text to express an alternative point of view.
- Analyse texts in terms of the author's purpose, focusing on who you think the text is written for, why you think so and what the text tells you about information if a factual text, or what it presents about social realities if a narrative text.
- Identify characters in narratives, in terms of their gender and role and address
  - what does each role do in the story?
  - who has the power in the story?
  - what does the author tell us about this character?
  - what doesn't the author tell us about this character?

- – what does the author want you to feel and think?
- Identify patterns across texts by the same author. For example, draw a character as you expect a particular author will and write/enact/illustrate what you expect the characters will do in this text. Or re-write a known text as if by another author.

Guided reading

Guided reading provides a setting for teachers to give greater control and responsibility of text analysts over to the children. As teachers and children together read and talk about texts, teachers may scaffold children's attention on how texts construct their underlying ideological meanings. For example, if reading Jeannie Baker's *Where The Forest Meets the Sea* (1987), children's attention may be focused on the finely detailed collage images. As they talk about how these images have been constructed, they may also be encouraged to reflect on how those images make them feel and why they think the author went to such lengths to construct these images of the environment. This may lead children into picking up the importance of the environment to the author, which may lead to further exploration of why that is so and what their own views are. Interactions such as this allow children to further see and explore the constructedness of texts and how this constructedness conveys particular messages to readers.

In guided reading, children's voices as text analysts are given greater opportunity and responsibility to be heard. It is important that their views are not overwhelmed by the teacher's views or those expressed in the text. It is important to heed the caution in Baker and Freebody's research (1988) that texts and teachers are most times given greater authority at the expense of children's own ideas and views. Thus, as teachers ask questions, it is important to convey that it is the individual's views that are being sought, for their own sake and not to measure that up against preconceived right or wrong answers. Using projection in a teacher's questioning is important – questions like:

- 'What do <u>you think</u> this text wants you to do or believe?'
- 'Do <u>you agree or disagree</u> with that? Why?'
- 'How do these pictures [or words] make <u>you feel</u>?'
- 'Why do <u>you think</u> the author wrote this text?'
- 'Have <u>you read</u> other texts like this?'

This is neither a definitive nor prescriptive list of questions for guided reading. It does, however, indicate aspects of a text analyst that can be the focus of guided reading and how we might bring these aspects into focus. Using projection in this way, teachers support and prompt children's functioning as text analysts, while sitting back to listen to what children say and observe how they are functioning as text analysts.

[handwritten margin note: Teachers should let chln explore how txt posits them a readers by inviting multiple perspectives from all chln w prompts such as]

As children are explicitly encouraged to voice their own views about texts, they need to be encouraged to elaborate on what they think, with prompts like 'Tell me more about that' and 'Why do you think so?' As children express their views and explore how texts position them as readers, teachers should also invite multiple perspectives from all children, with prompts such as 'That's one way of thinking about it. Are there other ideas?' This enables children to see that different readers take up different positions and the reasoning behind these positions. It also allows children to see that readers do not necessarily have to agree with the text and that there are different ways of either endorsing or challenging a text's position. Finally, it allows children to see how readers construct alternative positions – all of which is demonstrated during modelled reading.

The knowledge and skills related to text analysts which are developed during guided reading, may be further consolidated by appropriate activities such as those shown in Figures 3 and 4. For example, having focused in guided reading on texts which advocate an environmentalist perspective, children might be involved in deliberately adopting an alternative stand and writing a text from that standpoint – such as the text shown in Figure 4. Can you think of other activities which might suit this purpose?

Independent reading

Independent reading provides children with the responsibility of initiating and selecting their own reading materials, from the range which is available in the classroom and which should include texts from children's home and community contexts. Independent reading allows children to use, control and practices their own functioning as text analysts. This can be further pursued by teachers as they observe what children are reading and by holding individual or small group reading conferences to discuss the views children are forming about what they have read. Children may also be given opportunity to discuss their views among themselves. Again, independent reading can be consolidated with a range of activities shown in Figure 4.

For example, children may have read different narrative versions of texts about foxes and hens. They might then work on a chart or some other kind of visual display which identifies stereotypes of these characters, as illustrated in Figure 5.

Online shopping in the classroom

An interesting and useful activity for text analysts in classrooms would be to involve children in doing their own analyses and evaluations of a particular section of the internet (such as online book shops or other kinds of online shops), with criteria that are modelled, or criteria they jointly construct with expert guidance, or criteria they independently generate and compile their own consumer reports.

Figure 4

An example of a child's text written from an alternative position to texts which advocate environmental concerns

Hello. My name is David. My father is a land developer. He builds nice houses for people to live in.

My father works very hard clearing land to build houses on. He builds houses in places where you can stand and see hills and mountains for miles all around. The people who live in my Dad's houses are very happy and pay him lots of money for their houses. Mum says that pays for our clothes and education.

A little while ago, Dad's company built a large block of apartments and a convenience store and petrol station right next to a row of fast food places. I love KFC best. He paid for traffic lights to get taken out. He put a roundabout in, so it would be easier for people to drive their cars in.

Another project that my dad's company is working on is building a mariner. This is going to be so good. There will be lots of piers for people to park their boats and go sailing. There will be cafes and shops, too. There will be jumping castles and a visitors centre with lots of things for kids to do. I can't wait till it's finished.

The End.

This could be done in the framework of modelled, guided and independent reading:

- A teacher models reports which analyse and evaluate a particular section of the internet, such as online book shops (*Choice* magazines provide useful models). This would include modelling of the focus, criteria used, site samples and the structure of the report including tables, diagrams, facsimiles of the sites and formatting of the main text.
- A teacher then negotiates with the children the choice of another section of the internet (such as online sports shops). Criteria are jointly constructed and selection of sites negotiated, possibly as two intertwined processes. Children in

Figure 5

Children's analysis of stereotypes in five fox and hen narratives

	FOX	HEN
GENDER	male	female
ROLE	villain	heroine
WHERE THEY LIVE	cave in the woods	house with a fence or house in a tree or a hen-house on a farm
WHAT THEY DO	makes plans chases the hen	cleans the house gathers food
WHAT THEY LOOK LIKE	usually doesn't wear clothes or else wears a suit	usually wears apron and scarf and carries a basket
DESCRIPTION	sly and cunning greedy	tidy and kind foolish, but clever in the end
WHAT HAPPENS TO THEM IN THE END	falls into hot water and is either killed or frightened away	lives happily ever after

groups could then investigate these sites (such as one site per group) according to the criteria generated with the teacher. Their analyses completed, the class could then reconvene to pool outcomes and jointly construct the report.

• Children could independently carry out such reports – choosing a section of the internet, selecting samples of sites and generating their own criteria. Children could then work through drafting and revising of their final reports.

Text Analysts in Action in a Year Five Classroom

The following section describes text analysts at work in a Year 5 classroom. The classroom teacher, Terry, believes that children can really only understand critical literacy when they are forced to confront their own biases and prejudices as reflected in texts which deliberately have a hidden agenda of ideological construction. Only then, this teacher holds, can they understand how a text contains elements of power, social features, world views and personal constructions.

Every book that becomes the daily focus of Terry's classroom is carefully chosen so as to in some way confront the children in his class. The following example came from a period of time when he was teaching a class that was particularly adverse to anything different. Although, in his words, 'they were lovely children, they couldn't cope with anything in their world that was out of the ordinary. In particular they had no concept of the value that aged people could bring to society and had no contact with disabilities'. Hence he chose Colin Thiele's *Let the Balloon Go* as a means of developing critical perspectives through personal confrontation.

Figure 6 shows an extract from the first two weeks of his program.

Figure 6

The First Two Weeks of a Year 5 Teacher's Critical Literacy Program

	Literature Focus	**Class Demonstrations**	**Language Features**	**Writing**
Week 1	*Discussion Points* Impressions of various characters, children make predictions Does the title suggest anything? Relate character traits to own lives, e.g., nagging mother, daydreams, feelings towards people with disabilities.	Begin story maps and character sociograms. Discuss outcomes of character analysis.	Discuss language Thiele used to create the characters. Discuss episodes that were used to create sympathy without reader initially knowing it. How was this effect achieved?	Discuss the concept of narrator. Who is the narrator in this story? Rewrite the text with an explicitly identified narrator or a character's viewpoint. Discuss the language needed for the change.
Week 2	Gauge reactions when children find out John has a disability. Why didn't the author tell us this at the start of the story? Discuss the title in relation to the character John. Why did the author choose this title?	Identify changing relationships in the story. Why do these changes occur? How is surprise created at the revelation that John has a disability?	Discuss the beliefs that that are explicitly and implicitly created. How are these revealed in the narrative to the reader?	What are the writer's hooks?

Terry believes that being text analysts – or doing critical literacy – should involve children in a tripartite excursion into the text. By 'tripartite excursion', he means moving to and fro among talking, reading and writing in order to critically examine a text (after Britton, 1983). Thus Terry's program provides opportunities for reading the text, talking about it and using it as a model for children's own writing. This provides what the teacher believes is genuine integration as children are learning about text through text while gaining insight into the creation of text.

The fiction which Terry reads in serial form to his class on a daily basis often leads to a great deal of discussion and debate. Such is the climate created by this teacher: all views and beliefs are acknowledged by the teacher and there is an explicit understanding that there is no right or wrong answer. Children are free to express their opinion openly and honestly. While this process is aimed to be used as a lever to provide opportunities for the children to look into the text, their own values and those held in society at large, there is no overt force for anyone to accept the majority views of the class. This teacher has the view that 'genuine care begins with care for each other as a class members. While we talk about, hopefully, the bigger issues they will face and the prejudices they hold, it all begins here in this room. They have to see it all in action in here.'

The program sample in Figure 6 also demonstrates the questions that the teacher has designed. The layout and carryover into oncoming weeks is also intended to convey the ideal that while the teacher needs to prepare, one can never be sure of how long each discussion session will last as the teacher can never be sure of what the children will ask. For this teacher, the questions children ask form the pinnacle of critical literacy – in terms of what they choose or are guided to scrutinise and in terms of what their questions reveal about their developing understanding.

Terry always aims to read a large section of print every day as serial fiction. The children understand that this daily practice, accompanied by discussions, is necessary to gain understanding from what was read the previous day and begin to make links to the new section read. While the teacher stops at predetermined strategic points and asks questions, the children are also aware that they too can interrupt and generate comments, ask questions and make connections.

The following extract shows the nature of this interaction. After reading for approximately for two minutes with the intent of stopping and asking the question detailed in Week Two concerning why Thiele had not stated up front that John had a disability, a child interrupted – significantly, the teacher had not yet asked the question himself:

Child 1: Mr M. I think Thiele has set us up.
Teacher: What do you mean?
Child 1: Well, we had no idea John was a spastic? Did he know? And you think spastic is the right term?
Child 2: Yes he set us up and disabled people are called clients, my dad works with them.
Child 3: He does set us up because he wants us to realise that we're all normal, somehow.
Child 1: It like racism kind of. Its like in 'The Quay', we're all the same on the inside.

As stated before, this form of interaction is the pivotal element of critical literacy or reading as a text analyst in Terry's classroom – it allows children to make connections and develop their own understanding of the ideological and social fabric of the text.

The study of themes and issues of the book in focus was accompanied by careful scrutiny of the book's language. For example, in a discussion of Thiele's book title, *Let*

The Balloon Go, the class needed careful guidance to make the connection between the theme of the book and the careful choice of words:

Teacher: If Thiele has set us up, as K' decided, what has the title got to do with this?

Child 4: Well, he makes you think that John can do stuff like we can.

Child 5: Kind of, but what does he mean, let it go? Wouldn't you want to hang on to it?

Teacher: Remember when we read the opening pages and looked for the initial hook to draw us in, the language of ...

Child 6: Sympathy!

Teacher: That's right, he used those tools to make us think John was OK, but the real thing this book was about was hidden, right?

Class: Yeah.

Teacher: It was also in the title.

Child 7: Are you talking about being free and being able to run around?

Teacher: Yeah, buts its more than that as well.

Child 5: I think that its trying to tell us that we have to let go not keep...

Child 7: No it's about John this book, not us, he had to think he was normal.

The careful construction of the episodes which lead the reader to the realisation that this book is a deliberate attempt to confront the prejudices held by society in regard to people with disabilities and the language features which the author has used to draw the reader into the text, were an almost daily source of discussion in the writing segment of this teacher's timetable.

Assessing Readers as Text Analysts

Assessing children's reading as text analysts should be based on an understanding of knowledge and skills associated with text analysts, as we have described and summarised in Figure 2, along with developmental indicators summarised in Figure 3.

In terms of gathering information about how children are functioning as text analysts, it is important to observe children over time and in a number of different situations. Children should be observed with a variety of texts and text types, as well as reading alone and reading with the support of an expert other.

This information can be gathered by observations and work samples. Observations may be organised in a variety of ways, as described in Chapter 3. An example of an observational record which focuses on how a child is functioning as a text analyst is shown in Figure 7.

As shown in this sample, all assessment records should include the following information:

- name of child, name of observer and date of observation
- situation in which the child was observed – for example, modelled reading, guided reading, independent reading, related activity

Figure 7

A Sample of an Observational Record Focusing on How a Child is Functioning as a Text Analyst

Child's Name: Christine Bennett   Date: January 11, 2000   Observer: Ann Brown

Situation: Guided reading in a small group   Text: "Piggybook" by Anthony Browne

Checklist:	Not present	Emerging	Early	Competent
Knows that texts are culturally crafted objects			x	
Knows that texts construct ideological meanings			x	
Knows that texts position readers			x	
Knows that texts carry opinion, bias and point of view			x	
Knows that different texts may treat same topics or themes differently		x		
Knows that readers may agree or disagree with a text's position		x		
Knows that different readers might interpret a text differently		x		
Recognises and talks about opinion, bias and point of view in text		x		
Interrogates texts		x		
Discerns a text's position			x	
Takes and articulates a position		x		
Constructs alternative positions to those in texts	x			
Recognises and describes ways in which a text is crafted		x		
Understands why readers might interpret texts differently	x			

Comments: Christine could identify how the author put forward his ideas about family roles through his pictures. Christine spent some time commenting on the metamorphosis of images into pigs, and linked this quite clearly to how the father and two boys were behaving. With my prompting, Christine was able to explain that the author wanted the reader to believe that things weren't always fair in families. She related this to her own family experiences, when sometimes her Mum would remind her brother and herself about their chores. She was able to answer questions about who did what in this story's family, and what that said about family roles. Christine was able to express her position on the text - to paraphrase her words, it's important to behave fairly and be sure everyone shares the work in families. When asked to think about what other positions a reader might take on this text, and why, she was unable to comment. She needs more explicit encouragement and scaffolding to construct and support an alternative position. Also, it might be that she needs to be aware of how different families function before she can express alternative view points that others might hold. My next step will be to involve her in reading and talking about other narratives on families; and talking more explicitly with her peers about their family experiences and their viewpoints on texts about families.

- whether the child was reading alone or with the support of peers or teacher
- the name of the text being read
- the type of text, for example, narrative, information report, etc
- descriptive information detailing what happened
- interpretive information, wherein the teacher links the descriptions to developmental outcomes, Syllabus outcomes, and/or program objectives.

To facilitate the recording of observations, checklists based on indicators or outcomes can be devised by the teacher.

The sample in Figure 7 also illustrates the teacher moving from description to interpretation, to identifying future learning experiences for the child. As these experiences are implemented, teachers continue to monitor performance as text analysts.

Summary

When readers engage in text analyst practices, they are critically reading texts for their underlying messages. Learning to be competent text analysts is a crucial part of being a reader who functions effectively in society, as well as significant to individuals' sense of their own identities, roles, relationships and views about the world.

Key Concepts

- text analyst
- reader position
- constructedness of texts
- adopting reader position

- ideological meanings
- detecting text position
- text position

Tutorial Activities

A.   Figures 3, 4, 5, 6 and 7 describe teaching strategies and learning activities which support and promote the development of text analysts. In relation to developmental indicators shown in Figure 3, and/or in relation to Syllabus outcomes, develop a set of learning experiences based on a text or small collection of texts provided.

B.   Figure 4 summarises several learning activities which involve children in working with texts as text analysts. Working in small groups with texts provided in your tutorial, choose some of these activities and complete them. When finished, answer the following questions:

   •   How did you function as a text analyst?

   •   How did discussions with your group peers support your functioning as a text analyst?

   •   What different points of view came out in your group discussions?

   •   How did this activity further your understanding about text analyst and how to support them in the classroom?

   •   How might you use these activities in a classroom?

Further Readings

Davies, B. 1989, *Frogs and Snails and Feminist Tales – Preschool Children and Gender,* Allen & Unwin, Sydney.

Luke, A. 1993, 'The social construction of literacy in the primary school', in L. Unsworth (Ed.) *Literacy Learning and Teaching – Language as Social Practice in the Primary School,* Macmillan, Melbourne.

Luke, A. & Freebody, P. 2000, 'Critical literacy in Australia – a matter of context and standpoint', *Journal of Adolescent and Adult Literacy, vol.43,* no.5, pp.448-461.

Knobel, M. & Healy, A. (Eds.), 1998, *Critical Literacies in the Primary Classroom,* Primary English Teaching Association, Sydney.

Luke, A. & Gilbert, P. (Eds.), 1993, *Literacy in Contexts: Australian Perspectives and Issues.* Allen & Unwin, Sydney.

Widdowson, H.G. 1983, *Learning Purpose and Language Use,* Oxford U.P., Oxford.

Williams, G. 1991, 'Space to play: the use of analyses of narrative structure in classroom work with children's literature'. In Saxby, M. & Winch, G. (Eds.) *Give Them Wings: the Experience of Children's Literature (2nd Edn),* Macmillan, Sydney.

Yates Garden Guide – Centennial Edition 1895-1995, Angus and Robertson, Sydney.

Chapter 8

TOWARDS A BALANCED LITERACY PROGRAM

'The only truism in teaching is that nothing stays the same.'
(A Kindergarten teacher of 30 years)

Chapter Preview

This, the last chapter, focuses on the many factors that need to be in place in order to establish an effectively balanced literacy program in your classroom. It will identify the many factors that need to be considered and suggest possible ways of organising time, planning the classroom environment, choosing appropriate resources, organising groups, selecting appropriate strategies and organising assessment information. Finally it will introduce the teaching/learning cycle –the heart of a balanced literacy program.

Focal Questions

- What constitutes a balanced literacy program?
- How do I organise the students?
- How do I organise time?
- How do I plan my assessment?
- What is the teaching/learning cycle?

Introduction

As we come to the end of this book on reading we would love to be able to say, 'You have all the knowledge now about reading, you know how reading is best learned, you have a range of classroom strategies, you know how to assess your students reading needs and teach accordingly, so here is THE way of putting them altogether into a classroom literacy program that works for all teachers and all children!' Unfortunately it is not that easy. The Kindergarten teacher quoted above sums it all up in her statement. Not only do things keep changing in teaching, it is also fair to say that no two teachers teach in the same way and no two classrooms ever look the same.

While it may seem like we are stating the obvious here, such 'truisms' do not stop practising teachers constantly being on the look out for ideas, strategies, ways or organising their classrooms so that they have THE perfectly balanced literacy program that serves the needs of all the students in their care. It is these challenges that keep teaching exciting (sometimes frustrating) but always interesting.

We can, however, identify the key elements of a balanced literacy program so that you can use these as a guide when planning the literacy program for your class.

Much of what will be shared in this chapter has been said elsewhere in this book. What we will attempt to do here is 'pull the threads together' into an overview of what you need to consider. We also remind you that there are many useful books already written that have been referred for you at the end of each chapter. These books are full of ideas and strategies and we encourage you to begin to collect your own library of professional books. We also suggest that you join professional associations (see information at the end of this chapter). These associations are run by teachers for teachers and for your annual subscription you will be supplied with books and information that are seen to be 'the latest' in literacy teaching.

It is also important to point out again that while we have focused on the teaching of reading in this book, we acknowledge that reading, writing, speaking and listening are all important language components that need to be part of a 'literacy program'. (See definition of literacy in Chapter 1, p.18). Because we believe reading is also part of the overall literacy program, you will note that from here on we will talk about 'literacy' rather reading.

The question we now will address is: 'How can all of this be put into practice?'

How Can All of This Be Put into Practice?

In what follows we will share what we have found out from those teachers with whom we have worked over the years.

There are two distinct types of activity teachers typically engage in:
- planning
- organising the classroom for effective literacy teaching.

Planning involves knowing:
- what one is supposed to be teaching, i.e. what is required by the system
- what one needs to teach, i.e. what are the needs of students
- how one is going to teach
- why one is teaching this content this way.

Thus a key to effective planning is the ability of teachers to be able to make explicit the literacy objectives they aim to achieve with their students in their particular classroom settings.

In order to achieve these aims teachers will need to consider how they will go about:

- organising time
- organising space
- gathering a range of resources
- assessing and evaluating literacy learning.

Planning: Making Explicit Literacy Beliefs and Aims

At the whole school level

Ideally the starting point is to develop a whole school literacy plan which will support a whole school approach to the teaching of literacy. Such a plan needs to be inclusive of the different needs, backgrounds and skills of all students and provide a systematic approach to teaching literacy across the school which can then be interpreted in each classroom.

One way of doing this is to seek the whole teaching staff's commitment in individually answering these three general sets of questions (or variations of them) in writing and then providing time for the whole staff to share and discuss their responses.

Whole School Question 1:   What is effective literacy? Why do I think this?

Whole School Question 2:   How is this kind of effective literacy best achieved? Why do I think this?

Whole School Question 3:   After our students have achieved this kind of literacy what should they use it for? Why do I think this?

The aim of such an activity is <u>not</u> to develop a set of definitive, immutable answers. On the contrary, it is to begin the process of developing shared meaning and of clarifying and making explicit their values and beliefs about learning, about language and about literacy and its instruction. Our research and the research of others into teacher learning and school change show that if we want positive change to occur at the school level (Turbill, 1994; McKenzie & Turbill, 1999), a useful place to begin is the development of shared meaning around such issues as those embedded within these questions.

We acknowledge, however, that working at the whole school level may seem rather daunting for beginning teachers, so a 'second best' situation is to make sure you find out as much as you can about what already is in place with respect to school policies, grade expectations, as well as parent expectations. Some schools support beginning teachers by pairing them up with a 'buddy' or 'mentor' whose role it is to support the beginning teacher in not only learning about how the school 'works', but who also can provide guidance in the planning and the organisation of the classroom literacy program. If this support is not built into the school organisation then we strongly urge you to seek out a buddy who is willing to guide and share with you.

At the individual classroom level

It is important that you are able to respond to the three questions suggested above yourself. Responses to these questions will force you to make explicit your beliefs about literacy and the teaching of literacy. As we pointed out in Chapter 2 these beliefs, whether they be conscious or not, drive your practice. However, when you are conscious of the beliefs that guide or underpin what you want to achieve in your classroom, you are in a far better position to evaluate your teaching activities and thus be able to change them when needed.

TASK

Take some time to respond to these questions now:

1.   What is effective literacy? Why do I think this?

2.   How is this kind of effective literacy best achieved? Why do I think this?

3.   After my students have achieved this kind of literacy what should they use it for? Why do I think this?

A final question that is important for teachers to consider when planning is:

What do I want the children in my class to be able to do with respect to literacy at the end of this school year?

Again the research into teacher practice quite clearly shows that after teachers have 'had a go' at personally addressing and attempting to resolve questions like these, they can then begin to develop procedures for:

- teaching and learning reading, writing, talking and listening in meaningful and purposeful ways
- assessment and evaluation
- early intervention
- communicating accurate information on each student's progress to parents or caregivers.

(Mathie, 1994; Graham, 1994)

What has been described are starting points. They should not be seen as a 'lock-step' process – never to be repeated. Rather they are 'strategies' for beginning the reflection and discussion with your peers, your students and yourself. Once begun, such reflection and discussion will become a cyclic process and constantly inform both your planning and teaching, the outcomes of which in turn should become the focus of further reflection and discussion and so on.

Organising the Classroom for Effective Teaching of Literacy

Organising time

One of the most constant issue for teachers is the way they organise time for the teaching of literacy. Many have made the shift from a traditional organisational unit ('the lesson') to a significantly different one. Whereas the traditional lesson is typically a 15-30 minute time slot which has a pre-determined structure, ('motivation step, demonstration/explanation step, discussion step, application step, correction/revision step and closure step') and a set of one or two pre-determined purposes/aims, the newer unit is a bigger unit of time, typically called 'the language session' or 'the literacy block', which is made up of organisational units which are called 'episodes' (Cambourne & Turbill, 1994). These episodes are distributed across the one to two hour slots in different ways by different teachers. No two are exactly the same. On the following pages are some examples of what we mean.

The 'episodes' these teachers developed were teaching/learning events which had a specific overall purpose and a set of behaviours for achieving this purpose. Episodes are very predictable. Both teacher and learners know that episodes will proceed in a predetermined order with predictable purposes, processes and ways of operating.

Establishing predictable routines like episodes helps students in two ways. Firstly, they become aware of teacher expectations. Secondly, they have the supports and scaffolds they will need to successfully complete the tasks that are inherent in the episode. It needs to be pointed out that there is no one way to organise this time and the organisation should be modified as you observe the students at work. A balance needs to be established between whole classwork and small group instruction focused on a group's particular needs. Note how the session plans can also be used to identify the assessment opportunities that exist in these episodes as part of the regular routine. Understanding how assessment and teaching can co-occur enables teachers to gather information on students' progress during the course of teaching. Such understanding and practice maximise the use of teacher time and allow for students to be assessed within the context of their learning.

Organising space

In order to organise time in ways described above, one also needs to organise space as well. Such classrooms are characterised by learner movement and learner interaction, periods when the class becomes a single group with a single purpose ('whole class focus') and periods when the class becomes a series of discrete groups with a multiplicity of different purposes.

Classrooms which operate this way need desks and furniture arranged so that movement, interaction, group work, individual work, quiet times and whole class focus times are possible. The desks need to be set out so that children can move easily and

| \multicolumn{4}{c}{**Episode Organisation- Kindergarten Fully Integrated 90-minute Daily Language Session**} | | | |

TIMING	EPISODE/OVERALL PURPOSE	WHAT HAPPENS	WHAT I CAN ASSESS IN EPISODE
15-20 minutes	Whole Class Focus – Reading (Modelled Reading) Purpose: To demonstrate models of good reading and writing	Teacher reads to students; text on OH, chart or in enlarged book focusing on how text works and phonic awareness. Sometimes followed by a print walk.	• interest • attentiveness • oral response to teacher questions • ability to concentrate, sit still, participate • understanding of concepts being demonstrated
5-10 minutes	Drop Everything And Read (DEAR) time Purpose: Provide opportunities to practise reading skills independently (Independent reading)	Students choose own books (charts, big books etc) to read.	• depth of engagement with text • strategies used to choose texts • language used when talking about texts
15 minutes	Whole Class Focus – Writing Purpose: To provide demonstrations of the writing process	Teacher 'model writes' and makes connections with the focus from the earlier Whole Class Focus – Reading. Sometimes followed by a print walk.	• depth of engagement with demonstrations • oral response to teacher questions and comments • awareness of connections with reading episode
15-20 minutes	Writing Purpose: To provide opportunities to employ writing skills and knowledge	Students write individually, often collaboratively. Teacher conferences with as many as possible.	• understanding of processes and text conventions • control over text conventions and skills of reading/writing
20-25 minutes	Demonstration/ Reading Groups Purpose: To demonstrate & practice literacy strategies, skills, knowledge	Teacher demonstrates skills, understandings to whole class followed by small groups practice and teacher led guided reading.	• depth of engagement with demonstrations • oral response to questions etc • teacher observation of student reading behaviours
10-15 minutes	Sharing Time Purpose: To promote meta conscious awareness and communication skills	Children share insights, drafts, books, problems, issues with rest of class. Class respond and comment. Teacher listens, occasionally intervenes with comment or refocus.	• understanding of processes and text conventions • ability to use language to share • willingness to share • confidence when sharing • depth of engagement with previous demonstrations

Episode Organisation- Grade 5 Fully Integrated 2 Hour Daily Language Session			
TIMING	**EPISODE**	**WHAT HAPPENS**	**WHAT I CAN ASSESS IN EPISODE**
20-25 minutes	Whole Class Focus Purpose: To focus whole class attention on tasks, events, models, demonstrations. Modelled Reading	Teacher reads, models, demonstrates reading, writing, spelling etc. Children engage with demonstration in a range of ways.	• interest • attentiveness • oral response to teacher questions • ability to concentrate, sit still, • participate • understanding of concepts being demonstrated
10-15 minutes	Print Walk Purpose: To interact with, use, and become consciously aware of how print 'works'. (Modelled Reading)	Teacher takes students on guided tour of wall print in room and demonstrates structure and function. Children engage, respond.	• depth of engagement with demonstration • oral responses to teacher questions • understanding of connections being made explicit
20-30 minutes	Sustained Silent Reading (SSR) Purpose: Provide opportunities to practice reading skills independently.	Children select books and read silently.	• time taken to choose books • number of books completed • time taken to complete books • student evaluation of books read
50 minutes	Activity Time Purpose: To provide opportunities for students to make choices, practice and employ developing literacy skills, receive feedback and guidance from teacher.	Children work on contracts and activities individually and in groups, using the reciprocal reading strategy. Teacher conferences with groups organised for guided reading.	• understanding of text conventions • ability to organise time • ability to take responsibility for learning
10-15 minutes	Demonstration Time Purpose: To demonstrate literacy strategies, skills, knowledge.	Teacher demonstrates skills, understandings to whole class/small groups.	• depth of engagement • oral response to questions • connections made re text conventions
10-15 minutes	Sharing Time Purpose: To promote meta conscious awareness and communication skills.	Children share in-sights, drafts, books, problems, issues with rest of class. Class respond and comment. Teacher listens, occasionally intervenes with comment or refocus.	• confidence and willingness to share • control over oral language • listening skills • comprehension ability

From Cambourne and Turbill (1994, p.21-22)

talk to each other. Resources and materials need to be arranged so that children have ready access to them.

Such use of space allows for the teaching/learning strategies of modelled, guided and independent reading to operate successfully.

Gathering a range of resources

Written and oral texts are the tools of trade of balanced literacy classrooms. They are what learners are immersed in and the source of most of the demonstrations of how language is used and structured. Much has already been said about resources throughout the book. However, the following are some general points about creating and using resources in classrooms:

- Ask the school librarian to allow the students in your class to select three books each that they would like to have in the classroom for an extended period of time to resource the class library.
- Bulk borrow poetry books, picture books, collections of short stories.
- Beg, borrow and scrounge non-fiction texts and magazines.
- Ask students to bring in one or two of their own books and 'lend' them to the class collection for a while.
- Find authors who write for a range of ability levels so that readers of different levels of ability can share common authors.
- Try to build collections which feature different works by the same author.
- Look in the school store room for old reading programs and break them up so that the individual stories, poems and other non-fictional texts can me made into 'skinny books'.
- Print useful texts (poems, rhymes, information texts and many others) that you and the children find on the Internet and laminate them for the class collection.
- Flood the room with Wall Print.

Organising groups

There are many ways to organise students for learning. At one end of the continuum there is working as the whole class, at the other working individually. Groups can be pairs, in threes, fours and so on. Group size and make-up depend on the activity and the expected outcomes that the teacher wants the group to achieve. Children may be grouped according to perceived needs as assessed by the teacher. This form of grouping is advocated for Guided Reading. However, children can also be organised into 'social groups'. A social group can be teacher selected for various purposes, for example to mix children of different abilities, backgrounds, genders and so on. Social groups can also be organised to suit the children. In other words, the children select the group they want to work in.

A third type of grouping has been called 'activity grouping'. This type of group is dictated by the activity the children as asked to do. For example, the teacher may want the children to move into pairs to carry out a cloze activity together. When the 'pairs' have finished the task, they may be asked to pair up with another pair to share and justify their responses. At another time the activities that the teacher has selected for children may require a pair of children to work on one activity, while another activity such as a board game may require four children. What is important is that children do not always work in the same group for all activities. Moving in and out of different groups allows them to work with different students and to see and hear different opinions and ideas and learn from each other.

A concern with grouping children in 'ability groups', particularly when these groups rarely change, is that it sets up certain expectations (remember the Conditions of Learning in Chapter 1) that some children are 'dumb' and some are 'clever'. When children are moved around in their groups this is less likely to occur and children are seen by each other as all having certain expertise in a particular area. Children become less competitive and more likely to support each other when they work in more flexible groups. In such supportive environments learners are more likely to 'have-a-go' and learn from the responses and feedback they receive from their peers.

Assessing and evaluating literacy learning

The three major decisions made by teachers who seem confident with the issues of assessment and evaluation are:
- decisions concerning the kind of information that needs to be collected
- decisions on methods of collecting information
- decisions on routines for collecting and storing information.

Kind of information collected
Most teachers decide that there are two broad kinds of information they need to collect:
- information which allows them to draw conclusions about each student's attitude towards literacy and literacy learning
- information which permits them to draw conclusions about each learner's developing control the processes underpinning effective reading, writing, spelling and other forms of language use.

Methods of collecting information
Most teachers use three basic information collection methods:
- observations which are recorded as field notes and/or anecdotal records
- conversations, interviews, dialogue with students, conferences, from which relevant student responses are recorded
- sampling and collection of student products.

Routines for collecting and storing information

Most successful teachers examine their teaching episodes for opportunities to collect information as shown in the time lines above. Once collected, they then need to devise ways of storing this information. Some store them in folders often called 'portfolios'. Others use data bases. Many teachers record notes in their own Learning Journals.

It is important that teachers become conscious of the fact that they can collect a great deal of information on student learning during the normal teaching episodes. Once collected, this information needs to be stored and analysed. It becomes the data for making decisions about future teaching/learning experiences; that is, it not only informs teachers what students are achieving and therefore what they need to learn next, but also how effective the teaching has been and if necessary how it might be improved in order to further guide and support student learning.

A way of synthesising all that has been said here can be seen in the teaching/learning cycle below:

Teaching/Learning Cycle

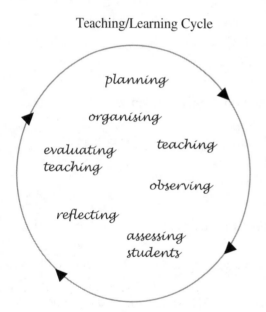

Teaching and Learning Cycle

It is difficult to state just where the teaching/learning cycle begins. For instance, teachers assess students needs and then plan teaching to meet these needs. Teachers reflect on their teaching activities such as a modelled reading activity and evaluate the effectiveness of the activity for teaching the students a specific skill such as use of speech marks. Such reflection and evaluation can lead to further planning and a change in organisation and so the cycle continues. The cycle is ever moving and can be likened to the heart of a balanced literacy program.

TASK

Choose a classroom setting (or a video of a classroom setting) and observe how the teacher:

1. organises time

2. organises space

3. organises resources

4. organises groups.

Professional Associations for Teachers of Literacy

1. Primary English Teaching Association (PETA)

    PETA's focus in on all areas of language and literacy for primary teachers. For an annual subscription members receive books and shorter very practical monographs called PENS.

    Web address: http://www.peta.edu.au/

2. Australian Literacy Educators' Association (ALEA)

    This association produces three research based journals each year (Australian Journal of Language and Literacy – AJLL), three practical magazines (Practically Primary) as well as books. ALEA runs a major conference each year that are very interesting to attend.

    Web address: http://www.alea.edu.au

Further Readings

Nicoll-Hatton, V. 1998, *Getting Started. Ideas for the Literacy Teacher*, Primary English Teaching Association, Sydney.

Cambourne, B. & Turbill, J. 1994, *Responsive Evaluation: Making Judgments about Student Literacy*, Eleanor Curtain Publishing, Melbourne.

References

Adams, M.J., Foorman, B.R., Lundberg, I. & Beeler, T. 1998, *Phonemic Awareness in Young Children*, Paul H. Brookes, Baltimore.

Ahang, S. 1999, 'Explicit processes and strategies using literature circles', in *Teaching Literacy Using Information Technology*, ed. J. Hancock, Australian Literacy Educators' Association, Carlton South, Victoria.

Anstey, M. & Bull, G. 1996, *The Literacy Labyrinth*, Prentice Hall, Sydney.

Australia's Language: The Australian Literacy and Language Policy, 1991, Department of Employment, Education and Training, Australian Government Publishing Services, Canberra.

Baker, C. & Freebody, P. 1989, *Children's First School Books*, Basil Blackwell, Cambridge.

Bleich, D. 1976, *Readings and Feelings: An Introduction to Subjective Criticism*, National Council for the Teaching of English, Urbana, IL.

Bloom, B. Ed. 1956, *Taxonomy of Educational Objectives, Handbook 1: Cognitive Domain*, McKay, New York.

Bourdieu, P. & Passeron, J.C. 1977, *Reproduction in Education, Society and Culture*, Sage, London.

Britton, J. 1970, *Language and Learning*, National Council for the Teaching of English, Hammondsworth.

Britton, J. 1983, Writing in the Story World, in *Explorations in the Development of Writing*, eds. B. Kroll, & G. Wells, Wiley Park, New York

Brown, H. & Cambourne, B. 1987, *Read and Re-tell*, Nelson, Melbourne.

Bruner, J. 1965, *On Knowing: Essays for the Left Hand*, Harvard University Press, Harvard.

Bruner, J. 1983, *Child's Talk: Learning to Use Language*, W.W. Norton and Company, New York.

Bruner, J. 1998, *The Culture of Education*, Harvard University Press, Cambridge, MA.

Cairney, T. 1990, Intertextuality: infectious echoes from the past. *The Reading Teacher*, March, 478-484.

Cairney, T. 1992, Fostering and building students' intertextual histories. *Language Arts, 69,* 502-507.

Cambourne, B. & Turbill, J. 1994, *Responsive Evaluation: Making Judgments about Student Literacy*, Eleanor Curtain Publishing, Melbourne.

Cambourne, B. 1988, *The Whole Story: Natural Learning and the Acquisition of Literacy*, Ashton Scholastic, Auckland, New Zealand.

Cambourne, B.L. 1995, 'Towards an educationally relevant theory of literacy learning: Twenty years of inquiry', *The Reading Teacher*, vol.49, no.3, pp.182-192.

Cao, W. 2000, 'Selection of electronic reference resources'. Unpublished document, State Library of New South Wales, Sydney.

Chambers, A. 1980, 'The reader in the book', in *The Signal Approach to Children's Books*, Kestrel, London, pp.250-273.

Chambers, A. 1991, *The Reading Environment: How Adults Help Children Enjoy Books*, Primary English Teaching Association, Sydney.

Chambers, A. 1993, *Tell me – Children, Reading and Talk,* Primary English Teaching Association, in association with Thimble Press, Sydney.

Choice Magazine, 2000, 'www.books!', November, pp.26-31, Australian Consumers' Association, Sydney.

Clark, M.M. 1976, *Young Fluent Readers,* Heinemann, London.

Clay, M. 1979, *The Early Detection of Reading Difficulties,* Heinemann, Auckland.

Clay, M. 1991, *Becoming Literate,* Heinemann, Portsmouth, N.H.

Clay, M. 1993, *An Observation Survey of Early Literacy Achievement,* Heinemann, Auckland.

Comber, B. & Simpson, A. 1995, 'Reading cereal boxes – analysing everyday texts', In *Texts – the Heart of the English Curriculum, Series 1,* Curriculum Division, Department for Education and Children's Services, South Australia.

Creenaune, T. & Rowles, L. 1996, *What's Your Purpose? Reading Strategies for Non-Fiction Texts.* Primary English Teaching Association, Sydney.

Davies, B. 1989, *Frogs and Snails and Feminist Tales – Preschool Children and Gender,* Allen & Unwin, Sydney.

Derewianka, B. 1990, *Exploring How Texts Work,* Primary English Teaching Association, Sydney.

Derewianka, B. 1998, *A Grammar Companion for Primary Teachers,* Primary English Teaching Association, Sydney.

Dillon. J.T. 1994, *Using Discussion in Classrooms*, Open University Press, Philadelphia.

Dixon, N., Davies, A. & Politano, C. 1996, *Learning with Readers Theatre – Building Connections.* Peguis Publishers, Winnipeg.

Education Department of Western Australia, 1994, *First Steps Reading Developmental Continuum,* Longman, Melbourne.

Elbow, P. 1973, *Writing Without Teachers.* Oxford University Press, Oxford.

English K-6 Modules, 1998, Board of Studies, Sydney.

Evans, R. 1993, 'Learning Schooled Literacy: The literate life histories of mainstream student readers and writers', *Discourse Processes*, vol. 16, pp.317-340.

Fairclough, N. 1989, *Language and Power,* Longman, London.

Farr, R. 1999, 'Putting it all together – solving the reading assessment puzzle', in *Reading Assessment – Principles and Practices for Elementary Teachers,* ed. S.J. Barrentine, International Reading Association, Newark.

Ford, D. 1980, *Daniel 8:14 The Day of Atonement and the Investigative Judgement,* Euangelion Press, Casselberry, FL.

Freebody, P. 1992, 'A sociocultural approach: Resourcing four roles as a literacy learner,' in *Prevention of Reading Failure*, eds. A. Watson & A. Badenhop, Ashton-Scholastic, Sydney, pp.48-80.

Freebody, P. & Luke, A. 1990, 'Literacies programs: Debates and demands in cultural context,' *Prospect: Australian Journal of TESOL,* vol 5, no.7, pp.7-16.

Frith, U. 1985, 'Beneath the surface of developmental dyslexia', in *Surface Dyslexia,* eds. K. Patterson, J. Marshall & M. Colheart, Lawrence Erlbaum Associates, London.

Geekie, P., Cambourne, B. & Fitzsimmons, P. 1999, *Understanding Literacy Development.* Trentham Books, London.

Gibbons, P. 1991, *Learning to Learn in a Second Language.* Primary English Teaching Association, Sydney.

Gilbert, P., with K. Rowe, 1989, *Gender, Literacy and the Classroom.* Australian Reading Association, Melbourne.

Goodman, Y. & Watson D. 1998, 'A sociopsycholinguistic model of the reading process and reading strategy instruction,' in *Practicing What We Know: Informed Reading Instruction,* ed. Constance Weaver, National Council for the Teaching of English, Urbana, Illinois.

Graham, J. 1990. *Pictures on the Page,* Australian Reading Association, Carlton, Vic.

Graham, J. 1994, 'Organising the classroom for responsive evaluation: Getting started K-3', *Making Judgments about Student Literacy,* eds. Brian Cambourne and Jan Turbill, Eleanor Curtain Publishing, Melbourne, pp.38-59.

Halliday, M.A.K. 1975, *Learning How to Mean: Explorations in the Development of Language, Edward Arnold,* London.

Halliday, M.A.K. 1978, *Language as a Social Semiotic: The Social Interpretation of Language and Meaning,* Edward Arnold, London.

Halliday, M.A.K. 1980, 'Three aspects of children's language development: learning language, learning through language, learning about language', Paper presented in Master of Education Course, Sydney University, Australia.

Halliday, M.A.K. 1985, *An Introduction to Functional Grammar,* Edward Arnold, London.

Hancock, J. Ed., 1999, *The Explicit Teaching of Reading,* International Reading Association, Newark.

Harris, P. 1998a, 'Mediating children's functioning as readers in a year one classroom', *Australian Journal of Early Childhood,* vol 23, no.4, pp.18-23.

Harris, P. 1998b, 'Intertextual strategies for making meaning in shared book experiences in the early school years', *Australian Research in Early Childhood Education,* vol 1, pp.24-37.

Harris, P. & Trezise, J. 1997, 'Rock-a-byes and spells, recipes and stories: an examination of competing intertextual agendas in reading instruction in the initial school years', *Australian Journal of Language and Literacy,* vol 20, no.3, pp.197-208.

Harris, P. & Trezise, J. 1999, 'Duckville and other tales', *Language Arts,* vol 5, pp.371-376.

Harris, T. & Hodges, R. 1995, *The Literacy Dictionary: the Vocabulary of Reading and Writing,* International Reading Association, Newark, Delaware.

Hartman, D.K. 1995, Eight readers reading: the intertextual links of proficient readers reading multiple passages. *Reading Research Quarterly, Vol. 30,* No.3, pp.520-561.

Hasan, R. 1996, 'Speech genre, semiotic mediation and the development of higher mental functions', in *Ways of Saying: Ways of Meaning. Selected Papers of Ruqaiya Hasan,* eds. C. Cloran, D. Butt, & G. Williams, Cassell, New York.

Hawisher, G. & Selfe, C. 1999, 'Reflections on research in computers and composition studies at the century's end', in *Teaching Literacy Using Information Technology,* ed. J. Hancock, Australian Literacy Educators' Association, Carlton South, Victoria.

Heath, S.B. 1986a, What no bedtime story means: narrative skills at home and school, in *Language Socialisation Across Cultures,* eds. B.B. Schieffelin & E. Ochs, Cambridge U.P., Cambridge.

Heath, S.B. 1986b, 'The functions and uses of literacy', in *Literacy, Society and Schooling,* eds. S. De Castell, A. Luke, & K. Egan, Cambridge U.P., Cambridge.

Heath, S.B. 1983, *Ways With Words: Language, Life and Work in Communities and Classrooms.* Cambridge U.P., Cambridge.

Hill, S. 1986, *Books Alive – Using Literature in the Classroom,* Nelson, Melbourne.

Hill, S. 1990, *Readers Theatre – Performing the Text,* Eleanor Curtain, South Yarra.

Holdaway, D. 1979, *The Foundations of Literacy.* Ashton-Scholastic, Sydney.

Holland, N. 1973, 'A letter to Holland', *Hartford Studies in Literature*, vol. 5, nos. 1-3, pp.9-30.

Ingvarson, D. 1997, 'Introduction to the Internet', in *A Teacher's Guide to the Internet – the Australian Experience,* ed. D. Ingvarson, Heinemann, Melbourne.

Iser, W. 1980, 'Interaction between text and reader', in *The Reader in the Text*, eds. S. Suleiman and I. Crosman, Princeton University Press, Princeton.

Jennings, P. 2000, 'The end of story', unpublished presentation, *Expanding the Literacy Agenda*, Australian Literacy Educators Association Conference, Melbourne.

Kress, G. 1985, *Linguistic Processes in Sociocultural Practice,* Deakin University Press, Geelong.

Kristeva, J. 1984, *Revolution in Poetic Language,* Columbia U.P., New York.

Lee, H. 1960, *To Kill A Mockingbird,* Heinemann, London.

Lewison, M., Leland, C. & Harste, J. 2000, '"Not in my classroom!"' The case for using multi-view social issues books with children, *Australian Journal of Language and Literacy,* vol.23, no.1, pp.8-20.

Luke, A. 1993, 'The social construction of literacy in the primary school', in *Literacy Learning and Teaching – Language as Social Practice in the Primary School,* ed. L. Unsworth, Macmillan, Melbourne.

Luke, A. 1994, *The Social Construction of Literacy in the Classroom*, Macmillan: Melbourne.

Luke, A. 2000, 'Critical literacy in Australia: A matter of context and standpoint', *Journal of Adolescent and Adult Literacy*, vol. 43, no.5, pp.448-461.

Luke, A. & Freebody, P. 1999a, 'A map of possible practices – further notes on the four resources model', *Practically Primary*, vol 4,no. 2, pp.5-8.

Luke, A. & Freebody, P. 1999b, 'Further notes on the four resources model', *Reading Online,* www.readingonline.org

Mailoux, S. 1977, 'Reader Response criticism?' *Genre*, vol. 10, Fall, Oklahoma, University of Oklahoma Press.

Manzo, A. 1969, 'The ReQuest procedure', *Journal of Reading*, vol 13, pp.123-126.

Marshall, J. 1999, 'Explicitly teaching the reading of non-fiction texts', in *Teaching Literacy Using Information Technology,* ed. J. Hancock, Australian Literacy Educators' Association, Carlton South, Victoria.

Massie, M. 1997, 'Intranets: spinning your own web', in *A Teacher's Guide to the Internet – the Australian Experience,* ed. D. Ingvarson, Heinemann, Melbourne.

Mathie, V. 1994, 'Making beliefs explicit: One teacher's journey', in *Responsive Evaluation: Making Judgments about Student Literacy*, eds. Brian Cambourne and Jan Turbill, Eleanor Curtain Publishing, Melbourne, pp.28-37.

McCourt, F. 1996, *Angela's Ashes,* Harper Collins, London.

McKenzie, B. & Turbill, J. 1999, 'Professional development, classroom practice and student outcomes: Exploring the connections in early literacy development'. Australian Association for Research in Education, Melbourne November 29 – December 2. www.swin.edu.au/aare/99pap/mck99328.htm

Meek, M. 1988, *How Texts Teach What Readers Learn,* Thimble Press, Stroud.

Meek, M. 1991, *On Becoming Literate,* Bodley Head, London.

Minns, H. 1990, *Read It To Me Now! Learning at Home and at School,* London: Virago Press.

Mooney, M. 1990, *Reading To, With and By Children,* Macmillan, New York.

Moore, P. 1999, 'Reading and writing the internet', in *Teaching Literacy Using Information Technology,* ed. J. Hancock, Australian Literacy Educators' Association, Carlton South, Victoria.

NSW Board of Studies, 1997, *Teaching Reading: a K-6 Framework,* Ryde.

NSW Department of School Education, 2000, *Focus on literacy – writing,* Sydney.

National Association for the Education of Young Children, 1999, 'The internet and young children', www.naeyc.org/resources/eyly/1998/18.htm, accessed 24th October, 2000.

Ninio, A. & Roskos, K. 1992, 'Literacy objects as cultural tools: Effects on children's literacy behaviour in play', *Reading Research Quarterly*, vol. 27, pp.203-225.

NSW Board of Studies, 1998, English K-6 Syllabus and Support Materials, NSW Board of Studies.

NSW Department of Education and Training, 1997, *Teaching Reading: A K-6 Framework,* NSW Department of Education and Training, Sydney.

O'Brien, J. 1998, 'Experts in Smurfland', in *Critical Literacies in the Primary Classroom,* eds. M. Knobel & A. Healy, Primary English Teaching Association, Sydney.

Olsen, D. & Bruner J. 1996, 'Folk psychology and folk pedagogy', in *The Handbook of Education and Human Development: New Models of Learning, Teaching and Schooling,* eds. D. Olsen and N. Torrance, Blackwell, Cambridge, MA.

Oyler, C. & Barry, A. 1996, 'Intertextual connections in read-alouds of information books', *Language Arts,* vol 73, no. 5, pp.324-329.

Painter, C. 1991, *Learning the Mother Tongue,* Deakin U.P., Geelong.

Pitt, J. 1997, 'A woman's week? Investigating women's magazines', in *Texts – the Heart of the English Curriculum, Series 2,* Curriculum Division, Department for Education and Children's Services, South Australia.

Plinker, S. 2000, *The Language Instinct*, Penguin, London.

Rapp Ruddell, M. 1993, *Teaching Content Reading and Writing,* Allyn & Bacon, Boston.

Reid, J. 1998, '"Show me a child before s/he is ...". Prior-to-preschool literacy experiences of children in Australia,' *Australian Journal of Language and Literacy,* vol.21, no. 3, pp.234-247.

Rhodes, L.K. & Nathenson-Mejia, 1999, 'Anecdotal records: a powerful tool for ongoing literacy assessment', in *Reading Assessment – Principles and Practices for Elementary Teachers,* ed. S.J. Barrentine, International Reading Association, Newark.

Rosenblatt, L. 1978, *The Reader, The Text and the Poem*, Southern University Illinois Press, Carbondale, IL.

Ruddell, R.B. & Harris, P. 1989, 'A study of the relationship between influential teachers' prior knowledge and beliefs and teaching effectiveness: developing higher order thinking in content areas', in *Cognitive and Social Perspectives for Literacy Research and Instruction,* eds. S. McCormick & J. Zutell, National Reading Council, Chicago.

Ruddell, R.B. & Speaker, R. 1985, 'The interactive reading process: a model', in *Theoretical Models and Reading Processes, 3rd Edn,* eds. H. Singer & R.B. Ruddell, International Reading Association, Newark, Delaware, U.S.A.

Ruddell, R.B. & Unrau, N.J. 1993, 'Reading as a meaning construction process: the reader, the text and the teacher', in *Theoretical Models and Processes of Reading,* eds. R.B. Ruddell, M.R. Ruddell & H. Singer, International Reading Association, Newark.

Rumelhart, D. 1994, 'Towards an interactive model of reading', in *Theoretical Models and Reading Processes, 3rd Edn,* eds. H. Singer & R.B. Ruddell, International Reading Association, Newark, Delaware, U.S.A.

Sanders, N.M. 1966, *Classroom Questions, What Kind?* Harper and Rowe, New York.

Shepherd, L. 1999, 'Building on cultural capital: linking home and school literacies with popular texts', in *Teaching Literacy Using Information Technology,* ed. J. Hancock, Australian Literacy Educators' Association, Carlton South, Victoria.

Simms, J. 1997, 'More than words: exploring comics and cartoons: speech, sound and movement', in *Texts: the Heart of the English Curriculum, Series 2,* Curriculum Division, Department for Education and Children's Services, South Australia.

Sloan, P., & Whitehead, D. 1986, 'Reading theories explained', P.E.N. 55. Primary English Teaching Association, Sydney.

Smith, F. 1981, Demonstrations, engagement and sensitivity, *Language Arts, Vol. 58,* No.1, pp.103-112.

Snyder, I. 1999, 'Using information technology in language and literacy education: an introduction', in *Teaching Literacy Using Information Technology,* ed. J. Hancock, Australian Literacy Educators' Association, Carlton South, Victoria.

Soderman, A.K., Gregory, K.M. & O'Neill, L.T. 1999, *Scaffolding Emergent Literacy: A Child-Centered Approach for Preschool Through Grade 5,* Allyn & Bacon, Boston.

Stauffer, R. 1969, *Directing Reading Maturity as a Cognitive Process,* Harper & Row, New York.

Todorov, T. 1980, 'Reading as Construction' in *The Reader in the Text,* eds. S. Suleiman and I. Crosman, Princeton University Press, Princeton.

Turbill, J. 1994, From a Personal to a Grounded Theory of Staff Development, unpublished PhD thesis, University of Wollongong.

Turbill, J., Butler, A. & Cambourne, B. 1999, 4th ed. *Frameworks: Literacy and Learning Staff Development Program,* University of Wollongong, Wollongong and Wayne-Finger Lakes Board of Co-operative Services, Newark, New York.

Valencia, S. 1999, 'A portfolio approach to classroom reading assessment: the whys, whats and hows', in *Reading Assessment – Principles and Practices for Elementary Teachers,* ed. S.J. Barrentine, International Reading Association, Newark.

Vialle, W., Lysaght, P. & Verenikina, I. 2000, *Handbook on Child Development,* Social Science Press, Australia.

Vizyak, L. 1999, 'Student portfolios: building self-reflection in a first grade classroom', in *Reading Assessment – Principles and Practices for Elementary Teachers*, ed. S.J. Barrentine, International Reading Association, Newark.

Wallace, C. 1992, *Reading*, Oxford U.P., Oxford.

Walton, C. 1993, 'Literacy in Aboriginal contexts: re-examining pedagogy', in *Literacy in Contexts: Australian Perspectives and Issues*, eds. A. Luke. & P. Gilbert, Allen & Unwin, Sydney.

Weir, R. 1962, *Language in the Crib*, Mouton and Co, The Hague.

Widdowson, H.G. 1983, *Learning Purpose and Language Use*, Oxford U.P., Oxford.

Williams, G. 1991, 'Space to play: the use of analyses of narrative structure in classroom work with children's literature', in *Give Them Wings: the Experience of Children's Literature, 2nd Edn*, eds. M. Saxby & G. Winch, Macmillan, Sydney.

Wilson. L. 2000, 'Reading for living in the Year 2000', unpublished presentation, *Expanding the Literacy Agenda*, Australian Literacy Educators' Association Conference, Melbourne.

World Book CD-Rom, Macintosh Edition, 1998, World Book Inc. and IBM Corp.

Yates Garden Guide, 1995, Harper Collins Publishers, Sydney.

Children's Books

Ahlberg, J. & A. 1986, *The Jolly Postman*, Heinemann, London.

Baker, J. 1987, *Where the Forest Meets the Sea*, MacRae, Sydney.

Baillie, A. & Bentley, J. 1999, *Archie the Big Good Wolf*, Red Fox, Sydney.

Browne, A. 1986, *Piggybook*, Julia Macrae, London.

Browne, A. 1998, *Voices in the Park*, Picture Corgi Press, London.

Burningham, J. 1977, *Come Away from the Water, Shirley*, Red Fox, London.

Cousins, L. 1992, *Maisy Goes to Playschool*, Walker Books, London.

Hutchins, P. 1968, *Rosie's Walk*, Bodley Head, London.

Hutchins, P. 1971, *Titch*, Puffin, Middlesex.

James, S. 1991, *Dear Greenpeace*, Walker Books, London.

Jorgensen, G. & Mullins, P. 1988, *Crocodile Beat*, Omnibus Books, Adelaide, S.A.

King, S.M. 1998, *Henry and Amy (Right-Way-Round and Upside Down)*, Scholastic Press, Sydney.

Milne, A.A. 1927, *Winnie the Pooh*, Methuen, London.

Munsch, R. & Martchenko, M. 1980, *The Paperbag Princess*, Annick Press Ltd, Toronto.

Nicoll, H. & Pienkowski, J. 1975, *Meg's Eggs*. Heinemann, London.

Potter, B. 1908, *The Tale of Jemima puddleduck*, Frederick Warne, London.

Sendak, M. 1967, *Where the Wild Things Are*, Bodley Head, London.

Viorst, J. 1972, *Alexander and the Terrible, Horrible, No Good, Very Bad Day*, Angus and Robertson, London.

Wagner, J. & Brooks, R. 1977, *John Brown, Rose and the Midnight Cat*, Puffin, Middlesex.

Guided Reading

Intro
- What is 'Guided Reading?
- How does G.R. works?
- Benefits of G.R.?
- Skills & Strategies
- 4 Reader Roles
- Conclusion

- G.R. + Bloom's Taxonomy
which thinkin category it falls into

Index